CREATIVE
APPROACHES TO
PROBLEM
SOLVING

3

This book is dedicated to the memory and work of Alex F. Osborn (1888–1966).
We are indebted to the pioneering efforts of Alex Osborn, Sidney Parnes, and Ruth Noller.
Alex Osborn's original work to outline explicit procedures for Creative Problem Solving (CPS), and
Sid and Ruth's efforts to build on this foundational work to establish an academic program,
are fundamental to our own efforts to continue the journey.

Osborn was a founding partner of Batten, Barton, Durstine, and Osborn (BBD&O),
an advertising firm that had to make use of the creative talents of its people to meet the needs
of its customers. Alex invented brainstorming as a tool to help groups generate ideas. He used
this tool within his company in the 1930s. Alex was one of the first to attempt to make
creativity something that could be deliberately understood and developed.

Without his personal passion about the human imagination, and his willingness to invest
energy in making his approach explicit, those who followed would never have made the progress
they have in moving our field forward. We have been inspired by Alex Osborn's intellectual curiosity
and open-mindedness. He made numerous changes and improvements in his own understanding of
CPS and published those refinements in an effort to reflect on and share his own continuous learning.

Alex set a high standard for blending scholarship with practice. Indeed, we will endeavor
to honor his original efforts and take forward the key ingredients of the Buffalo tradition
he started as we continue to learn and refine our own approach.

Further to our dedication, we would like to remember the friendship and colleagueship of
Allan Brooks. Although he left us on July 4, 2000, he has helped make a lasting impression
on those of us who work in this field. His sponsorship of CPS within Bull Worldwide Information
Systems, and the work he did following that, really made a difference. Allan will be greatly missed.

Finally, while preparing this update and revision, Dr. Ruth Noller passed away. Her positive
and powerful influence on our work is a part of a cherished legacy.

CREATIVE
APPROACHES TO
PROBLEM
SOLVING

A Framework for Innovation and Change

THIRD EDITION

3

Scott G. Isaksen
Creative Problem Solving Group, Inc.
The Norwegian School of Management

K. Brian Dorval
Think First Serve, Inc.

Donald J. Treffinger
Center for Creative Learning, Inc.

Los Angeles | London | New Delhi
Singapore | Washington DC

For information:

SAGE Publications, Inc.
2455 Teller Road
Thousand Oaks, California 91320
E-mail: order@sagepub.com

SAGE Publications Ltd.
1 Oliver's Yard
55 City Road
London EC1Y 1SP
United Kingdom

SAGE Publications India Pvt. Ltd.
B 1/I 1 Mohan Cooperative Industrial Area
Mathura Road, New Delhi 110 044
India

SAGE Publications Asia-Pacific Pte. Ltd.
33 Pekin Street #02-01
Far East Square
Singapore 048763

Printed in the United States of America

Library of Congress Cataloging-in-Publication Data

Isaksen, Scott G.
Creative approaches to problem solving: a framework for innovation and change / Scott G. Isaksen, K. Brian Dorval, Donald J. Treffinger. — 3rd ed.
    p. cm.
Includes bibliographical references and index.
ISBN 978-1-4129-7773-9 (pbk.)
  1. Problem solving. 2. Group problem solving. 3. Creative thinking. I. Dorval, K. Brian. II. Treffinger, Donald J. III. Title.

BF449.I73 2011
153.4'3—dc22   2009031779

This book is printed on acid-free paper.

10 11 12 13 14   10 9 8 7 6 5 4 3 2 1

Acquisitions Editor:	Lisa Cuevas Shaw
Editorial Assistant:	MaryAnn Vail
Production Editor:	Astrid Virding
Copy Editor:	QuADS Prepress (P) Ltd.
Typesetter:	C&M Digitals (P) Ltd.
Proofreader:	Scott Oney
Indexer:	Kathleen Paparchontis
Cover Designer:	Gail Buschman
Marketing Manager:	Carmel Withers

Brief Contents

Detailed Contents

Foreword

For Creative Problem Solving (CPS) to be relevant, useful, worthwhile, and impactful in application, it must be well modeled and understandable in theory and application. This current version of *Creative Approaches to Problem Solving* (CAPS) satisfies those criteria.

My fascination with the study of creativity and CPS dates back to 1964, with my participation in a week-long Creative Problem Solving program at the University of Buffalo (UB, now SUNYAB [State University of New York at Buffalo]). I had been teaching mathematics at UB for more than 20 years at that time, and I was curious about this program, and what I had heard about it in discussions among the faculty. I had heard some complimentary remarks but also many which were critical and quite disdainful. This, I discovered later, was because of a lack of understanding of the total process and the program's approach to creativity.

Many people assumed that I would naturally be tuned to CPS, since I had been dealing with mathematical problems of all descriptions. I met these problems in my teaching at UB and in my 2-year assignment as a mathematics-engineering officer stationed at Harvard University working on the Mark I Computer (the Automatic Sequence Controlled Calculator) in the United States Naval Reserve during World War II. I had decided to attempt to uncover the mystery of this process for myself. On finding initially that there were some aspects of CPS (format, terminology, etc.) that were both quite foreign, but at the same time exciting to me, I have continued over the years to search for sources that would clarify those foreign aspects. With each new publication of a version of CAPS, I have found additional clarification.

My own search for a better understanding of the creative process was further supported by my involvement in the Creative Studies Project. This unique experimental academic program was designed to teach techniques that would stimulate students to free their imagination, enabling them to increase and to apply their creative capabilities in academic studies as well as in their everyday lives. As I grew with CPS, I found that my life, as well as those of my students, was becoming greatly enhanced. Realizing

---

AUTHORS' NOTE: While we were putting together this edition of the book, our friend and colleague Ruth Noller passed away. Ruth had a profound impact on many of us in the field. As one of the key pioneers in Creative Problem Solving, she was an active supporter and mentor in our efforts to improve on the Osborn-Parnes tradition. We decided to honor her memory, in part, by keeping her foreword—as it was originally written for our 2000 edition.

how extensively all of us were using CPS, primarily as a coping tool, I continued to study the process and to more fully understand this nurturing of creative potential, always searching for fresh approaches to the well-established techniques and procedures. CAPS has provided these fresh views.

This current version of CAPS, the first update after 7 years of documentation of the authors' experience, research, and development in CPS in the worldwide arena of educational and business organizations, clarifies aspects of CPS that have confused practitioners as well as newcomers to the method. I have continued to reflect on the early original "cook-book," "run-through" approach to CPS, which, it seemed, often mystified newcomers as to "where they were" in the process. The lack of linearity of the current format is descriptive rather than directive, being more purpose driven and, therefore, refreshing in that it promotes "possibility thinking." We used to consistently model a nonlinear process with a linear model. This edition of CAPS introduces a more flexible, multidirectional model, which centers on "Planning Your Approach." Then, depending on the needs presented by the plan so devised, the problem solver moves to "Understanding the Challenge," "Generating Ideas," or "Preparing for Action."

The concept of including a special component of CPS that helps people manage their own way through the process helps ensure a deliberate movement away from the primarily linear application of the process. "Planning Your Approach" suggests an autonomy in thought and action, dictated by the experience of the individual(s). It is a natural part of the CPS process, especially if the focus is on real-life application and relevance, emphasizing thinking that is independent of the earlier "run-through" attitude and is, therefore, more personalized and flexible.

Another aspect of this current version is the change in language, which it is hoped would make it more understandable and approachable, based on feedback received over the years from many clients and colleagues. For example, in the study of mathematics, the terms *diverge* and *converge* are readily understood. However, because they must often be explained to the general public, the terms have been replaced here by the more commonly understood terms *generate* and *focus*. In addition, the terms for the former six "steps," usually described as ending in "finding," have been replaced by terms that the authors consider clearer, more user-friendly, and more descriptive of those aspects of the process.

I am confident that the material presented in this book will satisfy the criteria of helping CPS be relevant, useful, worthwhile, and impactful in application. I have no doubt that, by following the suggestions presented here, it will be well modeled and understandable in theory and in application. The authors have done a masterful job in presenting a fresh, comprehensive picture of creative approaches to problem solving.

Dr. Ruth B. Noller
Distinguished Service Professor Emeritus
Center for Studies in Creativity
State University College at Buffalo
New York
(Foreword to the 2000 edition of CAPS)

Preface

Preface to the Third Edition

The new millennium has highlighted and reinforced the demand for creativity and innovation. The increasing pace of change, the demand for dealing with complexity, and the pressure of global competition have underscored the need for Creative Problem Solving (CPS). The need has intensified for lifelong skills for individuals, team effectiveness strategies, and productive change methods for organizations. For business organizations, deliberately developing creativity-relevant skills is a matter of survival and growth. You may be able to have creativity without innovation, but you can't have innovation without creativity. For those concerned with education, there is increasing concern that our emphasis on testing the basics is a distraction from encouraging learners to develop their creative-thinking and problem-solving skills.

The need for a comprehensive description of the current version of Creative Problem Solving (CPS Version 6.1, which is a proprietary framework jointly developed and owned by the Creative Problem Solving Group, Inc., and the Center for Creative Learning, Inc.) prompted the update to the 2000 version of this book. The previous decades had seen numerous structural and technical changes to our approach to CPS. Over the past 8 years, we have noticed some stability in our framework. The emerging research in cognitive science, and our many and varied applications in both educational and organizational applications, have reinforced the design of the framework. The natural and descriptive language, the suite of thinking tools, and the guidelines for generating and focusing have withstood more than 8 years of application and research and are now widely accepted and used.

When the 2000 version of this book sold out, we decided to invest in preparing an updated edition that now included more up-to-date references and reflects our advances in understanding of styles of problem solving. The structure of the book has been maintained, so we have included the original preface to preview the contents of each chapter and to understand our rationale for writing the book in the first place.

We have maintained our focus on CPS, rather than attempting to review all other available methods. We continue to hope that you find this description helpful and useful on a variety of levels.

Preface to the 2000 Edition

Society needs new responses to many significant challenges. Learning how to solve problems creatively, meeting goals, and achieving a sense of personal satisfaction from dealing with life's challenges and opportunities are important for everyone. Schools are attempting to deal with preparing our youth for real-life problems and challenges in relation to personal life, careers, and good citizenship. Organizations work with those students, later as employees, to help them function more effectively in groups and teams to meet the challenges of an evermore competitive and changing marketplace. All these factors seem to be pointing toward the need to support the development of improved ways to think about opportunities, to generate fresh new perspectives, and to implement and follow through on those insights. CPS provides a very important and useful framework to help meet these needs.

The first edition of *Creative Approaches to Problem Solving* was completed in 1993 and published in 1994. Three printings later, we were faced with the challenge from our publisher to make some cosmetic changes and offer yet another reprinting. The three of us agreed to get together and make a few touch-ups and produce a slightly revised edition.

During the past 7 years, we have worked with thousands of people such as you who are interested in creativity and problem solving. We have had the good fortune to work with hundreds of educational, business, and not-for-profit organizations in many different countries. We listened to the feedback we received from our customers and colleagues. We continued conducting our research and providing workshops, training courses, and change programs. We studied the literature from other fields regarding creativity, change, and leadership. Through those efforts, we learned much about our approach to problem solving, its strengths and limitations, and believed that it would be beneficial to update our description of CPS.

We got together at a local hotel and began to summarize some of the feedback and insights we received over the years. Our original intent was to make small tweaks to the book, such as updating the language from divergent and convergent thinking to generating and focusing. We planned to make minor modifications to certain chapters and update key messages throughout the book. However, as we began working, we discovered that the recommendations were getting larger in scope and more significant. We quickly realized that we had moved from making "cosmetic updates" to making substantial changes to the entire CPS framework to its language, and to our approach to its application. The minor update turned into a major revision, which we hope will be a significant improvement.

We really started our journey in 1982, when we published the *Handbook for Creative Learning* (Treffinger, Isaksen, & Firestien). Later, we wrote *Creative Problem Solving: The Basic Course* (Isaksen & Treffinger, 1985). We then embarked on a number of research and development initiatives, beyond attempting to prove that CPS made a difference. As reflective practitioners, we were already convinced of the value and importance of CPS. We turned our attention to improving our understanding of how different people learned and applied CPS. We were interested in the conditions that provided for the best-case application of the method. These questions, and the research they promulgated, led us in important new directions. Through a variety of shared efforts at the Center for

Studies in Creativity, the Center for Creative Learning, and the Creative Problem Solving Group, Inc., we worked to make improvements and turn our insights from research into improved approaches to learning and applying CPS.

Throughout this journey, we followed the practice of laying out milestones. It is important to mark the path we have taken so that others can clearly see the way we have traveled. We worked to synthesize what we learned and read from science and forge these insights with those from our practical and applied work. There is real value in pursuing a framework from the perspective of scholarly inquiry and from successful real-life application. There is also a benefit if this work is done in collaboration with those who work with schools and academic institutions and those who work in corporations and industry. We hope that the result is a general framework capable of broad application and use. The major purpose of this substantially revised second edition is to describe our current view of CPS. This description is the most comprehensive statement regarding the CPS framework, language, and tools available.

Changes in the Second Edition

This book differs from the first edition in a number of ways. First, we changed the CPS language used to identify the elements of the CPS framework. This new, friendlier, and more purpose-driven language is more descriptive of what actually takes place during the different elements of the process. It does a better job of promoting the flexible application of CPS as well as encouraging "possibility thinking." The new language is also more natural, enabling you to integrate CPS more easily into your natural approaches to creativity, decision making, and problem solving.

Second, we made changes to the CPS framework itself. We integrated a new part of the process that helps you make better decisions about the use of the method and to plan to get the best results for different kinds of tasks. We also updated the graphic model we use to represent the framework, in order to make it clearer and more concise.

Third, we integrated more examples and real-life case studies to help bring the information in each chapter to life. The stories in the beginning of most of the chapters help establish the chapter's purpose. Then, the "Rest of the Story" at the end of each chapter demonstrates the effect you can have when you apply the information in the chapter. We used the stories to explore the main issues and content in each chapter.

The book focuses on helping you unleash your personal creativity. We describe the CPS framework, language, and tools in ways that will help you understand and apply them to individual topics. Try to use what you are reading shortly after reading about it. It is not necessary to read the entire book before using the framework, its language, or any of the tools.

The contents of this book can also be applied to help groups unleash their creative talent or to enable organizations to get more productivity from their creativity resources. You will also find the information, tips, and suggestions in this book helpful for facilitating groups and driving organizational change if you have previously developed facilitation skills or experiences with leading such efforts. If you want information about what to consider when facilitating CPS in a group setting, read Isaksen (2000).

The Chapter Structure and Flow

Each chapter begins with a purpose and list of objectives to assist you in pulling out and focusing on the key messages of the chapter. Use them as an outline before you read the chapter, as a guide to help you organize your thinking as you go through the chapter, and as a checklist to summarize your learning after you read the chapter.

Chapter 1: Creative Approaches to Problem Solving

Chapter 1 describes the meaning of "Creative Approaches to Problem Solving." We present you with the overall purpose of the book and set the foundation for the key concepts to be examined (i.e., What is creativity? What is problem solving? What is an approach to change?) and their interrelationship. It sets the stage for what is to come in the following chapters.

The next four chapters examine the CPS framework, language, and tools in detail.

Chapter 2: Creative Problem Solving

This chapter introduces you to Creative Problem Solving (CPS). It provides a definition and current description of the overall CPS framework, language, and tools. It examines the essential "heartbeat" of CPS (generating and focusing), overviews the guidelines for generating and focusing, and introduces the 19 tools to be examined in the book.

Chapter 3: Understanding the Challenge

This chapter provides you with an overview of the Understanding the Challenge component of CPS. It identifies the input you need to enter the component, the kind of processing that takes place within the component, and the kind of output you can get as a result of using the component. It also demonstrates the use of some of the CPS language and tools. Although we will introduce the tools in a particular component of CPS, it is important to remember that you can use the tools in any of the CPS components.

Chapter 4: Generating Ideas

This chapter overviews the Generating Ideas component. It identifies the input, processing, and outputs related to the component. It demonstrates the use of some of the CPS tools, particularly those for generating many, varied, and unusual options. It also provides you with a model for knowing when to use each generating tool based on the kind of change you want to create.

Chapter 5: Preparing for Action

This chapter provides you with information about the Preparing for Action component. It will help you understand when to use the component, what will happen when you do, and what you are likely to get as a result. It does this by examining the input, processing, and outputs of the component, and demonstrating the use of some of the

CPS tools, particularly for focusing options. It also provides you with a model for knowing when to use each focusing tool based on the quantity of options being considered.

The next five chapters examine the Planning Your Approach component of CPS. Chapter 6 overviews the component, while Chapters 7 to 10 examine the key issues associated with understanding a task and its appropriateness for using CPS.

Chapter 6: Planning Your Approach to CPS

This chapter prepares you for examining issues in a task that need to be considered in order to make a good choice about using CPS and developing a plan to optimize its use. It provides an overview of the Planning Your Approach component, including the Appraising Tasks and Designing Process stages. The chapter also identifies the general issues you need to understand to be productive when using CPS to make change happen.

Chapter 7: People as Creative Problem Solvers

This chapter explores in detail the key issues associated with understanding the people involved in the task. It defines and describes the issues of ownership, diversity, and task expertise and their impact on your application of CPS. Specific questions are provided to help you develop an appropriate understanding about people involved in CPS.

Chapter 8: The Context for CPS

This chapter examines the context for creativity necessary to support productive change. It identifies and describes how you know if a context is ready, willing, and able to support change. It examines the impact of climate, culture, and history; strategic priorities, change leadership, and energy; and time, attention, and resources. It illustrates how these issues have an effect on your use of CPS to manage change.

Chapter 9: The Role of Content

This chapter examines the role and importance of the task content in using CPS. It provides you with information about how to determine the kind of novelty needed in a task, the size of the change desired, and the best place to begin working on the task. It provides specific questions you can use to understand the content and prepares you for customizing your use of CPS for maximum effect.

Chapter 10: CPS as a Change Method

This chapter provides you with information about why and how CPS helps people produce change. It examines the unique qualities of CPS as a method and identifies the kinds of tasks on which it can be most effective. It identifies how you know you can be confident in the use of CPS, as well as the pros and cons associated with its use.

The last two chapters (Chapters 11 and 12) focus on helping you design your use of CPS and provide stories, tips, and suggestions for doing so effectively.

Chapter 11: Designing Your Way Through CPS

CPS is a flexible process that can be used on different kinds of tasks. This chapter helps you customize CPS to best fit the unique demands of a task. It helps you set the appropriate scope for CPS and select only those parts of the CPS framework that are appropriate. It also helps you plan how you will involve people and ready the context for best CPS application. We also provide tips for how to design your use of the process.

Chapter 12: Applying CPS

CPS works best when you consider the entire system of people, methods, context, and content. The chapter demonstrates this point by providing you with case studies of how CPS has been used successfully to meet the needs of groups and organizations. It also provides you with specific tips and suggestions for getting the most from your use of CPS.

We have also included a comprehensive listing of the references cited throughout the book and some additional suggested resources you might acquire to learn more about the topics presented to improve your impact from using CPS.

We hope that you find the information and approach in this book informative, productive, and enjoyable. Please feel free to contact us to share your own experiences as you progress on your own journey with creative approaches to problem solving.

Scott, Brian, and Don

Acknowledgments

Many people have influenced our work in the field of creativity and Creative Problem Solving (CPS). Those who have studied and worked at the Center for Studies in Creativity (CSC), particularly Sidney Parnes, Ruth Noller, Angelo Biondi, Dorothy Hunter, Fern Innes, Grace Guzzetta, and the many who came after them, provided the context for our early interactions and learning. The founding scholars of our field, J. P. Guilford, E. Paul Torrance, Donald W. MacKinnon, John Gowan, Moe Stein, and others made many contributions to us and to our emerging field of inquiry. The faculty and many fine students we have had the honor to work with in many academic settings through the years helped us refine and develop our interest in learning, writing, researching, and teaching about creativity and creative problem solving.

Each of us has had numerous opportunities to work with many clients who helped us extend our learning and our service to the world outside the academic arena. Some of the key organizational clients who have helped us see the relevance of CPS to business and industry include Bill Lambert, Mary Wallgren, and Susan Ede of Procter and Gamble; Frank Milton and Trevor Davis from PricewaterhouseCoopers; Don Taylor, Chuck Brandt, and George Saltzman of Exxon; Tom Carter of ALCOA; Don Betty, Nancy Hann, and Mary Boulanger of Armstrong World Industries; Russ Ward and Christopher Goodrich from Datex-Ohmeda (now GE Healthcare); David Dunkleman of Weinberg Campus; Simon McMurtrie, Greg Dzuiba, Samantha Stead, Alf Tönnesson, David Thatcher, Jillian Bruhl, and Debbie Clark-Nilsson of International Masters Publishers; Rita Houlihan, Bruce Esposito, Ed Lynch, and Will Husta of IBM; Gideon Toeplitz of the Pittsburgh Symphony Orchestra; Suzanne Merrit of Polaroid; Aggi Heinz of Bertelsmann; Mike King and colleagues from Ogilvy & Mather; Allan Brooks, Andy Wilkins, John Rees, and Paul Wright from Bull Worldwide Information Systems; Peter Lyons, Charlie Prather, and Dick Comer of DuPont; and Stan Gryskiewicz, Anne Faber, and others at the Center for Creative Learning, Inc.

Some of our educational and academic clients in recent years have included Bill Littlejohn, Priscilla Wolfe, Bonnie Buddle, Jackie Pitman, Gary Collings, and the CPS team at Indiana State University; Carol Wittig and all the G/T (Gifted/Talented) and Ideas Specialists in the Williamsville Central Schools; Cindy Shepardson and Yvonne Saner in the Newark, New York, schools; Grover Young and others from the Holt, Michigan, schools; the CPS team from the Lakewood, Ohio, school district; Jennine Jackson, Marianne Solomon, and Kathi Hume from the Future Problem Solving

Program; John Houtz, Giselle Esquivel, and Ed Selby at Fordham University; Pat Schoonover and her colleagues in OM (and now the Destination Imagination program); and Andi Williams, Jan Casner, Marion Canedo, Evie Andrews, and the late Leonard Molotsky from the National Inventive Thinking Association. These people helped us understand the crucial improvements that are necessary to keep CPS relevant and dynamic.

The many international scholars, practitioners, and clients with whom we have worked helped us understand the value and usefulness of CPS for other cultures, and in different ways. Marjorie Parker and Per Grohølt were the first to invite us to Norway. Luc De Schryver brought us to Belgium and the Netherlands. Wayne Lewis helped us learn about the United Kingdom and France, and Göran Ekvall and Rolf Nilstam introduced us to Sweden. Bob Swartz, Agnes Chang, Dennis Sale, Norah Meier, and others asked us to help them work on attaining the goal of "thinking schools and a learning nation" in Singapore. Lilian Dabdoub has brought us into Mexico and Helena Gil de Costa into Portugal. Anke Theile brought us into Germany. Guido Prato-Previde and Roberta Prato-Previde brought us into Italy. Many friends and colleagues in Canada have contributed actively to advancing CPS across North America, including Diane Austin, Lenore Underhill, and others from the Cowichan School Division in British Columbia; Tom Hengen and others in Saskatchewan; Ken McCluskey, Sé O'Hagan, and Phil Baker in Manitoba, Canada; and Gretchen Bingham, Gwen Speranzini, and Barbara Babij in different parts of Ontario, Canada.

When it comes to the writing of this revision of our earlier book, the network of researchers and friends within the Creativity Research Unit, including Geir Kaufmann, and the network of Creative Problem Solving Group-certified professionals, such as Glenn Wilson, John Gaulin, Kate Stuart-Cox, Lary Faris, Doug Reid, and Andy Wilkins, have been invaluable. Other professionals with whom we have enjoyed our colleagueship are Alex Britz, Tamyra Freeman, Alan Arnett, Jean-Marc le Tissier, Bill Shephard, and Maggie Kolkena. We particularly enjoyed the encouragement provided by Charlie Clark, one of Alex Osborn's colleagues. And now, for the third edition, even more researchers and practitioners have influenced our work.

Marves, Erik, Greg, Bill, Lee, and Kristin, as the core team at Creative Problem Solving Group, and others who support the team, and Carol, Carole, Pat, Ed, and Grover—the core team at the Center for Creative Learning—have worked tirelessly (and been very patient with us). Particular thanks go to Maarten Louwies for helping update the third edition of this book as part of his internship, and Hans Akkermans for helping us put the finishing touches on this edition.

From Scott: Don and Brian have been great friends and colleagues with whom to work on this challenging project. Marves, Kristin, and Erik and his wife, Krissy, have, as usual, done without me at home and enabled me to work late and on weekends (and put up with the occasional invasion of our family activities) in order to see this project through. Their love and acceptance is central to my life. To my Creator, I pray that this work can help release the creative human talent that You have given us.

From Brian: I have learned a great deal about my own creative process in collaborating with Scott and Don on this book. Thank you! I am indebted to Samantha for her keen insights, as well as the love and support she provides me every day. My hope is that this work helps people move toward God's intentions.

From Don: My long-standing collaboration with Scott and Brian has been, and continues to be, a source of energy, inspiration, and renewal. It is a joy to work together with colleagues who are also good friends! Judi's love and her tolerance for my eccentric working style are wonders for which I am always thankful. God works in powerful ways through human creativity, enabling faith and science to thrive together.

Creative Approaches to Problem Solving

Whether it is considered from the viewpoint of its effect on society, or as one of the expressions of the human spirit, creativity stands out as an activity to be studied, cherished, and cultivated.

—Silvano Arieti

The purpose of this chapter is to describe what we mean by "creative approaches to problem solving." As a result of reading this chapter, you will be able to do the following:

1. Describe the four basic elements of the system for understanding creativity.

2. Explain what the terms *creativity*, *problem solving*, and *creative problem solving* mean and their implications for managing change.

3. Describe how creativity and problem solving relate to making change happen.

The person who follows the crowd will usually get no further than the crowd. The person who walks alone is likely to discover places no one has ever been before.

Creativity in living is not without its attendant difficulties. For peculiarity breeds contempt. And the unfortunate thing about being ahead of your time is that when people finally realize you were right, they'll say it was obvious all along.

You have two choices in life: You can dissolve into the mainstream, or you can be distinct. To be distinct, you must be different. To be different, you must be what no one else but you can be. . . .

—Anonymous

The purpose of this chapter is to prepare you for using the information in this book to help you make decisions, solve problems, and use your creativity to change your world in the direction of your greatest aspirations. Let's examine the core concepts behind *Creative Approaches to Problem Solving: A Framework for Innovation and Change.*

One of our intentions in writing this book is to explore with you a creativity method you can use to productively and proactively manage change and produce innovation. However, one of our assumptions is that you already have experience with managing change. Therefore, let's start with you and your own thoughts about the main concepts in this book.

Activity 1.1 Defining Creativity and Problem Solving

Take a minute and write down a few of your first impressions when you see or hear the word Creativity.

Now write down a few of the first impressions when you see or hear the words Problem Solving.

The purpose of Activity 1.1 is to help set the stage for understanding what we mean by creative approaches to problem solving. It asks you to identify and list your perceptions of the key words in our book title. Take a minute to complete the activity before continuing to read the chapter.

What do you notice about the two lists you created? When we do this exercise in our training courses and workshops, we get plenty of different responses for each word. However, we also find strong themes in people's responses, even when we involve people from several different cultures. Let's examine how people have responded to the activity and use these responses to examine each topic.

What Is Creativity?

Creativity is a distinguishing characteristic of human excellence in every area of behavior.

—E. Paul Torrance

Most people can readily come up with informal definitions of creativity. They often associate creativity with words such as *new, unusual, ideas, out of the ordinary, imagination, unique, exciting, wacky, open, fuzzy,* or *something radically different.* It is common for them to relate creativity to the arts: composing or performing plays, making great sculpture, the paintings of the masters, writing great literature, composing and performing music, and the like. It's a word that often has a great deal of positive power and energy associated with it, within and across cultures.

On the other hand, it is unusual for people to associate creativity with words such as usefulness, value, and purposeful. When we probe further, we find that some people often perceive creativity as something not very worthwhile, and in some cases, even as something quite negative. We have identified three principal myths people hold about creativity. We call them the myths of mystery, magic, and madness.

Some people believe that creativity is something so mysterious it cannot be studied productively. They believe creativity comes from an external source over which the individual has no control. This becomes a problem when it inhibits or interferes with their desire or ability to make sense of their own creativity and how they might use it.

Other people believe that creativity is something that is magical, which only a few gifted people really have. This suggests that creativity is a trick that certain people know and if you talk about how the trick is done you will take away the "magic." If you hold this belief, you separate people into two groups: those who have it and those who do not. This myth also discourages people from discussing how they use their creativity or how they can nurture it in others.

A third common myth is that creativity is linked with madness. In other words, to be creative, you must be weird, strange, or abnormal. This suggests that creativity is unhealthy behavior, which should be avoided (Figure 1.1).

In the face of so many common myths and misconceptions, it is a wonder that creativity has been studied seriously at all. However, there is an alternative set of assumptions and beliefs that allow us to be more productive in learning about and developing creativity. Creativity is natural (present in everyone), healthy, enjoyable, important, and complex but understandable.

Although creativity is a complex and challenging concept, with no universally accepted definition, it is understandable. For more than 50 years, people have been studying, reading and writing about, theorizing about, and researching creativity. Many theories have been developed to help us understand and organize the complex nature of creativity. Many research studies have established a body of evidence to guide us in understanding, recognizing, and nurturing creativity.

Rothenberg and Hausman (1976) support the importance of studying creativity. They stated,

> The investigation of creativity is at the forefront of contemporary inquiry because it potentially sheds light on crucial areas in the specific fields of behavioral science and philosophy and, more deeply, because it concerns an issue related to our survival: our understanding and improvement of ourselves and the world at a time when conventional means of understanding and betterment seem outmoded and ineffective. (p. 5)

Creativity is a natural part of being human. It is not reserved for those people with some sort of special gift. This suggests that creativity exists in all people

Figure 1.1   A Common Perception of Creativity

SOURCE: Copyright © 2009. The Creative Problem Solving Group, Inc. Reprinted with permission.

(at different levels and various styles). The challenge arises from learning how to understand and use the creativity you have. This belief is fundamental for those who are interested in identifying what creativity is and understanding how it can be developed.

Accessing and using creativity can release tension and help people lead healthy and more productive lives. Much of the popular creativity literature tends to focus on those stories of unusual artists or scientists who were highly creative and known for rather exotic or strange behavior. We often overlook creative individuals who lead "normal" lives. It can be easy to fall into the trap of believing that people need to display unusual behaviors in order to be creative. In the research conducted on creativity, there is no evidence to suggest that in order to be creative one must be sick, abnormal, or unhealthy. To the contrary, there is some evidence to suggest that learning how to understand and use creativity can be mentally and physically healthy.

Creativity is enjoyable in that using it brings about a sense of satisfaction, accomplishment, and reward. When you learn about and apply your creativity, it can provide you with a sense of peacefulness and joy. Creativity is also important in that the outcomes and consequences of using creativity have benefits for individuals, groups, and organizations. Creativity provides important benefits for all people in their personal life, as well as in their work, and enhances the quality of life for society as a whole.

We are not the first authors to attempt to define creativity. Previous scholars have collected and synthesized dozens, and even hundreds, of different definitions offered by various writers and thinkers (e.g., Treffinger, 1996). For example, Gryskiewicz (1987) defined creativity as novel associations that are useful. This definition came as a result of interviews and analysis of stories of creative performance with approximately 400 managers in organizations. What we like about this definition is that it is simple and has a built-in tension between something being novel and useful. The novelty part of the definition appears to fit well with most people's perceptions of creativity. However, the usefulness part of the definition often stimulates questions in people's minds about whether something needs to be useful in order to be creative. It also raises questions in general about who determines if something is novel or useful, and therefore, who determines if creativity is present or not.

Ruth Noller, Distinguished Service Professor Emeritus of Creative Studies at Buffalo State College, developed a symbolic equation for creativity. She suggested that creativity is a function of an interpersonal attitude toward the beneficial and positive use of creativity in combination with three factors: knowledge, imagination, and evaluation (see Figure 1.2). Children are often viewed as naturally strong in imagination. They often need help in acquiring knowledge and expertise, as well as in understanding appropriate criteria for evaluating ideas or behavior. In comparison, practicing professionals often are seen as having a great deal of knowledge and evaluative strength but as needing help with imagination.

Figure 1.2 Noller's Symbolic Formula for Understanding Creativity

$$C = f_a(K, I, E)$$

Creativity is a function of Knowledge, Imagination, and Evaluation, reflecting an interpersonal attitude toward the beneficial and positive use of creativity.

You might learn a number of lessons from Noller's equation. One is that creativity is a dynamic concept. It changes through our experience. Also, creativity always occurs in some context or domain of knowledge. But, while expertise is important and necessary, it is not sufficient for determining creativity. Finally, creativity involves a dynamic balance between imagination and evaluation.

Despite the many different definitions of creativity, you can make some sense out of them. Just look back to what you wrote down during the first activity in this chapter. As Welsch (1980) indicated,

> The definitions of creativity are numerous, with variations not only in concept, but in the meaning of sub-concepts and of terminology referring to similar ideas. There appears to be, however, a significant level of agreement of key attributes among those persons most closely associated with work in this field. . . . On the basis of the survey of the literature, the following definition is proposed: Creativity is the process of generating unique products by transformation of existing products. These products must be unique only to the creator, and must meet the criteria of purpose and value established by the creator. (p. 107)

Rather than trying to subscribe to one single definition of creativity, we use a broad framework originally offered by Rhodes (1961) to organize the diverse and large numbers of definitions. Rhodes collected 56 definitions of creativity and reported,

> As I inspected my collection I observed that the definitions are not mutually exclusive. They overlap and intertwine. When analyzed, as through a prism, the content of the definitions form four strands. Each strand has unique identity academically, but only in unity do the four strands operate functionally.

Rhodes (like many other scholars) found it more productive to describe creativity within four overlapping themes. These themes include definitions of the characteristics of creative people, the operations within the creative process, the creative results and outcomes, and the context or place for creativity. Isaksen (1984) put these four themes into a Venn diagram (see Figure 1.3) to represent the interaction that occurs among the four elements and the need to consider the whole system to obtain the best picture of creativity.

There are some in the creativity field who feel that this framework is old and tired and that it should be retired or broadened. Unfortunately, most do not offer an alternative. We know of two alternatives that have been offered as general models for outlining inquiry for the broad field of creativity research. One is specifically focused on formulating research (Isaksen, Stein, Hills, & Gryskiewicz, 1984). The other is designed to provide a framework and name for the entire emerging discipline of creativity (Magyari-Beck, 1993).

Those who complain about the "4P's" (person, process, product, and press) model seen in Figure 1.3 present an argument that is similar to complaining about the periodic table of elements. These four broad themes are simply the way creativity has been defined and how it is found in the literature. We see value in this general way to classify our understanding of creativity because it provides a comprehensive model that embraces a number of different and important perspectives on this subject. It also provides a view of the entire system of creativity. We refer to it as a system because each of the four elements is a

Figure 1.3 Systematic Approaches to Creativity

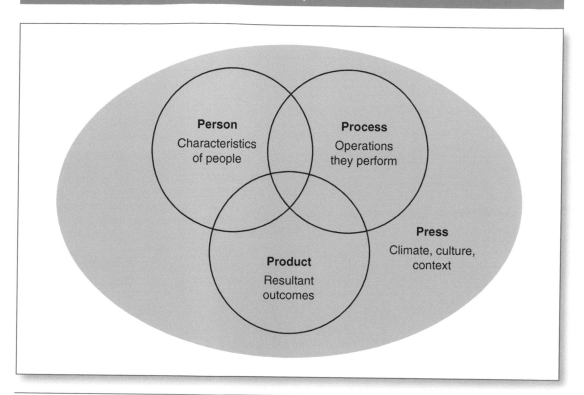

necessary and interrelated part of the whole concept of creativity. Each element influences the other elements. It is difficult to get a complete or true picture of creativity when one part of the system is left out.

The following four subsections will provide you with a short summary of each of the four P's.

Characteristics of Creative People

> *Creative personality is . . . a matter of those patterns of traits that are characteristic of creative persons. A creative pattern is manifest in creative behavior which includes such activities as inventing, designing, contriving, composing, and planning.*

> —J. P. Guilford

Much of the initial interest in creativity among psychologists and others working in applied settings started with curiosity about how highly creative people were able to demonstrate their creativity. Some of the initial approaches to understanding the characteristics of creativity in people involved finding and describing individuals who were generally agreed on as being highly creative. The major challenge facing investigators who followed this approach was in determining how much creativity the individuals had. As a result of this approach, we had a great deal of information regarding the cognitive and affective characteristics of highly creative people.

Early writers in this area often focused on describing creative geniuses, those people who have special and significant talents and gifts. More recently, scholars have taken a more inclusive approach and looked for extraordinary creativity in ordinary people. Most researchers and educators have emphasized the level aspect to creativity in people. The major question for them is "How creative are you?" It was easy with the historical geniuses, but much more difficult if we look at everyday creativity. For example, MacKinnon (1978) indicated that there were many different paths along which people travel toward the full development and expression of their creative potential. Rather than trying to put creative people into a single mold, he said, "the full and complete picturing of the creative person will require many images" (p. 186).

A great deal of this research led to the identification of a large number of characteristics associated with highly creative people (Puccio & Murdock, 1999; Treffinger, Young, Selby, & Shepardson, 2002). However, as you read the sample list in Figure 1.4, you will probably begin asking yourself some important questions such as:

- To be creative, is it necessary to demonstrate all the characteristics in the list? If not, how many?
- Does anyone really demonstrate all those characteristics? All the time? Isn't that a little unlikely?
- Are these "traits" (aspects of your personality that are "with you" all the time) or patterns of behavior that might describe how someone acts once in a while?
- Wouldn't many of the characteristics vary, depending on what task the person might be working on and how she or he feels about and reacts to that task? Might they not also change over time, or in different situations?

These are not easy questions to answer. The traditional view of traits in highly creative people fosters the belief that those characteristics are only held by those at the very top of the spectrum—geniuses and those who are famous for their productions. Clearly, these characteristics may be held by everyone, at all levels, to some degree.

Some people might also believe that these characteristics are fixed and cannot be modified or enhanced. Our experience and research indicate quite clearly that creativity characteristics are dynamic and changeable (see Isaksen, 1987; Isaksen, Murdock, Firestien, & Treffinger, 1993). Although many writers emphasize identifying high or low creativity, the challenge might be more appropriately posed as nurturing and developing creative characteristics within everyone.

A more recent approach to the study of creativity in people concerns how people show the creativity they have. Rather than asking the question, "How creative am I?" it

Figure 1.4   Some Characteristics of Being Creative

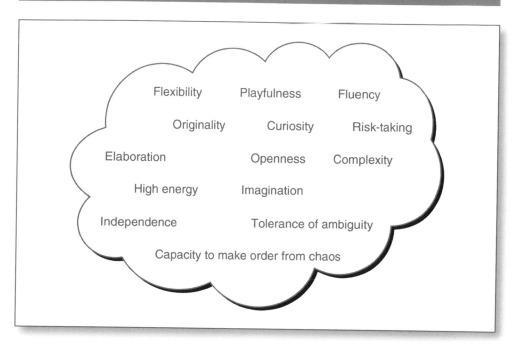

asks the question, "How am I creative?" This question deals more specifically with the form, kind, or style of creativity, rather than the level, degree, or amount.

We believe that it is important to recognize, understand, and access the full spectrum of creative talent in people. This includes the natural diversity in orientation that people have toward creativity, as well as the full range of knowledge, abilities, and skills people bring to the table when solving problems creatively. Understanding your personal creativity, and the creativity of those around you, will help you be more successful in deliberately using your creativity.

You will read more about this area of creativity and its relationship to Creative Problem Solving (CPS) in Chapter 7.

Operations Within the Creative Process

> *The art of thought, like the art of running, or the actor's art of significant gesture, is an attempt to improve by conscious effort an already existing form of human behavior.*
>
> —Graham Wallas

The creative process is also one of our four essential aspects of creativity. It is concerned with how creativity takes place. It examines the mental or cognitive processing, or the thinking that occurs, as people use their creativity. Much of our early research on the creative process involved reports of how highly creative people described the processes they went through to develop their products. This type of investigation is based on the assumption that we can

> take a single achievement or thought—the making of a new generalization or invention, or the potential expressions of a new idea—and ask how it was brought about. We can then roughly dissect out a continuous process, with a beginning and a middle and an end of its own. (Wallas, 1926, p. 79)

One of the challenges to studying the creative process was developing an accurate description of a person's internal thought processes. The goal was to help make the creative process more visible and understandable in order to improve creative thinking. Many different artists, scientists, composers, poets, and inventors made attempts to describe their creative moments. A variety of scholars during the 20th century became interested in productive or reflective thinking and the art of thought (Dewey, 1933; Ghiselin, 1952; Koestler, 1969; Spearman, 1931; Wallas, 1926; Wertheimer, 1945), resulting in many different attempts to describe the best thinking that humans could accomplish.

Wallas (1926) developed one of the early descriptions of the creative process (see Figure 1.5) based on numerous descriptions of famous artists and scientists. He suggested that the art of thought included four stages: (1) preparation (investigating the problem in all directions), (2) incubation (thinking about the problem in a "not conscious" manner), (3) illumination (the appearance of the "happy idea"), and (4) verification (validity testing and reducing the idea to an exact form). This demonstrated that you could deliberately identify the creative process.

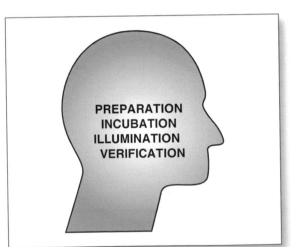

Figure 1.5 Wallas' Creative Process

PREPARATION
INCUBATION
ILLUMINATION
VERIFICATION

In the 1930s, Alex Osborn (1942, 1953) pursued his interest in the human imagination and began reading the research on and experimenting with practical procedures for encouraging creative thinking by the people with whom he worked. His initial description of CPS built on the work of Wallas, Spearman, and others, and helped change the perception that the creative process could only happen intuitively or implicitly. He also worked to develop deliberate strategies for its use in groups.

Another outcome from pursuing an improved understanding has been a diversity of strategies and methods that can be helpful to anyone who is attempting to be deliberately creative. These strategies can include deliberately shifting your perception about a problem by using analogies or metaphors, setting aside the problem to allow for incubation and insight, or seeking inspiration from great works of music or art. There are as many strategies as there are stories from highly creative people about their creativity.

Removing Blocks and Barriers. Many of the strategies for increasing your personal creativity come from an understanding and removal of your personal barriers or blocks to creative thinking. You may notice that in some situations you feel confident about yourself and your ability to succeed in a particular task, while in other situations you do not. As depicted in Figure 1.6, one aspect of your approach to creativity is your awareness of blocks to creative thinking and behavior.

It is only natural to have some resistance to novelty. Novelty requires you to change the approach, behavior, or way of thinking. It requires new learning and may increase the possibility of failure. Your internal climate is most likely formed as a result of some interaction between who you are and the environment or situation in which you operate. One of the ways to reduce the effects of blocks and barriers is to increase the likelihood of developing your strengths. Another way to overcome barriers is to

Figure 1.6   Blocks to Creative Thinking

SOURCE: Copyright © 2009. The Creative Problem Solving Group, Inc. Reprinted with permission.

know what they are and whether or not they are keeping you from productively making use of your strengths. You will overcome obstacles more effectively when you are conscious of their presence and impact.

There are three broad, overlapping categories of blocks: personal, problem solving, and environmental (situational). Examples of personal blocks include lack of self-confidence or self-image; a tendency to conform; a need for the familiar, habit-bound thinking; emotional numbness; saturation; excessive enthusiasm; various values and cultural influences; and lack of imaginative control.

As an example of personal blocks, Jones (1987) discovered four major categories of barriers in the literature. These included strategic, value, perceptual, and self-image barriers. Strategic barriers relate to the inability to see and use a variety of possibilities for problem solving. Examples of strategic barriers include resistance to using imagination, an inability to tolerate uncertainty, and the inability to keep an open viewpoint to new ideas.

Value barriers reflect the lack of flexibility displayed in applying personal values, beliefs, and attitudes. Examples of this kind of barrier include being rigidly custom bound, having a strong desire to conform to preexisting patterns, and having dogmatically negative attitudes toward creative thinking.

Perceptual barriers relate to seeing things in rigidly familiar ways and usually involve aspects of sensual acuity and awareness of the environment. Having difficulty in seeing a problem from a variety of viewpoints, imposing unnecessary constraints, failing to use all the senses, and stereotyping are examples of this kind of barrier.

Self-image barriers describe conditions where people do not assert themselves or make use of available resources. Sometimes, people have an extreme fear of failure, have a reluctance to exert influence, or simply fail to take advantage of resources around them. These barriers are easily related to other problem-solving and situational blocks.

Problem-solving blocks are strategies, skills, or behaviors that inhibit your ability to focus and direct problem-solving activities, generate and identify options and alternatives, or turn ideas into action. Some problem-solving blocks include solution fixedness, premature judgments, habit transfer, using poor problem-solving approaches, lack of disciplined effort, poor language skills, various perceptual patterns that limit intake, and rigidity.

Environmental blocks are those factors in your context, situation, or setting that interfere with your problem-solving efforts. Environmental (situational) blocks to creativity include the belief that only one type of thinking is required for creative outcomes, resistance to new ideas, isolation, a negative attitude toward creative thinking, autocratic decision making, reliance on experts, various strategic blocks that limit the use of resources, and an overemphasis on competition or cooperation. We will look more deeply into these barriers and the conditions necessary for their removal in the section on the context for creativity.

We believe that most creativity methods today share common core foundations and relate to the creative process outlined by Wallas and Osborn. Although these methods may appear distinct on the surface, they are likely to be guided by solid foundational principles associated with how highly creative people naturally use their creativity.

Work on understanding the creative process continues today. Beyond the work of those who follow the tradition established by Osborn, there are practical books such as *Creating Minds* (Gardner, 1993) and *The Mind's Best Work* (Perkins, 1981). In addition, there have been advances in cognition and neuroscience that can provide even further insight into the nature of the creative process (Boden, 1991; Carroll, 1993; Dietrich, 2007; Kaufmann, Helstrup, & Teigen, 1995; Ward, 2004, 2007).

This book is mainly about a particular approach to understanding the creative process, called Creative Problem Solving. An overview of this approach is more fully described in Chapter 2.

Creative Results and Outcomes

Creativity may be defined, quite simply, as the ability to bring something new into existence.

—Frank Barron

Creative products or outcomes come in a variety of sizes and shapes and from many different contexts. Many people think of an outstanding play or novel, an inspiring painting or song, or a significant invention or discovery when they think about creative products. They are not limited to either the arts or the sciences. Creative products can be found in the arts, the sciences, the humanities, or any other discipline or domain of human endeavor. They can be the result of the efforts of individuals or groups. They may have varying degrees of novelty and usefulness.

Creative products can be both tangible and intangible. They may be concrete or "touchable," such as an invention or marketable product. Other creative outcomes can be intangible, such as learning and personal development, the development of a new service or improvement of an existing one, social technology, or the design of a new process or methodology.

For many people, this area of study has been called "innovation" rather than "creativity" because of the focus on product rather than process (see Figure 1.7 for other distinctions). Since innovation is often considered to be the commercialization of a new idea, we see it as a part of the creativity system outlined above. The reasons some prefer to use the term *innovation* over *creativity* include the need to focus on obtaining concrete

Figure 1.7 Creativity Versus Innovation

CREATIVITY	INNOVATION
Imagination	Implementation
Process	Product
Generating	Developing
Novelty	Usefulness
Soft	Hard

results, preferring to stay focused on what is useful and easier to understand, and the need to avoid such fuzzy concepts as people and process. Our position is simple. You can have creativity without innovation, but you cannot have innovation without creativity (see Isaksen & Tidd, 2006).

MacKinnon (1975) pointed out the importance of studying creative products. He stated:

> In a very real sense . . . the study of creative products is the basis on which all research on creativity rests and, until this foundation is more solidly built than it is at present, all creativity research will leave something to be desired. . . . In short, it would appear that the explicit determination of the qualities which identify creative products has been largely neglected just because we implicitly know—or feel we know—a creative product when we see it. (pp. 69–71)

An interesting approach to examining the characteristics of creative products or outcomes has been developed by Besemer (Besemer, 1997; Besemer & O'Quin, 1987, 1993, 1999; Besemer & Treffinger, 1981). She and her colleagues developed ways to assess the creativity in a particular product or outcome, using a paper-and-pencil rating scale. Their assessment, initially called the Creative Product Analysis Matrix, and subsequently changed to the Creative Product Semantic Scale (Besemer, 2006; O'Quin & Besemer, 1989), is based on asking people to identify the characteristics required in a product for it to be considered creative.

As shown in Figure 1.8, creative products and outcomes can be evaluated on the three dimensions of novelty, resolution, and style. The novelty dimension examines the amount of newness or originality contained in a product. The resolution dimension examines how well the product solves the problem for which it is developed. The third dimension, style, focuses on the extent that a product extends beyond the basic requirements needed to solve a problem. The style factor examines the kind of elaboration or synthesis that has gone into creating an outcome with simple elegance. It considers, for example, factors such as packaging and presentation, how well crafted or attractive it is.

Many organizations involved in new product development have a similar process for analyzing and developing new concepts. One of the Dun and Bradstreet companies conducted a study of 51 U.S. companies. Figure 1.9 shows the results of the study. Note that, on average, it took more than 50 ideas to get one successful new product. These were

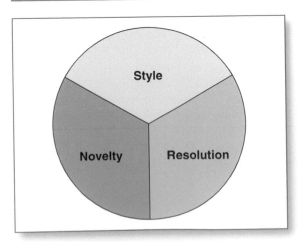

Figure 1.8 Besemer's Characteristics of Creative Products

Figure 1.9 Creative Product Decay Curve Identified in Dun and Bradstreet Study

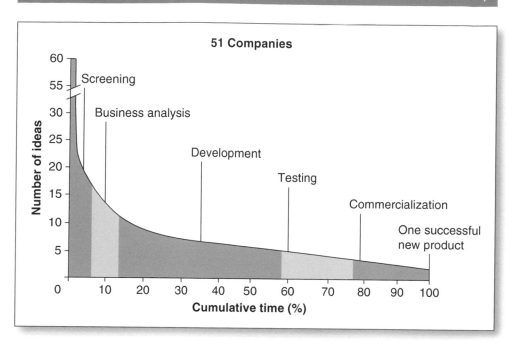

ideas that were screened or selected for further business analysis. More recent research from the private sector indicates that those organizations that are very successful in commercializing new ideas generate and nurture more than 100 ideas per day (Davis, 2000). Still others have found that it depends on when you start to count the ideas. For example, Stevens and Burley (1997) found that it can take as many as 3,000 raw, unwritten ideas to result in about 300 ideas submitted to a more formal idea-screening process. Evidently, it takes an idea-rich environment to produce creative products.

Current trends in many of the organizations within which we work point to some interesting implications for new concept and product development. Many organizations are trying to shorten the amount of time it takes to come up with successful new products. They are also trying to push more ideas through the entire process so that more than one successful new product will result.

This is having an effect on the kinds of new products being developed. Decreasing time, increasing throughput, and other demands on the new product development process appear to be reducing the occurrence of highly novel products. Instead, this trend seems to promote an increase in the frequency of useful and stylistically modified products. For example, Tide™ was a very new product for Procter & Gamble when it was first produced. Tide with Bleach™ is a new product, which is lower in novelty but emphasizes usefulness. The net result of the trend is that we are able to see more and more modifications and improvements on existing product lines (within many markets). Examining product and services lines, as well as examining customer demands, can be fruitful applications of the measure developed by Besemer. Inventors and companies can target the kind of new development they desire to meet market needs.

The development and nature of creative products and outcomes offers a fruitful and important aspect within various conceptions of creativity. Inventions, discoveries, innovations, and the development of new and improved services and products offer both tangible and intangible evidence of the significance and value of understanding creativity and its many applications. Recent developments in this area of creativity help to go beyond the traditional emphasis on products being new and useful. The third dimension of stylistic elaboration and synthesis, made evident through recent research, has expanded and extended our view of creative outcomes. The development of creative products and inventions is increasingly seen as a collaborative effort. Many organizations are attempting to shorten the product development cycle by involving all the relevant areas in cross-functional teams. This illustrates how creative people can work together to create products or outcomes in particular places using a certain kind of creative method. This serves as just one example of how the four areas of the system are related.

The Context for Creativity

Be brave enough to live creatively. The creative place is where no one else has been. You have to leave the city of your comfort and go into the wilderness of your intuition. You can't get there by bus, only by hard work, risking and by not quite knowing what you're doing. What you'll discover will be wonderful—yourself.

—Alan Alda

The creative context concerns the environment, place, situation, or climate in which creativity takes place. It examines those factors that promote or inhibit creative behavior. Those conducting inquiry into the creative climate ask questions such as, "What stops people from using their creativity?" "What is the environment, context, or situation that is most conducive to creativity?" "How can someone establish a climate that encourages the release and development of creativity?"

Press was the early word used to describe this broad area because it meant the interaction between the person and the situation. Factors in the environment pushed or pulled the person, while factors, actions, and qualities within the person pushed and pulled on the environment. When you consider the kind of blocks and barriers listed earlier that come from the situation (such as those identified in Figure 1.10), you can see how the climate can exert pressure on the individual. The entire interaction was labeled "press."

What is the environment like in which creativity can flourish? Research on organizational obstacles to creativity done by the Center for Creative Learning, Inc. (Burnside, Amabile, & Gryskiewicz, 1988) yielded a variety of barriers to innovation,

Figure 1.10 Barriers to Innovation

SOURCE: Copyright © 2009. The Creative Problem Solving Group, Inc. Reprinted with permission.

including various organizational characteristics (inappropriate reward systems being overly bureaucratic, lack of cooperation across functions, etc.), lack of freedom in deciding what to do or how to approach a task or problem, perceived apathy toward task accomplishment, poor project management, perceived inappropriate evaluation systems, insufficient resources, insufficient time, and emphasis on the status quo.

The same research approach identified a variety of organizational stimulants to creativity. These include freedom in deciding what to do or how to accomplish the task, good project management, sufficient resources, management exhibiting enthusiasm for ideas—creating a generally nonthreatening and open environment, a collaborative atmosphere across levels and divisions, a general sense that creative work will receive appropriate feedback, recognition, and reward, sufficient time, challenge due to the intriguing nature of the problem, its importance to the organization, or the context of the problem, and a sense of urgency that is internally generated.

Our research on the environment supporting creativity is built on the dimensions of the climate for innovation and creativity studied by Ekvall of the Swedish Employment Security Council and the University of Lund (Isaksen & Ekvall, 2007). We will provide more information regarding the context for creativity and how it affects CPS in Chapter 8.

The following list of suggestions for creating or maintaining a climate for creativity draws on the research of many scholars. It is not a totally comprehensive or conclusive list. In short, these suggestions provide recommendations to help you shape an atmosphere conducive to creativity and innovation. The items on this list are necessary for creativity to take place, although other factors may need to be present as well.

1. Provide freedom to try new ways of performing tasks; allow and encourage each individual to achieve success in an area and in a way possible for him or her; encourage divergent approaches by providing resources and room rather than controls and limitations.

2. Point out the value of individual differences, styles, and points of view by permitting the activities, tasks, or other means to be different for various individuals.

3. Establish an open, safe atmosphere by supporting and reinforcing unusual ideas and responses of individuals when engaged in both creative/exploratory and critical/developmental thinking.

4. Build a feeling of individual control over what is to be done and how it might best be done by encouraging individuals to have choices and involving them in goal-setting and decision-making processes.

5. Support the learning and application of specific CPS tools and skills in the workplace and on tasks that are appropriate.

6. Provide an appropriate amount of time for the accomplishment of tasks; provide the right amount of work in a realistic time frame.

7. Provide a nonpunitive environment by communicating that you have confidence in the individuals with whom you work. Reduce concern of failure by using mistakes as positives to help individuals realize errors and meet acceptable standards and provide affirmative feedback and judgment.

8. Recognize some previously unrecognized and unused potential. Challenge individuals to solve problems and work on new tasks in new ways. Ask provocative questions.

9. Respect an individual's need to work alone or in groups. Encourage self-initiated projects.

10. Tolerate complexity and disorder, at least for a period. Even the best organization and planning requires clear goals and some degree of flexibility.

11. Create a climate of mutual respect and acceptance among individuals so that they will share, develop, and learn cooperatively. Encourage a feeling of interpersonal trust and teamwork.

12. Encourage a high quality of interpersonal relationships and be aware of factors such as a spirit of cooperation, open confrontation and resolution of conflicts, and the encouragement of expression of ideas.

The four themes for understanding creativity (people, context, method, and outcome) will be examined throughout the book. We will keep these four perspectives in mind to help ensure that we take a comprehensive and holistic perspective to providing you with creative approaches to problem solving. As Rhodes (1961) concluded, the themes overlap and intertwine. The best and most comprehensive picturing of creativity will require the interaction of all four themes. In short, creativity is not a simple thing—it is multidimensional. Although we have made some progress in introducing some science to the field, we will never reduce the wonder inherent in human creativity. We believe that taking a holistic approach will increase your chances of successfully solving problems. However, what is problem solving and how does it relate to creativity?

What Is Problem Solving?

> *Nothing is more interesting for humans than human activity and the most characteristically human activity is solving problems; thinking for a purpose, devising means to some desired end.*

> —George Polya

In the Creativity and Problem Solving word listing activity, we often get a wide variety of words associated with problem solving. In some situations, people associate problem solving with overcoming a difficulty or avoiding some sort of pain. They focus their attention on the word *problem* and perceive it as a bad thing or something to be removed. However, in other situations, people associate problem solving with words such as logic, analysis, structure, closing a gap, meeting a need, overcoming difficulties, making something work better, mathematics, and science.

We take the stance that problem solving is a process of closing the gap between what is and what is desired. It is the act of answering questions, clearing up uncertainties, or explaining something that was not previously understood. You engage in problem solving while conducting day-to-day activities such as adding up grocery totals or figuring out how to find a particular building, office, or product. You may try to remember important birthdays, figure out what to do for someone special in your life, or try to find information to help you with a school project. You may also face more important or significant issues that require problem solving. For example, you may need to replace your car or home, make decisions about family holidays, determine the best courses to take at a university, or give tough feedback to an employee.

Problem solving generally involves devising ways to answer questions and to meet or satisfy a situation which presents a challenge, offers an opportunity, or is a concern. It involves closing the gap between what you have and what you want. The search for answers is often based on your expertise or existing knowledge. Many times, the area of the challenge is well-defined, with clear pathways and methods for solution. The opportunity may also offer clear-cut boundaries, priorities, roles, and directions for effective or even "correct" answers. There are a number of highly effective approaches you can use for problem solving in situations with these characteristics. Here are some examples:

- Check the literature (Has someone else already provided a perfectly appropriate and useful solution to this problem, or to one very similar to it?)

- Use existing or previous solutions from history (What has been successful for other people in similar circumstances?)

- Hire a consultant (Can an outsider bring a new perspective that will reveal a good option that was too obvious for you to see yourself? Will a consultant's past experience save you time, effort, and money?)

- Delegate the task (Should this situation be handled by someone else? Even though it seems like it's just "passing the buck," might that be the best response?)

- Just do it (If you really know what you ought to be doing, but you have been procrastinating or avoiding it, why not just get it over with?)

- Research it (Might the situation be handled effectively by conducting an experiment, a field study, or a pilot project?)

- Form a committee or task force (Might a few key people come up with a productive strategy efficiently and promptly?)

- Read the manual (As the sign says, "When all else fails, try reading the directions.")

- Use existing algorithms (Is there a formula or existing set of procedures that has been designed specifically for situations just like this?)

These approaches can be powerful in a variety of situations. However, when might you need a creative approach to problem solving?

What Is a Creative Approach?

We say that this book is about a creative approach to problem solving. What does that mean? An approach is simply the way you move toward, advance, or come closer to something. In the context of this book, an approach is a way of making change happen. There are at least two different kinds of approaches to making change happen; creative and non-creative. A creative approach implies that you are attempting to advance toward an outcome that is new, unstructured, and open ended. These situations often involve an ill-structured problem and unknown solutions. Although you need to use your knowledge and skills for evaluation, a creative approach requires you to engage your imagination, as well as your intelligence, during your approach because no ready-made answer exists. It also requires you to take a more comprehensive view and use the entire system of people, method, content, and context in the approach.

Using a creative approach also implies that you have a courageous attitude; one that includes being open to new experiences, embracing ambiguity, and venturing into new and unfamiliar territory. This attitude is often necessary because creative approaches are about helping you move from a place with which you are familiar to one that is different and potentially unknown, and the results of your efforts are potentially uncertain. To demonstrate what we mean by creative approaches to problem solving, consider the approaches identified in Table 1.1.

Table 1.1 Examples of Creative Approaches to Problem Solving

Actively constructing many and varied opportunities and identifying the more promising ones to explore and examine more fully. Being open to many different possibilities and maintaining a positive attitude. Solving future-focused problems that do not even exist today.
Examining facts, impressions, feelings, and opinions from many different points of view. Being willing to dig deeper under assumptions.
Seeing the problem or challenge from many different viewpoints. Being able to play with possibilities.
Generating many, varied, and unusual ideas that have high potential to address the problem or meet the challenge in a fresh and valuable way. Being able to think up and suspend judgment when needed. Having idea power.
Investing energy and talent in taking a wild or highly unusual idea and shaping, refining, and developing the idea into a workable solution. Being persistent.
Considering aspects of the situation surrounding the solution to enable agreement of your solutions by others. Being sensitive to the context and the people who may be involved with your solution and working to obtain support and acceptance.
Having a variety of possible approaches to take for any given situation, challenge, or problem. Being aware of the power of process.
Reflecting on many different factors in determining your approach.

Let's also illustrate what we mean by a noncreative approach to problem solving. Table 1.2 contains specific examples of what we would judge to be noncreative approaches to problem solving.

Table 1.2   Examples of Non-Creative Approaches to Problem Solving
Mindlessly defending the status quo. Being resistant to exploring new opportunities.
Making and acting on faulty assumptions or incorrect data.
Seeing the problem or challenge in only one way.
Applying worn-out or habitual responses that don't have the desired effect or fail to solve the real problem.
Overlooking the need to improve, develop, or refine a tentative solution.
Moving on before ensuring agreement and acceptance by others (premature completion or conclusion).
Using an approach uncritically, just because it may have provided relief or results before.
Reacting to a situation before reflecting on alternative ways of responding.

Creative approaches to problem solving enable you to better use the knowledge and skills you already have. They deliberately link creativity and problem solving.

Linking Creativity and Problem Solving

When we present our approach, some people become concerned about the relationship between the concepts of creativity and problem solving. They often ask, "Are you saying that creativity is the same as problem solving?" This idea of linking creativity and problem solving seems to create some tension for some people. One of the challenges we faced in writing this book was to demonstrate the productive links between creativity and problem solving that will help you get the best from both forms of thinking.

Researchers have explored links between creativity and problem solving before and have come up with a variety of answers (Isaksen, 1995). For example, Guilford (1977) suggested that problem solving and creative thinking were closely related. Creative thinking produced new outcomes, and problem solving involved producing novel responses and outcomes to new situations. Problem solving often has creative aspects, but creativity is not always problem solving. Newell, Shaw, and Simon (1962) suggested that "creative activity appears . . . simply to be a special class of problem-solving activity characterized by novelty, unconventionality, persistence, and difficulty in problem formulation" (p. 63).

Rather than keeping creativity separate from problem solving, our approach has been to deliberately link the two. Our approach is designed to apply both your imagination and your intelligence, to generate as well as focus, to use logic and memory as well as emotion and synthesis. The opportunity created by linking these two concepts is that you have a very diverse collection of strategies, tools, and approaches, enabling you to handle a wide variety of challenges and opportunities.

Linking creativity and problem solving is an example of Janusian thinking. This kind of thinking is named after the Roman god Janus. The reason Janus was chosen as the inspiration behind Janusian thinking is that he had to look in two opposing directions at the same time. As the god of doorways, he looked outside and inside at the same time. Rothenberg (1971) used this attribute to coin the phrase Janusian thinking. He (Rothenberg, 1999) described the Janusian process as

> actively conceiving multiple opposites or antitheses simultaneously. . . . During the course of the creative process, opposite or antithetical ideas, concepts, or propositions are consciously conceptualized as simultaneously coexisting. Although seemingly illogical and self-contradictory, these formulations are constructed in clearly logical and rational states of mind to produce creative effects. They occur as early conceptions in the development of scientific theories and artworks and at critical junctures at middle and later stages of the creative process; these simultaneous antitheses or simultaneous opposites usually undergo transformation and modification and are seldom directly discernable in final creative products. (p. 103)

Rothenberg (1979, 1996) provided evidence that this kind of process exists in both the arts and sciences, and in most creative endeavors. He has collected historical and anecdotal evidence, as well as a large amount of data from his psychiatric practice, to support his theory (Rothenberg, 1998).

Active and simultaneous consideration of opposites appears to be a key aspect of creating new and useful responses across a variety of fields. We find support for this idea from a number of key creativity researchers and writers, particularly those who are interested in the creative process. At the core, Janusian thinking is an attempt to describe an aspect of the creative process, a process that is in motion and is dynamic. Deliberately linking creativity and problem solving allows you to take a Janusian stance when you face challenges and opportunities.

A Framework for Change

We often hear the expression, "Change is inevitable, growth is optional." Unfortunately, we do not know who originally said it. However, it fits nicely when talking about a framework for change. This book provides our current description of CPS, a system that organizes creative approaches to problem solving. The system contains an explicit, yet flexible, framework, language, and suite of tools you can use to productively guide the changes you want throughout your life—at home, at school, and at work.

Change will happen. That is a given. CPS is designed to help you address change in a way that enables you to grow and prosper. Whether you are stimulating changes yourself, or responding to changes brought on by others, the CPS framework provides you with a flexible structure you can use to enhance your effectiveness at using your creativity to make change productive. You can use the framework to address your need for change on a personal level. You can use it to work more effectively with others in a group or team to make change happen. The framework can also be used to change and improve the quality of life and work within organizational settings, and indeed, for society as a whole.

Part of the CPS system is an explicit framework containing components and stages. The components will help you gain clarity about the change you need to make, help you create ideas for what the change might look like, and help you develop powerful solutions and plans for making the change happen. They will also help you take into consideration the whole picture surrounding a desired change to help you be more effective at making the change happen. Whether it takes 10 minutes to complete or multiple years to plan and initiate the change, the CPS framework is flexible enough to support your efforts.

You will find that the CPS framework serves as a menu from which you can choose specific components, stages, tools, and language. You only need to use the part of the framework that suits your needs for a given change you want to create. You can use the elements of the framework in any order or sequence, depending on your specific needs at the time. Therefore, we will show you the items on the menu in the initial chapters of the book, and then demonstrate how you can put the elements of the menu together in the later chapters of the book. Now let's look more closely at the framework of CPS.

Putting This Chapter to Work

This chapter has been focused on defining what we mean by CPS. We examined some of the conceptions of creativity and problem solving, and then linked the two to better understand creative approaches to problem solving.

Activities to Guide Reflection and Action

Work on one or more of the following activities to review your understanding of the material in this chapter and to practice applying the content in real situations. If you are using this book as part of a course or study group, you may wish to work individually and then compare your responses or to work collaboratively as a team.

1. Become a myth spotter. Be on the lookout for when people use the term *creative* or *creativity*, and see if they are holding on to any of the nonproductive conceptions of creativity.

2. Try generating a list of things that might benefit from a more creative approach to problem solving versus a more traditional approach. Try keeping a journal or create a blog to record or share these creative challenges.

3. Think about someone who strikes you as a creative person. Then list those characteristics that support your impressions. Compare those you listed against some of those included in this chapter.

4. Think about a time or place in which you felt particularly creative. List the characteristics of that occasion—what supported your creativity? Compare your answers with the description of the creative environment included in this chapter.

Creative
Problem Solving

The creative process is the emergence in action of a novel relational product growing out of the uniqueness of the individual on the one hand, and the materials, events, people, or circumstances of his life on the other.

—Carl Rogers

The purposes of Chapter 2 are to provide you with an introduction to Creative Problem Solving (CPS) and a brief overview of the specific components, stages, phases, and tools within CPS. After studying Chapter 2, you should be able to do the following:

1. Define creative problem solving.

2. Create an illustration, diagram, chart, or drawing to represent your own natural creative problem-solving process.

3. Describe the three process components and six stages of CPS, and explain ways in which these are similar to or different from your personal creative problem-solving process.

4. Offer reasons why the management component called Planning Your Approach is different from the three process components.

5. Describe the relationship between generating and focusing as two complementary kinds of thinking used during CPS.

6. Identify four important guidelines for generating and four important guidelines for focusing.

7. Identify the principal CPS tools used for generating and focusing.

In this chapter, we will introduce and examine CPS as a framework for thinking, problem solving, and managing change. CPS provides a basic structure to guide people in two complementary kinds of thinking—generating possibilities and focusing their thinking—when working to solve problems or manage change. The structure of CPS also includes a variety of tools to assist with understanding and focusing on challenges, generating ideas, and preparing to take action on new opportunities. The framework provides a menu to help you organize and choose tools, helpful language, and approaches. You will be able to use CPS on a wide variety of challenges and opportunities requiring useful novelty.

We will define the basic structure of the framework and explain its current graphic format. In this chapter, we will introduce the concepts of generating and focusing, the key guidelines for using CPS, and several specific tools you will be applying in the rest of the book.

What Is Creative Problem Solving?

Early interest in the creative process focused on the natural approaches highly creative people took in using their creativity in problem solving. One of the challenges for researchers and professionals over the years has been to help make these creative processes more visible, explicit, and deliberate. This challenge has guided our efforts through several generations of work on the creative problem-solving process. Parnes, Noller, and Biondi (1977) equated CPS with creative decision making, suggesting that "we first speculate on what 'might be' . . . we sense and anticipate all conceivable consequences or repercussions . . . and we choose and develop our best alternative in full awareness" (p. 14). Noller (1979) defined creative problem solving by offering a definition of each of the three main words: creative, problem, and solving.

> By creative we mean: having an element of newness and being relevant at least to you, the one who creates the solution. By problem we mean: any situation which presents a challenge, offers an opportunity, or is a concern to you. By solving we mean: devising ways to answer or to meet or satisfy the problem, adapting yourself to the situation or adapting the situation to yourself. Creative Problem Solving or CPS is a process, a method, a system for approaching a problem in an imaginative way resulting in effective action. (pp. 4–5)

CPS is a broadly applicable framework for organizing specific tools to help you design and develop new and useful outcomes. The structure of CPS provides an organizing system. Using the system involves applying productive thinking tools to understanding problems and opportunities; generating many, varied, and unusual ideas; and evaluating, developing, and implementing potential solutions. The system includes the framework of components, stages, phases, and tools, as well as considering the people involved, the situation or context, and the nature of the content or the desired outcomes. CPS enables individuals and groups to recognize and act on opportunities, respond to challenges, and overcome concerns.

The Origins and History of CPS

We credit Alex F. Osborn as the person who originally developed CPS. He was a founding partner of the Batten, Barton, Durstine and Osborn advertising agency and was very interested in the human imagination. He was also very concerned about releasing creative human talent in individuals and within organizations. He began experimenting with CPS in the 1930s and is well-known for originating brainstorming. In his book *Applied Imagination* (1953), he described the initial model of CPS. Osborn continued to read extensively about creativity and to apply the process and tools he developed with a variety of colleagues and friends.

Osborn's work had a profound influence on those interested in the deliberate development and use of imagination. *Applied Imagination* was reprinted many times and translated into many languages. It has become a classic for anyone interested in the subject of creativity. He founded the Buffalo-based Creative Education Foundation in 1954, with the vision of bringing a more creative trend to education. A journal dedicated to the subject of creativity was launched in 1967. That same year, an academic program was founded in Buffalo that provided the unique opportunity for some important experimental research and development.

Our view of CPS emerged through more than 50 years of research, development, and experience in many different programs and settings. We have been part of three generations of collaborative work through which many colleagues applied and advanced Osborn's original ideas. The historical development of our CPS framework is documented in greater detail in Isaksen and Dorval (1993), Isaksen, Dorval, Noller, and Firestien (1993), Isaksen and Treffinger (1985, 2004), Isaksen, Treffinger, and Dorval (1997), Parnes (1992), Treffinger (2000), and Treffinger and Isaksen (2005).

In this book, we focus on the CPS framework as it has evolved through our research, development, and field experience across several decades. There are also other variations of CPS that share the same historical roots as ours and other change models based on different foundations. A detailed explanation and comparison of those is beyond the scope of this book, although we will provide an overview of them in Chapter 10.

Personal Process Activity

All of us face problems to solve, decisions to make, and opportunities to pursue on a daily basis. You encounter these situations on the job, at school, and at home. In dealing with them over time, you have learned some specific problem-solving approaches or strategies that work well. In other situations, you may have learned what does not work well and you may need to acquire additional strategies to be more effective.

Our purpose in this book is to help you understand CPS as a means to broaden and strengthen your personal problem-solving approaches or strategies. It does not ask you to leave behind all the learning, practice, and experience you have had in using your creativity to solve problems. We challenge you to find ways to use CPS to enhance your personal problem-solving process.

Activity 2.1 Draw Your Natural Creative Process

1. Think back to a problem situation that was . . .
   - real.
   - in need of a new approach.
   - challenging.
   - motivating.
   - something you could influence.
   - dealt with successfully.

2. Design, illustrate, or draw your personal creative process.

3. Share your drawing with your group.

4. Identify similarities and differences.

5. Share key findings with the larger group.

Because our goal is to enhance and extend your process, not replace it, it may be helpful for you to examine your own natural problem-solving process before we talk further about CPS. Activity 2.1 asks you to think about a problem that you have solved and describe the process you went through to solve it. Rather than describing it in words, the activity asks you to design, illustrate, or draw the process in the space provided. Once your process is on paper, you will be able to see how it relates to other drawings of natural processes.

We have asked hundreds of students, scientists, artists, and professionals to do this exercise. We have observed similarities and differences among the wide range of creative process drawings produced by this diversity of people. Some similarities include using similar symbols or words to describe the process; identifying similar stages in the process; and being able to identify a specific process used on a task. Some differences include the number of stages involved in a process; the time taken in each process stage; and the amount of emotion present in the process. Table 2.1 contains the most

---

Table 2.1 Similarities and Differences Among Natural Creative Processes

SIMILARITIES	DIFFERENCES
Problems were identified	Amount of words and pictures
Used common symbols	Level of detail in process
Successful action was taken	Nature of the task
Able to identify a process	Amount of time spent in process stages
Generated ideas to solve problem	Levels of emotion displayed in process

common similarities and differences between processes participants have generated as a result of completing this activity.

You are likely to have more than one creative problem-solving process available to use, and the process you use may depend on the kind of task, the deadlines, your need to involve others, or the amount of support available. These factors will influence the kind, sequence, and duration of different activities involved in your processes.

Having a comfortable, natural framework helps you use your creativity more effectively to solve problems. The framework should be designed to support your personal process, not replace it. It should share some common elements with the processes used by others but also be flexible enough to meet the unique needs of different situations or varying groups working together.

Did you find at some point in your personal process that you generated ideas to solve the problem? Did you determine what the problem was that you were trying to solve? Did you implement the ideas you developed? Although the order, description, and amount of time spent in each activity may have been different, these aspects of problem solving often appear in many different illustrations of process. Any effective process framework should identify these components of the activities as well as provide a common language with which they can be described. However, in behavior, the process may not play out in the same way. How you actually use your creative process may depend on the factors identified in Figure 2.1.

Figure 2.1   Some Factors That Influence Your Creative Process

FACTORS INFLUENCING PROCESS

The process you use depends on:

- The number of people involved
- Where you are in the hierarchy
- Who is responsible
- What skills you need to learn
- How important it is to you

- The other methods being used
- Whether you have tried something already and failed
- The other things you are doing in parallel
- How you got into the mess
- Whether you have strategy

- Your objective
- What you want or need
- How you know when you're done
- How well you know the problem
- The kind of change you need

- The culture around the issue
- The level of strategic priority
- Your budget
- How much time you have
- The roadblocks you see

The CPS Framework

CPS can be described at several different levels. At the most general level, CPS is composed of four components (three *process* components and one *management* component). *Components* are general areas or categories of activity people deal with when they are solving problems creatively. The process components of CPS include Understanding the Challenge, Generating Ideas, and Preparing for Action; the management component is Planning Your Approach.

Within each component, there are specific stages. A *stage* is a smaller, more specific level of operation within CPS. The CPS framework includes eight specific stages, within the four components. The stages within Understanding the Challenge are Constructing Opportunities, Exploring Data, and Framing Problems. Generating Ideas includes only one stage with the same name as the component. Preparing for Action includes Developing Solutions and Building Acceptance. The Planning Your Approach management component includes the two stages of Appraising Tasks and Designing Process.

At the next and more specific level, each CPS stage in the three process components has two *phases*. One is a *generating* phase in which you come up with or generate many, varied, and unusual options. The other is a *focusing* phase in which you analyze, develop, or refine options. Together, these phases emphasize the dynamic balance between two different kinds of thinking we call "generating" and "focusing."

Finally, the most specific level of the CPS framework involves tools for generating or focusing options. We use the term *tool* to describe any structured approach used in performing an operation as part of a CPS effort. Tools guide your behavior during the generating and focusing phases of CPS. The CPS toolbox, included later in this chapter, describes the generating and focusing tools that are often used during any application of CPS.

Knowing the specific language we use for the various parts of the framework will help you learn and apply CPS effectively and efficiently. In particular, when everyone knows and uses the same names for things, confusion is minimized. This is important particularly when individuals need to work together to solve novel problems.

Having a common language is not enough for an effective problem-solving framework. An effective framework should be able to assist your communication by using a common set of symbols and figures as well as words and phrases. We depict the CPS framework as a graphic model in the following figures. As indicated in Figure 2.2, the illustration of CPS graphically identifies the framework's four main components.

Problem solvers do not necessarily apply these components, stages, or tools in any particular order or for any predetermined, fixed length of time. As we noted in the personal process activity, the order or sequence of steps and stages in natural problem solving is not always the same. The CPS framework should be used to describe the kinds of activities that might take place during natural problem solving, not to specify a fixed or rigid order or sequence of their application.

Figure 2.2   CPS Version 6.1™

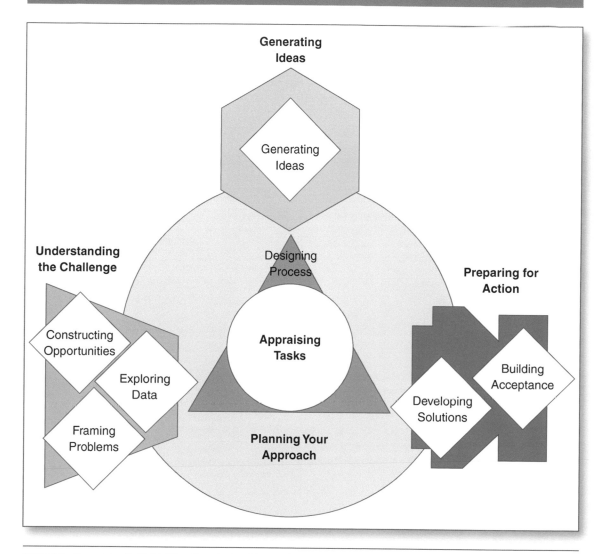

In the next sections of this chapter, we will overview the components of CPS and the stages contained within them. Each of these components will also be considered in greater detail in succeeding chapters (Understanding the Challenge in Chapter 3, Generating Ideas in Chapter 4, and Preparing for Action in Chapter 5). We will provide an overview of the Planning Your Approach component and the Appraising Tasks and Designing Process stages in Chapter 6.

Understanding the Challenge

This component deals with gaining a clear focus for your problem-solving efforts. Often a major breakthrough can occur by simply ensuring that you are working on the right problem. Preparing and stating the problem, challenge, or opportunity is very often what helps you find and use productive answers. The function of the three stages of this component (Constructing Opportunities, Exploring Data, and Framing Problems) is to help you develop a clear area of concern or well-defined opportunity. They are depicted in Figure 2.3.

Figure 2.3   Stages and Phases of CPS

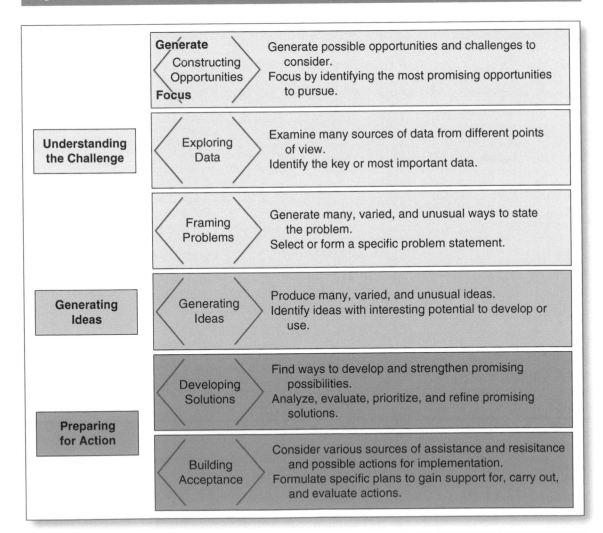

Constructing Opportunities. Constructing Opportunities deals with the question, "What is the challenge, opportunity, or concern on which we are going to be working?" The word *opportunity* means that, at this stage, the situation is fuzzy, broad, general, and ill defined. You are almost always confronted with a wide variety of tasks. Within any broad task, there are many potential opportunities. The major purpose of this stage is the identification and selection of a broad, brief, and beneficial goal for you to pursue.

For example, on August 28, 1963, the Reverend Martin Luther King delivered his "I Have a Dream" speech during a march on Washington for civil rights. Despite the shameful conditions for most African Americans at that time, he offered words and wishes for a future state. He described these in one of the most famous speeches of the 20th century that offered a shared focus for the entire civil rights movement. His description of a dream as a constructive opportunity remains a challenge today (even with the 2008 election of our first president of African American heritage) and continues to guide people in working for civil rights. King's dream, as a CPS opportunity statement, might be that "we seek to expand and enhance equality of opportunity for all Americans."

Exploring Data. In the Exploring Data stage, your efforts are aimed at seeking as much and as varied information as possible that will be important for you to consider in examining your opportunity or in helping you state problems. During this stage, you examine the situation to gather information, impressions, perceptions, and feelings from a variety of points of view. Then you determine which data seem to be most important to gain a better understanding of the problem.

For example, Jackson Pollock is well-known for his unique approach called drip painting. Rather than using the paintbrush in the typical way, he would use it (and other items) to drip paint onto the canvas. During his acts of creation, Pollock would combine the main themes from his memory with his emotions and their interaction with his materials and images. His unique approach, ability, and style in integrating so many different sources of data made him one of the most well-known American artists of the 20th century.

Framing Problems. The Framing Problems stage is designed to help you develop workable, stimulating, and specific problem statements. You engage in Framing Problems when you want or need to pose a specific problem. During this stage, you generate a variety of problem statements and then select or construct a specific statement. This will help prepare you for idea generation by providing a firm and well-defined problem statement that will stimulate many new ideas and possible solutions. This stage of CPS helps you identify a pathway to help you move toward your image of the desired future.

For example, Marie Curie worked her way from Poland to Paris to study at the Sorbonne at the turn of the 20th century. Becquerel had already discovered that uranium was giving off strange rays. Marie Curie picked up this topic as a part of her doctoral dissertation, and while measuring some pitchblende, she found that it was giving off much more energy than uranium. She had discovered radium. Marie reframed her discovery to mean much more than just the discovery of an element. She saw the process she used, measuring the amount of radioactivity materials were giving off, as a way to identify new elements. This use of radioactivity provided clues to the nature of matter and opened the doors to the nuclear age.

Generating Ideas

While the Understanding the Challenge component involves three stages, each with a distinct purpose and activity, this component contains one major stage called Generating Ideas and is depicted in Figure 2.3. You use this stage when you need many, varied, new, or unusual ideas to solve a problem that you have already defined.

For example, Thomas Alva Edison was responsible for 1,093 patents over the course of his lifetime. To obtain this number, he generated many ideas in a very systematic way. Edison set up a laboratory in Menlo Park in 1876 (one of the first formal research and development laboratories). Before long he had 40 different projects going on at once and was generating 400 patent applications a year. Edison is well-known as a persistent idea generator.

Preparing for Action

The purpose of the Preparing for Action component is to translate interesting and promising ideas into useful, acceptable, and implementable actions. The end result of your work in this component is a plan of action for carrying out the refined and developed solution. The Preparing for Action component involves the two stages, Developing Solutions and Building Acceptance, depicted in Figure 2.3.

Developing Solutions. The Developing Solutions stage involves working on promising ideas to analyze, refine, and improve them. Sometimes, this stage emphasizes sorting, narrowing, and selecting options, and at other times, the main need might be to generate and apply criteria. Developing Solutions provides the opportunity to examine your promising ideas carefully and then to strengthen them. Just having ideas is often not sufficient. Novel ideas, by definition, take some time and deliberate development to be understood and accepted.

For example, Sir Alexander Fleming is famous for his discovery of penicillin in 1929. It is not as well-known that it took a number of other key people (and many years) to isolate, purify, test, and then direct the widespread production and use of penicillin. It actually took the team of Baron Howard Walter Florey, a professor of medicine at Oxford who served at the Radcliffe Infirmary, Sir William Dunn (of the school of pathology in Oxford), and Ernst B. Chain (the head of biochemistry) until 1941 to accomplish effective implementation of Fleming's idea. Their medals are quietly displayed at the Ashmolean Museum in Oxford. The team of Fleming, Florey, and Chain was awarded the Nobel Prize in medicine in 1945.

Building Acceptance. The Building Acceptance stage challenges you to look at options through the eyes of others and to examine your potential solutions in ways that will lead to effective action. Building Acceptance deals with making and managing change or actually implementing the solutions that have been developed. This is the stage during which your major concerns are follow-through, commitment, and obtaining support for the solutions while minimizing or counteracting potential or actual objections and resistance. The result of this stage is a plan of action.

For example, Charles F. Kettering was head of research and development for General Motors. By his retirement in 1947, he held 147 patents. One of Kettering's famous stories is about his idea that cars should be painted in under an hour at a time when it took about 3 weeks to complete the job. Kettering not only wanted the time to be drastically reduced; he also thought cars should be available in many different colors. At the time, cars were only available in black. To overcome the many sources of resistance, he secretly had some key stakeholders' cars painted in their own favorite and chosen colors while they were out to lunch. After proving his point, Kettering encountered much less resistance.

Planning Your Approach

We describe Planning Your Approach as a management component because you will always be thinking about it when you are applying CPS. This component involves keeping track of your thinking while it is happening to ensure that you're moving in the direction you want to go. Planning Your Approach includes your efforts to monitor your own thinking, manage your choices about tools and location in process, and then modify your approach to allow for maximum effectiveness. This component includes two stages, called Appraising Tasks and Designing Process.

Appraising Tasks. In the Appraising Tasks stage, you determine whether CPS is a promising choice for dealing with any particular task. During this stage, you take stock of the commitments, constraints, and conditions you must consider to apply CPS effectively. You consider the people involved, the results you desire, the context in which you are working, and the methods that are available.

For example, we were working with the CEO of a global publishing organization on a leadership development program. We shared the results of an organizational climate measure we had developed to help organizations understand their readiness for change. The results were very meaningful for the group of senior managers with whom we were working, and the CEO requested that we conduct a study and program throughout the entire organization. During the program, we had learned that there were some major changes in the presidencies of a number of locations. It was simply not appropriate to offer this sort of measure or program until there was at least some stability within these positions. We had to advise the CEO to wait and reconsider his request.

Designing Process. In the Designing Process stage of the Planning Your Approach component, you use your knowledge of the task and your needs to plan your use of the CPS components, stages, or tools that will be best suited to help you reach your goals. During this stage, you customize your approach to applying CPS.

For example, we were working with the staff development team of a suburban school district. The leaders were enthusiastic about a summer curriculum development institute that would be targeted to secondary (high school) teachers. Through our initial collaborative planning, we decided that the team leaders had a well-defined task for which they had already formulated several promising ideas for a solution. As a result, our work focused on helping them to refine and develop those ideas (Developing Solutions), to anticipate areas of support and possible resistance among the target group, and to create a detailed Action Plan for promoting, carrying out, and evaluating the summer institute (Building Acceptance). The institute attracted a large group of participants, was well received, and led to a number of major new initiatives in the secondary curriculum.

Planning Your Approach allows you to consider carefully the people who are involved in your task, the situation, the need, and the desired outcomes. What you learn from these areas can help you modify the method you will apply. The four broad factors (people, context, content, and method) you consider when preparing your approach are described in more detail in later chapters. Chapter 7 will examine the aspect of people. Chapter 8 explores the area of context. Chapter 9 details the method, and Chapter 10 explores the content of your desired results.

The Heartbeat of CPS

Your heartbeat provides an audible signal of a complete pulsation of your heart. It is a vital and natural sign of your health and life. The heartbeat of CPS involves a dynamic balance, or pulse, of two complementary kinds of thinking: *generating* (stretching your search for many, varied, and unusual possibilities; often associated with "creative" thinking), and *focusing* (analyzing, refining, developing or selecting options; often associated with "critical" thinking). This dynamic balance involves separating generating from focusing and encouraging the most effective and appropriate use of each. It is a pulse that expands your thinking during generating and contracts during focusing. A healthy stretching of the arteries can prolong your life, and a healthy stretching of both kinds of thinking can improve your CPS.

Our approach to CPS emphasizes using *both* creative and critical thinking in harmony because we believe that problem solvers must be able to employ both kinds of thinking to be effective. Creative and critical thinking work together in a complementary way during CPS. Creative thinking has to do with making and expressing meaningful new connections. When you are using creative thinking, you perceive gaps, challenges, or concerns; think of many, varied, or unusual possibilities; or elaborate and extend alternatives.

Critical thinking has to do with analyzing, evaluating, or developing options. When you are using critical thinking, you screen, select, and support possibilities; compare and contrast options; make inferences and deductions; and improve or refine alternatives to make effective judgments and decisions.

Neither creative thinking nor critical thinking alone would be sufficient to help you solve a problem. Just generating many wild ideas might result in no sense of action or direction ("I have 50 ideas, but I still don't know what to do"). On the other hand, if you have only a sparse set of common, everyday ideas, even the most determined and persistent analysis will not breathe excitement or vision into them. Clearly, a more appropriate and productive approach is to use both your creative and critical thinking in harmony.

Knowing how to maintain effective balance between generating and focusing is an important factor in using CPS successfully. Just as creative and critical thinking are mutually important, generating and focusing are also necessary and important teammates in CPS. The balance may be delicate or hard to manage at times, but it is still important to remember that these two types of thinking will be used in concert to meet your needs in CPS. Although the balance depicted in Figure 2.4 appears to have reached equilibrium or stability, you will more likely experience this balance as dynamic and constantly shifting.

Figure 2.4   The Dynamic Balance or "Heartbeat" of CPS

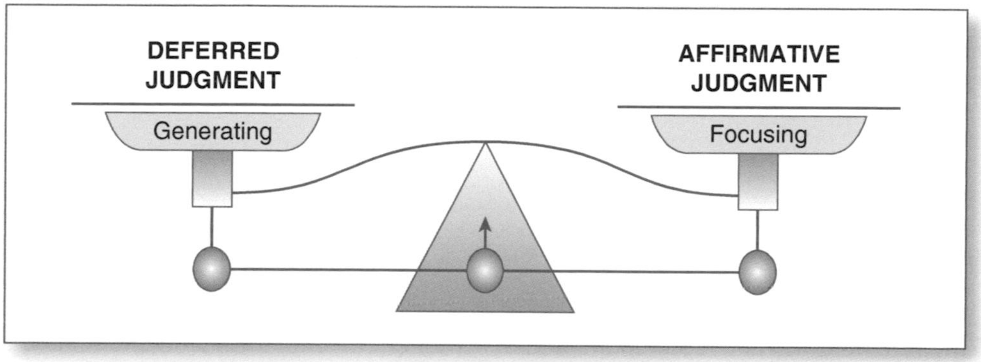

SOURCE: Copyright © 2009. The Creative Problem Solving Group, Inc. Reprinted with permission.

The harmony you will seek between these mutually supportive kinds of thinking and problem solving will help you decide when you have stretched enough or evaluated sufficiently. Some situations may call for a greater emphasis on generating and may require additional time and energy on generating options. Others may require more emphasis on focusing, where the need is primarily for analysis, evaluation, and improvement. The balance you will need and experience in your use of CPS will depend on a variety of important factors, but most of all the needs of the situation and the task. One of the best ways to seek and reach this harmonious balance is to be able to distinguish these two different kinds of thinking and to create conditions that are uniquely appropriate for each.

Guidelines for Generating

When you want to generate options, evaluation is likely to get in the way. Evaluating alternatives as you generate them tends to inhibit the flow of generating. It is more effective to let the options flow, without any criticism or praise. The major principle of deferred judgment, holding back evaluation while generating options, is the foundation for generating options.

This principle provides the foundation for the four guidelines for generating. A guideline is a general rule or suggestion. Together, following these four guidelines (see Figure 2.5) helps establish the conditions for generating alternatives and for the best use of the generating tools.

Figure 2.5	Four Guidelines for Generating Options

Defer judgment. Deferred judgment serves as the foundation for all the generating guidelines. It suggests postponing judgment and analysis until after you have generated a full menu of possibilities. Judgment is an important part of problem solving, but it is more appropriately done as a separate activity. Deferred judgment includes both positive and negative judgment (both praise and criticism are judgments!) and refraining from internal or external judgment. Judging your own options (internally) before you say them might inhibit you from considering them as options. Judging other people's options (externally) as they generate them may cause them to "shut down" or stop their generation.

Strive for quantity. Quantity often breeds quality, in that the more options you generate, the greater the possibility that at least some of them will be original and promising for you. This guideline suggests looking for a large quantity or number of options. To help raise the quantity of options generated, try to express them concisely, in just a few words (as in the "headline" of a newspaper or "telegram"). Do not write a whole book or elaborate too much.

Freewheel. This guideline emphasizes capturing or recording every option that comes to your mind, without being concerned that some might seem too wild or silly. Give yourself permission to be playful. Strive for uniqueness or originality. Sometimes the wildest options serve as springboards for other new options for you or someone else if you are working in a group. The unique connections between the wild options and the new options might not have been possible if the wild ones were held back.

Freewheeling should also remind you of the importance of stretching your imagination. It is all too easy for anyone to become mentally lazy, drifting along with the most common or familiar options or habits, or operating on "mental cruise control."

Seek combinations. This suggests modifying, altering, or building on previously generated options. You have probably observed many times, even in informal conversations, how one idea can lead to another. We often say, "Oh, yes . . . that reminds me of something else . . ." when someone says something that triggers a new idea in our own mind. We try to make good use of that same experience individually or when using CPS in a group. So we encourage you (or those in a group) to be alert for new ways to connect one option to another. This is also known as "piggybacking," or "hitchhiking."

The generating tools frequently used within the CPS framework are identified later in this chapter. Brainstorming is the basic CPS tool most closely associated with the generating guidelines. We will consider it in detail, since it is often the foundation for many other tools.

Brainstorming

Although some individuals believe that brainstorming is synonymous with CPS, it is really only one of many idea-generation tools within the framework (Treffinger, Isaksen, & Young, 1998).

Brainstorming was originally outlined by Alex Osborn as a set of guidelines for creative collaboration by groups (Figure 2.6). It is perhaps the best known, yet least understood, item in the CPS toolbox.

The Brainstorming tool can be used effectively in every stage of the CPS process. For example, Brainstorming is often used to generate a list of possible opportunity statements in the Constructing Opportunities stage of CPS. It can be used to generate data during the Exploring Data stage, possible problem statements during the Framing Problems stage, ideas in the Generating Ideas stage, criteria during the Developing

> ### Figure 2.6   An Illustration of Brainstorming in Action
>
>

Solutions stage, or sources of assistance and resistance during the Building Acceptance stage. In short, it is one of the most versatile tools in your toolbox!

Brainstorming is not the same as having a group discussion. We have often been invited to "brainstorm" with someone who destroys our ideas right after we share them! It is important to be clear about the basic guidelines and practice their use. Brainstorming involves more than just the four guidelines outlined above.

Brainstorming includes having someone lead the session. Just telling a group to follow the rules for brainstorming is not enough to ensure a successful session. Osborn included a leadership role within his design of the tool. Since brainstorming is a group tool, you need to have a trained or qualified individual to manage the use of the tool in a group of about five to seven individuals from diverse backgrounds. This leader works to manage the group's interaction and energy and to ensure that the guidelines are followed.

Brainstorming includes recording all options generated. When Alex Osborn originally developed the tool, he suggested that each brainstorming group have a dedicated session secretary to help with the technology and writing of each alternative suggested by members of the group. Having this person involved in the session means that participants will not need to wait or lose focus until they can offer their next suggestion.

Brainstorming involves extended effort. Parnes (1961) found that, when using the guidelines for generating options, those generated earlier in the session tended to be more typical, obvious, or familiar responses. As time goes on during generation, options become more novel or unusual. In the later stages of generation activity, the familiar options often blend with the highly unusual or novel options to make *novel and useful* options. He suggested that it is helpful to extend your effort while generating options because it often takes time for better options to be generated. Encouraging extended effort is one of the key responsibilities of the leader or facilitator of the session. The facilitator can often accomplish this by asking some stimulating questions or introducing another tool to help keep the energy going.

Brainstorming supplements individual ideation. Brainstorming is a tool for use in groups. It is simply not possible to follow the guidelines if you work alone, particularly the hitchhiking on the ideas of others guidelines. However, when you decide to use the guidelines to ideate individually, you may need to rely more heavily on using "enhancers" that work well for you. For example, while you or a group are generating options and it begins to slow down, you may wish to use other tools for generating options (see Table 2.2), such as forcing relationships or checklists (such as SCAMPER [substitute, combine, apply, modify, put to other uses, eliminate, rearrange]) to stimulate the production of more unique options.

Table 2.2   The CPS Toolbox With Generating and Focusing Tools

GENERATING TOOLS

- **Attribute Listing** Breaking down a problem to generate change.
- **Brainstorming.** Enables a group to generate many, varied, and unusual options.
- **Brainstorming with Post-its®.** Increases the number of options generated by allowing group members to record and share aloud their own options.
- **Brainwriting.** Allows individuals to systematically, and more anonymously, build on each other's options.
- **Forced Fitting.** Stimulates connections between the challenge and things that are seemingly unrelated.

FOCUSING TOOLS

- **Advantages, Limitations, Unique Qualities, and Overcoming Limitations (ALUo).** Provides an affirmative approach to strengthen new options.
- **Evaluation Matrix.** Uses a structured approach to evaluate options against specific criteria.
- **Criteria.** Help to generate specific standards to evaluate options.
- **Selecting Hits.** Identifies and selects promising options using personal experience and judgment.

(Continued)

Table 2.2 (Continued)

GENERATING TOOLS	FOCUSING TOOLS
• **Imagery Trek.** Involves taking a journey far from the challenge and developing novel relationships as a result. • **Ladder of Abstraction.** Helps to make the search more abstract, broad, and general; or more concrete, narrow, and specific. • **Morphological Matrix.** Provides a structured way to identify and combine elements of a task in new ways. • **SCAMPER.** Organizes six concepts (one for each letter) used to categorize idea-spurring questions that stimulate options. • **Visually Identifying Relationships (VIR).** Stimulates original responses and new perspectives by using visual sense to gain distance from the challenge.	• **Musts/Wants.** Sorts options based on importance. • **Paired Comparison Analysis (PCA).** Prioritizes options by comparing them against each other. • **Highlighting.** Compresses a large number of options into a manageable number of themes. • **Short, Medium, Long (SML).** Organizes options along a timeline from short term to long term.

Brainstorming is a tool designed to get the maximum generative productivity from a group. Osborn (1953) outlined detailed procedures to ensure the best results. He suggested that groups be prepared with a formal written invitation that includes background on the task at hand. This would allow individual ideation prior to the brainstorming session and give time for some incubation. For other suggestions, see Isaksen, Dorval, and Treffinger (1998) and Isaksen and Gaulin (2005).

Guidelines for Focusing

Focusing options, at which time evaluation and critical thinking become primary, constitute another, complementary set of guidelines. Unfortunately, many people seem to know only one way to evaluate ideas: with great vigor! It's as though, in driving a car, they only knew one way to stop, by slamming on the breaks and stopping as soon as possible. When it comes to options, they say, "Well, I deferred judgment about as long as I possibly could. Now it's time to get rid of some of these dumb ideas." They slam on the mental brakes. By finding fault with options, and limiting their view to a search for just one right answer or best solution (as depicted in Figure 2.7), they often trap themselves into unproductive "either-or" thinking (we can only do it this way or that way; it is possible, or it is likely impossible), rather than looking for possible ways to look at ideas carefully, constructively, and with an eye toward developing and strengthening those that seem intriguing or promising.

Figure 2.7 Affirmative Judgment Is an Important Guideline for Focusing

SOURCE: Copyright © 2009. The Creative Problem Solving Group, Inc. Reprinted with permission.

To help overcome the natural and sometimes overwhelming tendency to crush out the novelty in new possibilities, it is important to remember and use the principle of Affirmative Judgment. This principle serves as the underlying focal point and major emphasis in all the focusing phases of CPS. Using the principle helps overcome the reflexive "no" response that often results when considering novelty.

After generating many, varied, and unusual options, you could easily be overwhelmed with the quantity and diversity. Following these guidelines encourages you to stay open and consider the novel possibilities. They are designed to help you analyze and evaluate your options in a way that promotes building them up, not tearing them down.

Affirmative judgment serves as the foundation for three other guidelines for focusing identified in Figure 2.8. These are Be Deliberate, Consider Novelty, and Stay on Course.

Figure 2.8 Four Guidelines for Focusing Options

USE AFFIRMATIVE JUDGMENT

BE DELIBERATE

CONSIDER NOVELTY

STAY ON COURSE

SOURCE: Copyright © 2009. The Creative Problem Solving Group, Inc. Reprinted with permission.

Use affirmative judgment. This guideline suggests looking for the strengths or positive aspects of an option first. Then, focus your attention on its limitations or what should be done differently. However, when you identify its limitations, avoid pronouncements that kill ideas. Rather, state your concerns in the form of questions that promote the development and strengthening of the options. For example, start the statement by asking "How to . . ." or "How might . . ." These questions should invite you to think further about the options as opposed to discarding them. Using affirmative judgment should remind you, then, that evaluation and decision making are developmental processes, intended to get the best out of your options, not just ways to criticize options.

Be deliberate. This guideline promotes the planful use of specific tools or strategies for focusing. It means being systematic in your approach to analyzing, developing, and refining your options. Effective focusing often involves making choices and decisions about alternatives. Being deliberate about your focusing efforts can often help avoid conflict or controversy associated with making decisions in a group setting. Put your specific plan for decision making out in the open. This can help avoid "hidden agendas" or decision-making criteria that are not common or shared among a group. Having your plan out in the open can also encourage a more effective use of power.

Consider novelty. If you want new and useful results, then you must actively engage and embrace novelty. Often, when it is time to focus, people simply skip over options that are highly novel and choose something that is less threatening or more closely associated with their original line of thinking. As a result, these people often learn that generating is meaningless or unimportant. Considering novelty is a guideline designed to ensure that the novelty or newness you generated is nurtured and developed during focusing.

Stay on course. This guideline emphasizes the importance of remembering the goal or original purpose for focusing on the options. Like any navigator, you need to keep your eyes on your destination, making decisions and correcting your course as you travel. Particularly after deliberate generating, the excitement and enthusiasm you have experienced can lead you to lose sight of your initial purpose. If all your options are fascinating, your focus or vision for what you want to happen will be your most important "guidepost" for selecting and developing options.

Just as it is important to extend your effort in generating options, devoting deliberate time and energy to focusing will pay you dividends. In Figure 2.9 you can see that if

Figure 2.9 Focusing on Novelty Takes Time and Effort

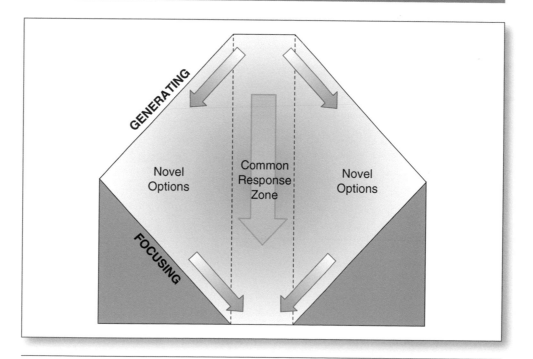

SOURCE: Copyright © 2009. The Creative Problem Solving Group, Inc. Reprinted with permission.

you have done a good job and extended an appropriate effort in generating options, you will have many and varied options outside the common response zone. We have seen sessions and meetings use nearly all their time to generate alternatives and fill up many flipcharts. Those responsible for these meetings often find themselves with little time to devote to focusing. In a sense, they slam on the brakes and will often avoid picking a highly novel response. Those hosting these meetings often resort to selecting an option that is well within the common response zone. This leads people who have participated in the generating with the feeling that their efforts were not used well. Over time, if this is how focusing is managed, people begin to believe that generating is a waste of time.

These are the reasons for the focusing guidelines and tools. They help preserve the novelty from the generating phases of CPS and encourage the deliberate screening, selecting, and supporting necessary for the development of new concepts. All the focusing tools used within the CPS framework follow these guidelines. The CPS tool that is most closely associated with the guidelines for focusing is called ALUo (Advantages, Limitations, Unique Qualities, and Overcoming Limitations).

ALUo (Advantages, Limitations, Unique Qualities, and Overcoming Limitations)

When focusing, it is often the case that options that represent high novelty are overlooked, disregarded, or even openly criticized or attacked. ALUo (see Figure 2.10) is a tool that provides a structured approach for productively managing the analysis and development of novelty while avoiding the more common idea, "slaughtering," which occurs when novelty is shared. (You will find that, particularly in educational settings, this tool has also been described as "ALoU." The tool is the same, despite the slight variation in notation.)

Figure 2.10   An Illustration of the ALUo in Action

ALUo is the tool that most clearly uses the guidelines for analyzing, developing, and refining options:

- *Identifying the advantages, strengths, or strong points:* ALUo uses the affirmative judgment principle by examining the advantages, strong points, pluses, or strengths of an option first. The examination of advantages encourages active involvement in the analysis of the option and assists in avoiding the reflexive "no" response to novelty. To identify the strengths of the option, it must temporarily but truly be accepted for consideration. Be careful to avoid trivial pluses or disguised weaknesses (strengths that are really weaknesses). It is important that the advantages be clearly legitimate. You may need to stretch to find them. That's exactly why this part of the exercise comes first!

- *Identifying limitations or areas for improvement:* Few options are perfect. ALUo deliberately considers the limitations, weak points, or challenges associated with an option. However, when considering the limitations, ALUo avoids the "dumping" of negatives by asking for limitations to be formed as questions beginning with How to . . . or How might . . . By turning limitations into questions (problem statements), you are encouraging the development of the option by overcoming weakness through idea generation.

- *Identifying unique qualities:* ALUo consciously considers the new or unusual elements of options by identifying unique qualities of the option(s). This deliberate consideration of novelty acts as a "safety net" for the development and analysis of novelty. It deliberately asks the questions, "What does this option have that no other option has?" "What are some of the unique qualities or aspects to this option?" This helps you preserve the novelty and can help focus attention on retaining those novel aspects of the option that are useful and valuable. It is not necessary to generate a large number of unique qualities. In fact, you will find it easier if you only identify the core or key elements of uniqueness within the option.

- *Overcoming limitations:* An important application of the ALUo tool is to be certain to identify the limitations that are most important to overcome. Once identified, time and energy should be focused on actually developing ways to strengthen and overcome these limitations. In this way, the ALUo tool leverages the analysis and increases the likelihood of a novel and useful outcome. As you work to overcome the key limitations, you can examine the advantages to help you generate ideas and ways to enhance or develop the option under consideration. You will also want to remember those elements of novelty that you wish to retain as you select the ideas you generated to overcome the limitations.

Generating and Focusing Lead to Creativity

The alternating attention to generating and focusing in any stage provides the energy system and natural flow of the process. This alternation is the reason the graphic we chose for each stage looks like a diamond. Each stage contains a generating and a focusing stage. How much time, energy, and effort you spend on each phase depends on many factors and will result in something we call the "dynamic balance." If you do not employ enough energy in generating, then you may invest your focusing energy on tired and worn-out ideas. All the analysis and evaluation in the world will not introduce the novelty needed to effectively respond to those messy and challenging situations. Establishing conditions for generating validates the use of your imagination; it invites incubation and illumination.

On the other hand, if you don't invest enough energy in focusing, then you may find that the options you choose to run with are not developed well enough or are unacceptable to others. Some really wild ideas need to be tamed down before they are shared or acted on. The conditions for focusing create opportunities to let an option germinate, ferment, or mature, until it is ready for use or harvesting.

We are often delighted to look at examples of high-level creativity and find evidence of this dynamic balance. Frank Lloyd Wright was responsible for nearly 11,000 architectural drawings over his career. Of these drawings, only about 1,000 were ever actually constructed. Of those constructions, Wright is credited with having 10 of the 100 most important structures ever built.

The same observation can be made within the arts. Pablo Picasso is probably one of the most famous artists of the 20th century. His career lasted more than 75 years, and he created thousands of paintings, sculptures, prints, and ceramics using all sorts of materials. While visiting the Picasso Museum in Barcelona, you will be able to see his interpretation of a particular little girl. He was evidently inspired by a painting he saw in the Prado done by Velasquez of the Dutch royal family. He focused on the little girl in the painting and made about 44 different paintings of her until he finally came to the one he chose. One of the reasons people may be able to identify a few of his works (Guernica, Las Meninas, etc.) is because he had produced so many over his career.

The guidelines and tools for generating and focusing create a certain mental attitude that is necessary for their effective use. Following them will not necessarily make you a Frank Lloyd Wright or a Pablo Picasso, but you will learn about your own creative talents and the conditions that help bring them out. The evidence is that by doing this and practicing the tools associated with CPS, you can increase the level of your creativity.

The Tools of CPS

Brainstorming and ALUo represent two basic tools for generating and focusing. However, there are hundreds of tools to help you generate and focus options. Table 2.2 identifies most of the basic CPS tools we will explain and illustrate in this book.

There are a number of additional sources you may want to consult to learn more about these and other tools, including Bognar et al. (2003), Couger (1995), Davis and Roweton (1968), Elliott (1987), Fobes (1993), Foster (1996), Geschka, Schaude, and Schlicksupp (1973), Hall (1995), Higgins (1994), Isaksen, Dorval, and Treffinger (2005), Keller-Mathers and Puccio (2000), Michalko (1998), Parnes et al. (1977), Ray and Wiley (1985), Straker and Rawlinson (2003), Treffinger (2008), Treffinger, Nassab, et al. (2006), Treffinger and Nassab (2000, 2005), VanGundy (1992), and van Leeuwen and Terhürne (2002).

How Do We Know CPS Works?

There are two broad ways that we know CPS works. One is derived from our own experience and practice over the years. A few of these examples are included in many of the chapters throughout this book. You will also see in Chapter 11 that CPS is useful for a variety of levels of application. The second way we know that CPS makes a difference is that there is a vast amount of evidence in the literature to document its effectiveness and impact.

Knowledge From Practical Experiences

We use CPS to help groups and organizations with such challenges as developing visions and missions, designing school curricula, establishing effective work teams, long-range planning, total quality management, continuous improvement, and developing new products and services. We train and certify people as well as license organizations to use the CPS process and its support materials within many national and international organizations. We continually receive positive feedback from a wide diversity of people about the value and productivity they experience from using CPS in their work at home or in school.

One of the most frequently cited reasons we hear for people deciding to use CPS is the extensive amount of field testing and empirical validation that has been conducted on the framework. We know CPS works on a practical level in that there are many practitioners using the framework in a variety of settings. We are often asked to use CPS in a number of educational, business, and not-for-profit organizations. (We will share several examples of these varied applications in Chapter 11.)

Knowledge Derived From the Literature

We can demonstrate that nine broad themes or categories in the literature, incorporating hundreds of citations, support the conclusion that CPS actually makes a difference to individuals, groups, and organizations (Isaksen & DeSchryver, 2000). We know that CPS makes a difference because:

A solid and explicit conceptual foundation exists. There are numerous writings to point out the historical foundations and development, various theoretical approaches, and general philosophical support for understanding and developing creativity.

There is continuous research and development. CPS begins its research and development through Buffalo-based foundational work done by the Creative Education Foundation and the Center for Studies in Creativity. This work continues today with other organizations and scholars around the globe.

Formal courses are available. Since the early course work developed in Buffalo, many courses have been developed and approved for academic, governmental, and industrial use around the world. These include courses for young children, older students, students in colleges and universities, and adult professionals offering certification.

Courses and programs have been evaluated. Experimental research, case studies, and formal evaluations have been conducted on these courses and programs, providing evidence that they work. In addition, many theses and dissertations across the disciplines have been completed.

Communities exist to advance knowledge. There are numerous edited collections, published bibliographies, handbooks, scholarly syntheses, and reviews documenting varying degrees of collaboration and knowledge exchange. There are also dedicated journals for those interested in the subject.

Communities exist to advance practice. There are numerous international networks and other organizations that, as a part of their mission, hold meetings, distribute materials, and exchange information on best practices.

There is a documented need. There is literature from a variety of disciplines illustrating the nature of knowledge, the importance of creative-thinking skills, and the transferability of these skills, and showing that situations demand creativity and that it can be enjoyable, is natural, and builds on knowledge.

There is experimental evidence. Early foundational experimental research is complemented by a large amount of research on brainstorming and experimental evidence of course impact.

CPS has been widely applied. There are many documented examples of CPS applied to special populations such as gifted students, students with disabilities, very young children, and a variety of adult populations. In addition, there are published case studies illustrating how CPS has been applied to a variety of issues and needs.

The Creative Problem Solving Group, Inc., maintains an up-to-date compendium of the evidence that CPS works on its Web site. You can download this free resource (*Compendium of Evidence on Creative Problem Solving*) by visiting www.cpsb.com.

Evidence that CPS works takes a variety of forms. The best way to know that it works is to try it out and apply it for yourself. If you wish to explore some additional help or resources, look over the suggestions in Chapter 12: Applying CPS.

The purpose of this chapter was to introduce the CPS process as a framework for enhancing your natural problem-solving process. The overview of the framework's language, structure, guidelines, and tools is designed to provide you with the "big picture" about the framework, language, and tools and how we know they work. The next three chapters will examine the three process components included in the framework: Understanding the Challenge, Generating Ideas, and Preparing for Action.

Putting This Chapter to Work

Our goals in this chapter were to provide you with a concise introduction to CPS and a brief overview of the specific components, stages, phases, and tools within CPS.

Activities to Guide Reflection and Action

Work on one or more of the following activities to review your understanding of the material in this chapter and to practice applying the content in real situations. If you are using this book as part of a course or study group, you may wish to work individually and then compare your responses or to work collaboratively as a team.

1. Think about one or more situations in which you have been a participant or leader of an effort to manage change or deal with a complex, open-ended problem or challenge. Consider the CPS components, stages, phases, and tools discussed in this chapter. Identify some specific ways in which the situation(s) you're considering included (or omitted) any of the elements of the CPS framework.

2. As you reflect on your experiences in responding to Question 1, how might knowledge of CPS and deliberate efforts to apply that knowledge have added value or contributed to the success of your efforts?

3. Identify some aspects of your current personal or professional setting that you believe may be fruitful opportunities for applying CPS components, stages, phases, or tools as you continue to learn more about CPS and seek opportunities to put it to work for you. Begin to formulate a plan to incorporate CPS into your "working repertoire."

4. With a group of peers or colleagues, discuss one of the following two questions: (1) When people talk about attempting to "solve a problem," do you find that what they do can often result in a Band-Aid type of effort that fails to get to the underlying or "root" issue or concern? How would knowledge of CPS help them to be more productive? (2) We propose that CPS deals with managing change; do you agree that change can actually be managed, and that we would actually want to do that? Why or why not?

Understanding the Challenge

Sometimes it's only a change of viewpoint that is needed to convert a seemingly tiresome duty into an interesting opportunity.

—Albert Flanders

The purpose of Chapter 3 is to examine the Understanding the Challenge component of Creative Problem Solving (CPS) and its use in developing clarity and direction for problem solving. After studying this CPS component, you will be able to do the following:

1. Work within a task domain, define many specific opportunities or challenges that might be addressed using CPS, and identify a broad opportunity or goal on which to focus your CPS efforts.

2. Explore the task in many ways and from varied perspectives, consider your current reality in relation to a desired future state, and determine the most important data.

3. Generate many different problem statements for a given task, and construct or select an appropriate and invitational problem statement.

Understanding the Challenge includes three specific CPS stages: Constructing Opportunities, Exploring Data, and Framing Problems. The specific objectives for each of these stages are listed below.

Constructing Opportunities

The objectives for this stage are for you to be able to do the following:

1. Define many specific opportunities or challenges that can be addressed using CPS.

(Continued)

(Continued)

2. Apply three important standards (broad, brief, beneficial) and three criteria for ownership (interest, influence, and imagination) in formulating opportunity statements.

3. Construct or choose specific opportunity statements for a specific task.

Exploring Data

The objectives for this stage are for you to be able to do the following:

1. Describe Exploring Data and explain its importance in CPS.

2. Define and use five different sources of data, giving examples and differentiating among them.

3. Describe and use a variety of methods and tools for generating and analyzing data, to determine the key data that need to be considered.

Framing Problems

The objectives for this stage are for you to be able to do the following:

1. Define and give examples of four essential elements of a problem statement (invitational stem, ownership, action verb, and problem-solving goal or objective).

2. Generate many different problem statements for a given task.

3. Broaden and redefine problem statements by using different levels of abstraction, changing key words, or identifying subproblems.

4. Select or construct effective problem statements based on the application of specific criteria (brief, concise, relevant focus, free of criteria, idea-finding potential).

Ahuman resources manager in a large systems software development division of a global computer company was working with his senior management team to address impending problems with their competition. The team was in a difficult position at the time because their division had one major product that brought in most of their revenue. Unfortunately, in 5 years, patents protecting the intellectual property rights for that product would expire. Other organizations might then introduce products that would compete with this group's main product. Making the situation even worse, competing organizations already had similar, but less expensive, products ready to flood the market. This would certainly damage the research and development facility's position in the marketplace, perhaps to the extent of closing their research and development facility and laying off more than 750 people.

The senior management team knew that continuing to follow their current approach would result in closing the plant within 3 years. Therefore, they needed to create a different future scenario than "business as usual." They needed an approach that didn't tie them to the impending problems of no patent protection and extensive competition. How do you turn this threat into an opportunity for change and growth? Can CPS help you (or this research and development facility) create a new direction or vision of the future? Can CPS help you identify the key problems to address for implementing a more promising vision?

This chapter will address these kinds of questions. We will examine a component of the CPS framework that can help you gain clarity about the future, understand your current situation, and identify the core problems that need to be addressed to accomplish your goals and objectives.

Many people believe that *getting ideas* is the major focus of CPS. Although generating new and useful ideas *is* important, to be successful, you must be certain the ideas respond to the right question! It doesn't do any good to think up dozens of responses to a question for which no one wants any answers.

All the process components of CPS add value to your problem-solving efforts. Generating Ideas, which we will consider in Chapter 4, leads to ideas—building blocks for creative solutions. Preparing for Action, in Chapter 5, will help you transform intriguing possibilities into workable solutions—the building blocks for creative action. In this chapter, we will deal with asking the questions that will help you to be sure that your problem-solving efforts are heading in the "right" direction (the way you really want to go)—the building blocks of creative purposes and directions. We will also describe the Understanding the Challenge component, its three stages, and examples of tools you can use when working with this component.

Understanding the Challenge in a Nutshell

The primary emphasis of the Understanding the Challenge component is to use the language and tools of CPS to focus on the results you want. The tools in these stages will help you identify and understand gaps that may exist between the current realities and your images for a desired future state, as illustrated in Figure 3.1 (based on Fritz's [1999] structural tension model). The typical input, processing, and output of this component are summarized in Figure 3.2.

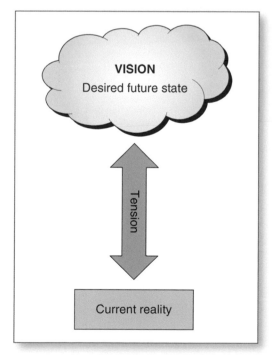

Figure 3.1 Fritz's Model of Structural Tension

VISION
Desired future state

Tension

Current reality

SOURCE: Adapted from Fritz (1999).

Figure 3.2 Understanding the Challenge in a Nutshell

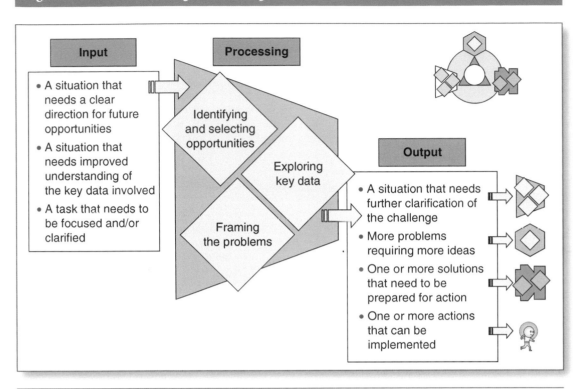

SOURCE: Copyright © 2009. The Creative Problem Solving Group, Inc. and The Center for Creative Learning, Inc. Reprinted with permission.

Input

Enter the Understanding the Challenge component when you need to focus your problem-solving efforts relating to a general task, improve your understanding of the current situation for the task, or identify specific pathways you might take to move the current situation in the direction of your desired situation.

Understanding the Challenge is the appropriate CPS component to help identify a variety of opportunities and then focus on a few key options. It can also be applied to clarify current reality by identifying and focusing on key data. Finally, this component can be used to generate and then focus on specific problem statements that clarify the issues or gaps between current reality and your desired future. This problem-finding effort provides a clear target for idea generation.

Processing

There are three stages in the component: Constructing Opportunities, Exploring Data, and Framing Problems. In Constructing Opportunities, the goal is to conduct a general search to identify the broad challenges and goals that exist in a particular task or situation. The results of that search help you to set the direction of your problem-solving efforts. In Exploring Data, the aim is to develop a clear understanding of the current situation, by gathering data (information, impressions, opinions, and questions). Identifying key data helps you pinpoint and interpret critical issues. In Framing Problems, the goal is to identify the pathways to close the gap(s) between the current situation and a preferred future situation. After generating many problem statements, identify those with potential for stimulating many new and useful ideas.

The three stages in the Understanding the Challenge component might be used independently, or in a variety of different combinations, orders, or sequences. The specific task, the context, the people involved, and the desired outcomes will determine which stage or stages to use, and the appropriate order or sequence to follow. For example, if the task requires a broad image or direction, enter at the Constructing Opportunities stage. If you need to improve your understanding of the current realities, enter at the Exploring Data stage. If you need to clarify and define problem statements that will help you move from your current situation to a desired future situation, enter at the Framing Problems stage.

Output

Using the Understanding the Challenge component can result in a variety of outcomes. You might have identified a specific problem for which you need new ideas, so that this component might lead to work on Generating Ideas. Alternatively, you might discover that the situation is bigger, more complex, or not as clear as you first thought; this might lead to additional, deeper, or more focused work in any of the specific stages in Understanding the Challenge. You may also find that your work in Understanding the Challenge enables you to move into Preparing for Action, or even to exit from CPS and proceed directly to action. The following sections of this chapter will help you understand each of the three stages in this component in more detail. You will be introduced to the language and tools that will help you construct opportunities, explore data, and frame problems.

What Is the Constructing Opportunities Stage?

Each stage in the Understanding the Challenge component plays a unique role in the process of Understanding the Challenge. We use several specific stems, which we present in Table 3.1, to help you think in ways that reflect the unique purpose or role of each stage in this component.

The aim of Constructing Opportunities is to help clarify the focus or direction for your problem-solving efforts. An opportunity is a broad, fuzzy, and ill-defined situation, challenge, concern, or goal. The opportunities or challenges you face at work, school, or home do not always arrive in nice, neat packages. As Figure 3.3 illustrates, they often come your way as complex, unclear situations that require untangling and organizing before you can work effectively on solving them.

In Chapter 2, we said that each CPS stage includes a generating phase and a focusing phase. In this chapter, we will discuss both phases separately as we present each

Table 3.1   The Language That Guides Your Thinking in Understanding the Challenge

Constructing Opportunities	Exploring Data	Framing Problems
Wouldn't it be nice if . . . ? (WIBNI . . . ?) To generate opportunity statements	Data—no stems needed To generate richer knowledge than simply gathering facts	How to . . . ? (H2 . . . ?) To generate problem statements
Wouldn't it be awful if . . . ? (WIBAI . . . ?) To generate challenges or obstacles	Who? What? Where? When? Why? and How? Facts and opinions	How might . . . ? (HM . . . ?) To generate problem statements
		In what ways might . . . ? (IWWM . . . ?) To generate problem statements

Figure 3.3   The Constructing Opportunities Stage

stage to illustrate how the dynamic balance between generating and focusing actually occurs. For each stage, we will describe several specific tools (from the CPS toolbox in Chapter 2) that can be very helpful to use during the stage, using a case study to illustrate their application. Keep in mind that all these tools can be used effectively in any of the CPS stages.

Generating When Constructing Opportunities

In the generating phase of Constructing Opportunities, your aim is to map out the broad domain of the task, or to seek many possible opportunities or challenges that you might pursue. Think about the history of mapmaking. The first mapmakers, limited to standing on the earth, relied on the stars to develop their maps. Since they weren't able to stretch the distance between themselves and what they were mapping, the results of their efforts were often limited in perspective and usefulness.

Today, mapmakers use satellites to take pictures from many miles above the surface of the earth. Stretching the distance between the surface of the earth and their point of reference enables them to have a more comprehensive picture or image of the earth's surface and, as a result, develop more accurate maps. Taking a broad view of the task as you map it out means being able to extend your field of view or your perspective, to gain enough distance from the task to be able to see it very broadly or with a "wide angle" view, or to see the task differently or more accurately. If you are too close, or too limited in your field of vision, you will hamper your ability to search for creative directions or possibilities.

Opportunity Statements. The generating phase of Constructing Opportunities involves producing *opportunity statements*. These statements (which we ordinarily pose in the form of questions) express the general goals, wishes, concerns, or challenges associated with the task, as summarized in Figure 3.4.

Figure 3.4 The Definition of an Opportunity Statement

A description of a broad, fuzzy, ill-defined challenge,
opportunity, or desired goal

INVITATIONAL STEMS FOR:

OUTCOMES
WIBNI ... = Wouldn't it be nice if ...

OBSTACLES
WIBAI ... = Wouldn't it be awful if ...

Figure 3.5 Guidelines for Writing Opportunity Statements

- **Broad** – General; an opportunity statement does not need to be specific
- **Brief** – Short; statement in "book title" form
- **Beneficial** – Positive; focus on what you want

They are *broad*, *brief*, and *beneficial* statements that help you explore and clarify possible directions for your problem solving to follow (see Figure 3.5).

By "broad," we mean designing opportunity statements that state general goals and that avoid limiting or restricting your initial thinking prematurely. If the focus for problem solving is unclear and you try to define a specific direction too quickly, you might miss the most important opportunity or challenge in the task. For example, if your task deals with getting a career, limiting yourself by saying "I have to get a job with a new employer" might prevent you from thinking about improving or modifying an existing job, creating a career of your own, or moving in a totally new direction in your life.

Describing an opportunity statement as "brief" means stating it in a few words. Rather than writing a story or paragraph about the opportunity, state it as a "headline" (a concise statement that communicates its main point quickly and clearly). Keep it clear and simple. For example, one effective opportunity statement might be, "Wouldn't it be nice if my team could be more productive?" In contrast, a poorly worded opportunity statement for the same challenge might be, "Wouldn't it be nice if I had a project plan that helped me focus the energy of my team members in a direction that is mutually beneficial and productive for all those involved and helped my boss see that the energy of the group is being used in an effective and efficient manner?" Although it might be an accurate description of your situation, it does not convey the creative opportunity effectively and probably contains several different opportunity statements.

"Beneficial" means that opportunity statements identify what you want to move toward or accomplish—the goal you hope to attain or the direction you hope to follow, not what you want to avoid or the dismal failure you might fear. For example, saying "Wouldn't it be nice if I could maintain my health" is more positive than saying "Wouldn't it be nice if I avoided being sick?"

As we demonstrated above, language for Constructing Opportunities includes specific stems for generating opportunity statements. These include "Wouldn't it be nice if . . . ? (WIBNI)" and "Wouldn't it be awful if . . . ? (WIBAI)." People often think about a task as a concern, or a situation in which something is bothering, worrying, or troubling them, or holding them back. It's common to see challenges more as concerns than as opportunities, and it's true that life does present us with any number of concerns; it would be naive to deny it. Many tasks contain real threats or obstacles that need to be removed, avoided, or overcome. Use what you want to avoid to help identify what you want to accomplish! Constructing Opportunities calls for you to use what you want to avoid, prevent, or overcome as a starting point for examining what you really do wish, hope, dream, or imagine might be the case in the future. It is much more powerful and helpful to work toward a positive, desirable goal than to linger in the unhappiness of what's wrong now. An opportunity statement encourages you to begin the journey toward your goal, but being locked in on the negative makes you feel like you're sinking in quicksand.

We use the WIBAI stem to express those concerns, and to bring them out in the light for examination. However, to move toward creative opportunities, ideas, or actions, we've learned that it is much more powerful and effective to look at where you want to go and to be forward-looking and constructive, rather than locking yourself into what's wrong, unhappy, or deficient about where you are now. So, even when we start with a concern (WIBAI), we search for the constructive WIBNIs that it contains or suggests.

For the "making my team more productive" example of a challenge, some possible opportunity statements might be:

- WIBNI . . . my project team members had clearly defined roles?
- WIBNI . . . I had a project management system?
- WIBAI . . . our team failed to meet its goals? (Then: turn it around: WIBNI . . . our team was on top of its goals?)
- WIBAI . . . all our team members lost their jobs? (Turn it around: WIBNI . . . all our team members were so successful that we earned rewards and recognitions?)

Opportunity statements might use a number of other stems too; don't feel limited to WIBAI and WIBNI alone. For example, consider these opportunity statement starters:

- If I had my way . . .
- If I were queen (or king) . . .
- I would really like to . . .

Instead, you might ask,

- Why don't we . . .
- I wonder if we could . . .

Now, consider these starters:
Wouldn't it be awful if . . .

- We couldn't prevent . . .
- I couldn't avoid . . .

Instead, you might ask . . .

- Wouldn't it be unpleasant if . . .
- Wouldn't it be terrible if . . .
- Wouldn't it spoil my day if . . .

(If you start with a negative, remember to flip it around to find the positive opportunity!)

Sometimes it can seem difficult to "stretch" your imagination in generating possible challenges and opportunities that might exist within a task. To stimulate your thinking about possible opportunity statements, consider the following word checklist:

- What would you like to . . .

correct?	minimize?	change?	turn around?
overcome?	invent?	discover?	move forward?
restore?	resolve?	reverse?	wish or hope for?

put to other uses?	eliminate?	improve?	convince others?
optimize?	maximize?	mechanize?	revise?
computerize?	humanize?	do away with?	develop?
enhance?	produce?	stimulate?	restructure?
present?	verify?	test?	produce?
adapt?	capture?	locate?	find?
show?	tell?	make?	

- Are there opportunities for . . .

experiments?	presentations?	organizations?	procedures?
programs?	productions?	campaigns?	tests/instruments?
publications?	policies?	public impact?	plans?
services?	models?	proposals?	awards?
networks?	newsletters?	publicity?	laws?

Opportunity statements can be generated using any of the tools described in the CPS toolbox in Chapter 2. Frequently, it is helpful to begin generating opportunity statements using brainstorming, although you might also use many other generating tools to stimulate varied results or outcomes.

Focusing When Constructing Opportunities

When you use the focusing phase in Constructing Opportunities, your aim is to channel or direct your efforts toward the key opportunities and challenges you want to address. Your initial step is to be clear about ownership, or the responsibility for implementation. It is always important to look for opportunities that you (individually, or with a group) can actually use, apply, or do something with to move forward to an effective outcome or solution. Ownership is an important consideration through-out the CPS components and stages, and you will read more about it in Chapters 6, 7, and 11. In the Constructing Opportunities stage, being clear about ownership is extremely important to guide effective focusing. The three I's of ownership (interest, influence, and imagination) are reviewed in Chapter 7.

Identify the opportunity statements from your list for which you have interest (motivation and commitment). If you have no motivation or interest in working on the situation, you will most likely not have the energy or commitment necessary to work through the tough points along the way. Next, look for the opportunity statements for which you have influence. This means that you have responsibility or authority to do something with the results of your problem-solving efforts. If you do not have influence, your energy might be wasted because you do not have the necessary authority, power, or control to follow through from ideas to actions. Finally, look for opportunity statements that call on you to use your imagination to create change or improvement. Lacking a need for novel or unusual outcomes or results, there would be little or no need to use CPS, and other approaches or methods might be better suited to the task.

You can use these three criteria to screen, sort, or sift your opportunity state-ments, and to turn your focus away from ones that might be inappropriate for CPS, making it easier to identify the most attractive, interesting, or promising opportunities for your work.

After you have generated many, varied, and unusual opportunity statements, and then applied the three tests for ownership, it is still likely that some of the remaining statements might seem more appropriate than others for addressing a particular issue. Look for the options that tend to "stand out" or "bounce off the page" at you. When focusing your thinking, your intuition, instincts, experience, feelings, or hunches will often guide you in identifying the opportunity statements that are most interesting or intriguing to pursue. We find that it is more often helpful to trust those personal impressions and judgments than to distrust them because "they aren't objective enough," precise enough, or scientific enough. It is important to work at being honest with yourself, and then to have confidence in your ability to locate and recognize the promising challenges and opportunities in front of you. You can also use many of the focusing tools from the CPS toolbox in Chapter 2 to help identify, construct, or choose an effective opportunity statement.

Constructing Opportunities: A Sample Application

Figure 3.6 is a copy of an actual article that appeared in a newspaper. It is a story about an inmate named Vernon Williams who was causing a lot of problems in a prison. Vernon

Figure 3.6   The Vernon Case Study

Inmate is Giant of Problem

New York (UPI) - "A giant inmate, who prison guards claim can break his handcuffs at will, has Rikers Island prison in a state of terror," said a spokesman for the guards' union Friday.

Correction officials admitted that they don't know what to do with Vernon Williams, who stands 6-foot-3 and weighs 375 pounds.

Williams, who is in jail waiting trial for four different charges, including assault and robbery, has been charged with assaulting six prison officials and two nurses during his stay at Rikers Island.

After Williams was charged with assaulting the nurses in October, prison officials ordered that he be handcuffed whenever leaving his cell, and accompanied at all times by no fewer than five guards.

"It would be funny if it wasn't so serious," said one correction official.

On Friday, Williams allegedly attacked officer Jose Aponte, breaking his nose.

After that incident, Phil Seelig, president of the Corrections Officers Benevolent Association, announced that his men would not go near Williams any longer.

VERNON CASE STUDY

was a very large inmate who, when angered, was strong enough to break handcuffs and hurt people. The warden and employees of the prison had to find a way to deal with Vernon and bring prison life back to order. This article will be used in Chapters 3, 4, and 5 as a case study to demonstrate applications of the CPS stages and several CPS tools.

Remember that the goal of Constructing Opportunities is to help you identify the general direction you want to pursue for a given task. In the Vernon Case Study, for example, the warden might have been thinking about general challenges associated with life in the prison (see the top half of Figure 3.7). However, after the Vernon incident took place, the warden might have shifted his attention to a particular set of prison issues related to Vernon (see lower half of Figure 3.7). After thinking about a variety of opportunity statements, the warden could have identified the most important and urgent issue as being the safety of the prison officials. As a result, he might have selected the opportunity statement in bold type in Figure 3.7.

Figure 3.7   Examples of Opportunity Statements From the Vernon Case Study

---

Opportunity Statements

Possible opportunities on the mind of the warden before the incident:

- WIBNI we had an improved correctional system?
- WIBNI we could improve our resources?
- WIBNI we had more counseling programs?
- WIBNI we had a better relationship with the governor's review board?
- WIBNI we had multiple sources of funding?
- WIBAI the state cut our funding?
- WIBNI we had more cooperation between different prison programs?
- WIBNI the prison was viewed as an important part of society?
- WIBNI the review board and prison officials had common goals?

Likely opportunities on the warden's mind after the incident:

- WIBNI we had better ways of restraining Vernon?
- WIBNI the correction officials could work safely?
- WIBAI violence spread throughout the system?
- WIBAI the correction officials were continuously harmed?
- WIBNI the prison was undisturbed by Vernon's situation?
- WIBAI prison funding was cut off because of the incident?

 VERNON CASE STUDY

What Is the Exploring Data Stage?

Developing the focus or direction for your problem-solving efforts requires a clear and accurate understanding of the current circumstances in which you find yourself.

Gathering data about the current circumstances of the task under consideration can provide a better understanding of where to focus your energy. The Exploring Data stage, as illustrated in Figure 3.8, helps you take a closer look at your context, the people involved in the situation, and your desired outcomes, and to find out what issues might really be at the "heart of the matter."

Figure 3.8 The Exploring Data Stage

Generating When Exploring Data

Often, many of the important factors to consider in any situation can be ambiguous, uncertain, or not out in open view. The purpose of generating in Exploring Data is to help ensure that you have a thorough and complete understanding of your present situation both at and below the surface of the situation. Generating helps avoid overlooking important or essential data that might influence your understanding of a particular task. By "data," we mean your awareness and understanding of important elements in a situation. We use the word *data* because it is a general term that encompasses many different sources of information or kinds of input. Figure 3.9

Figure 3.9   The Sources of Data Available for Understanding Your Situation

Information	Feelings	Observations	Impressions	Questions
Knowledge	Emotions	Notice	Intuitive guess	Inquiry
Facts	Sentiment	Perception	Hunch	Doubt
Intelligence	Awareness	Comment	Image	Perplexity
Memory	Affectiveness	Take into account	Reasonable expectation	Difficulty
Comprehension	Desire	Watch	Belief	Uncertainty
Recollection	Sensitivity		Vague notion	Curiosities
	Sympathy/ empathy			

identifies five different kinds and sources of data that might be generated when Exploring Data.

Information: Recognition, recall, and use of knowledge derived from study, experience, or instruction; knowledge of specific events, people, places, or situations; news; what is known and can be perceived, calculated, verified, discovered, or inferred

Impressions: Images or effects retained from past experiences; beliefs; hunches, notions, or intuitive perceptions or thoughts; what your "sixth sense" tells you

Observations: The act of noting, taking into account, and recording information through all your senses (see, hear, touch, taste, or feel) and from many vantage points

Feelings: Sensitivity or awareness of information through emotions, sentiments, or affective responses. Concerns for harmony, relationships, and effects on people

Questions: Areas of uncertainty or confusion, lack of clarity or information; areas of curiosity; paradoxes; perplexing experiences or events

A Tool for Exploring Data: 5WH

To assist you in generating data, use the Exploring Data tool known simply as "5WH." The 5WH tool involves six basic categories of questions to use in order to evoke different kinds of data. Five of the categories begin with W, and one with H. They are as follows:

- Who? and Who else?
- What? and What else?
- Where? and Where else?
- When? and When else?

- Why? and Why else?
- How? and How else?

For example, asking "Who?" identifies the key players (present, past, and future) associated with your situation. Asking "What?" calls for important data about things—materials, resources, or actions—related to the situation.

You can use the 5WH Exploring Data tool with the five sources of data to generate many different questions, as illustrated in Figure 3.10. For example, the following list includes samples of questions generated by asking one question for each type of data.

Figure 3.10   Questions for Exploring Data

Kinds of Data	Who?	What?	Where?	When?	Why?	How?
Information						
Impressions						
Observations						
Feelings						
Questions						

- Who? (Identifies the people involved)
  - ○ Who can provide me with information about my situation?
  - ○ Who has impressions different from my own?
  - ○ Who can I talk to about their observations?
  - ○ Who has strong feelings (positive or negative) about the current situation?
  - ○ Who can I go to, to answer critical questions?

- What? (Identifies things, materials, resources, etc., involved)
  - ○ What information can I recall about the situation?
  - ○ What impressions do I get from the context I am in?
  - ○ What observations can I or others make about the situation?
  - ○ What feelings are being generated by the current situation?
  - ○ What unanswered questions do I have about my context?

- Where? (Identifies places, locations, or events to consider)
  - ○ Where should I go (or not go) for information?
  - ○ Where are my, and other people's, impressions coming from?
  - ○ Where can I go to make accurate observations about my context?
  - ○ Where is the most harmony/disharmony in the context?
  - ○ Where can I go to get my unanswered questions resolved?

- When? (Identifies time frames or situations related to the situation)
  - ○ When is the best/worst time to gather information about the situation?
  - ○ When is my impression about the task strongest/weakest?

○ When should I observe the situation to get the most clear understanding?
○ When do feelings get strong (positively or negatively) in the situation?
○ When should I get my questions answered?

- Why? (Identifies reasons regarding the importance or need for the issue at hand)
  ○ Why has this information become an issue?
  ○ Why do I (or others) get the impressions they do about the task?
  ○ Why has what we observed happened?
  ○ Why are my (or other people's) feelings being influenced?
  ○ Why do the questions I have still remain about the task?

- How? (Identifies steps, activities, or actions involved in the situation)
  ○ What information can I gather about how this task became an issue?
  ○ How do my impressions about the task get formed?
  ○ How can I make observations about what is going on?
  ○ How do my (or other people's) feelings get hurt/supported in the task?
  ○ What questions can I raise about how this became an issue?

Focusing When Exploring Data

Identifying and paying close attention to every specific issue or detail in a task would require tremendous amounts of time and energy. When generating data, you will come up with many different pieces of information, questions, feelings, observations, or impressions. However, some pieces of those data will have more (or less) value, importance, and meaning in trying to understand your current reality. The purpose of focusing when you are Exploring Data is to help screen, sort, and organize the data in ways that guide you in understanding your current reality. Some of the data might distract your attention rather than clarifying your understanding of the task. While the generating phase in Exploring Data helps you bring out and be aware of as much data as possible, the focusing phase helps you summarize or sort the data so that you are able to see the current reality clearly and to understand the most important elements of the situation.

Figure 3.11   The Many Characteristics of a "Hit"

An option "hits" you when it is . . .

- On target
- Relevant
- Interesting
- Clear
- Intriguing
- Fascinating
- Workable
- Right "on the money"

Or when it . . .

- "Sparkles" at you
- Feels right
- Solves the problem
- Goes in the right direction

Identify Key Data. To identify critical or key data, *Selecting Hits* is an example of a tool that can be quite helpful. Selecting Hits is a focusing tool used to screen a large number or a wide variety of options. A hit is an option that seems interesting or intriguing. Figure 3.11 illustrates that an option can be a "hit" for you for a number of reasons.

When you apply Selecting Hits, you will use internal criteria, experience, and personal judgment in selecting options. Marking the hits forces you to examine all options. The first step is to identify the most promising or appealing options, or hits (often represented by a dot or other mark), as illustrated in Figure 3.12.

Figure 3.12 An Illustration of Selecting Hits in Action

SOURCE: Copyright © 2009. The Creative Problem Solving Group, Inc. Reprinted with permission.

Using the Selecting Hits tool to focus in the Exploring Data stage involves asking "What pieces of data give me the most important picture or understanding of my task?" or "To what data should I pay the most attention?" When you observe patterns or clusters of hits, you might also consider applying additional tools, such as Hot Spots and Highlighting. These will be discussed later in this chapter. In general, data can often be sorted into the following three categories:

• *Know:* These are data that are currently known and available to you. They are accessible with or without major effort or energy.

• *Need to know:* The "musts" that are needed to help you understand your current situation. These data provide key pieces that "unlock" the puzzle and provide you with valuable insights regarding the picture of your current reality.

• *Like or want to know:* The "wants" that would help you fill in the details or refine your picture and understanding of the current situation.

Exploring Data: A Sample Application

Figure 3.13 provides an illustration of the Exploring Data stage as it might have been applied in the Vernon Case Study. In the example, you will see a variety of sources of data, use of the 5WH Exploring Data tool, and marking hits (which are noted as bold-face type in the figure).

Figure 3.13 Examples of Data From the Vernon Case Study

Examples of Data

Who might be involved?
- **Vernon**
- Guards
- Handcuff manufacturers

What?
- Rikers Island
- **375 lbs., 6′ 3″**
- **Breaks handcuffs**

Where?
- **Prison**
- On an island

When?
- **Needs handcuffs only when walking between buildings**
- When does he need to be moved?

Why?
- To stop the terror
- To protect nurses, guards, etc.

How?
- Constrain
- Transfer
- **Understand motivations**

Who else?
- Vernon's mom
- Other prison staff
- Warden

What else?
- In jail temporarily
- **Needs to wear handcuffs when leaving cell**

Where else?
- In the nurses' office
- At home

When else?
- October, November
- **How long can the staff tolerate his behavior?**

Why else?
- To help Vernon
- **To keep peace at the prison**

How else?
- Protect
- **Channel energy**
- Buy stronger handcuffs

VERNON CASE STUDY

What Is the Framing Problems Stage?

Most people face problems of differing sizes or importance on a daily basis. By "problem," we mean a specific gap between what you currently have or do, and an opportunity or need to create or do something new or different in the future. Problems require you to use your imagination to generate and identify options or possibilities that do not currently exist. They are situations for which there is no "answer book" or "recipe" that can be used to close the gap or find a simple solution or answer. A *problem*, as we will use the term, differs from the broad or general opportunity or challenge that you might describe in the Constructing Opportunities stage. A problem identifies a specific gap between the opportunity you want to create in the future and your current situation. It is a question that invites you to generate new, exciting possibilities that will be powerful as you move forward toward a desired future. Some people have a negative reaction to the word *problem*. They see a problem as something to be avoided rather than as an issue they can solve, change, or deal with productively. Don't think of problems only as something wrong, deficient, or needing repair or correction; look at them instead as questions that pave the way for new and useful options.

A certain amount of tension accompanies your recognition of a gap between what you have or do now and what you would like to have or do in the future. It might be an uncomfortable or uneasy tension, but it can also be a stimulating, enthusiastic tension, too. Such tensions are often the starting points or "triggers" for problem solving. You can use your problem-solving skills, talents, and motivations to reduce or resolve the tension in two ways. First, you might resolve the tension by changing your image of what you want to create in the future—making it closer to what you already have or do now. This reduces your expectations about what you will have or do in the future and so reduces the tension. Second, you can seek to change what you currently have or do now into what you want to create in the future—moving your current reality closer to your desired future image. This also reduces the gap or difference between the two states (present and future) and helps resolve the tension. Effective problem solvers (that means you!) work to close gaps and resolve tensions by changing their current realities so that they move in the direction of their desired future states.

The purpose of the Framing Problems stage of CPS is to help you identify specific pathways to help you move your current reality closer to your desired future state. Before you can clearly identify gaps, however, you must have an understanding of what you want to create in the future, and what you currently have, as well as an understanding of their position in relation to each other. When you understand both the opportunity you want to create and the current reality of the task, and you need to identify pathways to guide you in moving forward, then you will benefit from using the Framing Problems stage of CPS.

Constructing an Effective Problem Statement

As John Dewey, a well-known educational philosopher, once stated, "A problem well stated is a problem half solved." The way a problem is stated has a strong impact on its ability to stimulate ideas for solving it. For example, like most people, you have probably sat in many groups or meetings or had conversations with people and heard statements such as

I don't have enough time to do my class work.

It's too expensive, we don't have the money.

We don't have the support we need to get the job done.

or

It has never been done like that before.

What we're doing now works just fine.

We need a task force to study it first.

Why aren't these satisfactory or helpful problem statements? First, they are all negatively worded. Most people report that these kinds of discussions are rather depressing. Before anyone even begins to do anything, many of the people are already discouraged or have a self-defeating attitude. Second, these statements turn thinking off, rather than turning it on. They tend to give people more reasons not to act than to try to do something. A problem statement should identify the specific pathways you might take to close the gap, move forward, or solve the problem. We prefer to structure problem statements in a way that directs your thinking toward a productive pathway for idea generation. They should motivate you to think about what might be done to transform your current reality into your desired future state, not about what can't be done or why you won't be able to do it.

Effective problem statements have *idea-finding potential*. By "idea-finding potential," we mean that problem statements are about searching for possibilities—a "can do" outlook, not about impossibilities, or a "can't do" attitude. Problem statements with idea-finding potential:

Invite ideas: They are phrased to invite many new ideas and possibilities or actions. They draw you naturally into the flow of generating.

State the issue for which you really want ideas: There are usually many different ways to look at the problem in a given task domain. Problem statements identify the specific issue that needs to be addressed.

Are concise: They are brief statements (5–7 words) that come right to the point, so they will be easy to understand and use as a starting point for idea generation.

Locate ownership: They identify the person or people who have ownership for the specific problem.

Are free of criteria: They do not "box you in" or limit your thinking by being filled with restrictions, limitations, or qualifications. Keeping them free from criteria opens up the range of possible answers, instead of closing it down (as shown in Figure 3.14).

Figure 3.14 Effective Problem Statements Are Free of Criteria

SOURCE: Copyright © 2009. The Creative Problem Solving Group, Inc. Reprinted with permission.

We suggest that you write problem statements that will follow a specific format or structure to help ensure that they deal with the five elements of an effective problem statement. The format we recommend, illustrated in Figure 3.15, develops in these steps:

An invitational stem: Begin with a stem that opens up, or invites, many possible responses. Three stems (and their abbreviations) that we have found particularly helpful include: How to . . . (H2 . . . ?), How might . . . (HM . . . ?), and In what ways might . . . (IWWM . . . ?).

An owner: Next, identify clearly the person or people who will be responsible for working on or following up with the problem. Be specific about stating whose problem you are working on! Ownership is often closely linked to the invitational stem. For example, "How might I . . ." suggests the problem belongs to one person. "In what ways might we . . ." suggests group ownership. The stem might be followed by the name of a specific person or group. For example, "In what ways might Harry . . . ?" or "How might our team . . . ?" The stem "How to . . ." implies that ownership belongs generally to the person or people who will participate in generating the problem statements.

An action verb: The next step is to identify a specific and positive course or direction invited or envisioned by the statement. For example, a problem statement might be, "In what ways might we increase the membership of our group?" The word "increase" is a constructive, positive action verb that describes the desired action.

An objective: To complete the problem statement, identify the target or desired outcome and direction for your problem-solving activity. In the statement "In what ways might we increase the membership of our group?" the objective is what you're seeking to increase— "the membership of our group."

Figure 3.15   Guidelines for Writing Effective Problem Statements

- An invitational stem (How to . . . ? How might . . . ? In what ways might . . .?)
- Owner (Who?)
- Verb—Action (Do?)
- Object (What?)

The following problem statements are samples of the kinds of problems on which people in our programs and classes often choose to work. The examples include several different kinds of issues or task domains.

- Some of the problems focus on people issues:
  - IWWM I motivate my students' learning?
  - H2 prioritize the use of my work time?
  - H2 increase my contributions to my team?
  - H2 get clients to consult with me earlier?
  - H2 create and maintain effective teams?

- Others focus on products or outcomes:
  - H2 develop a new consumer product?
  - H2 build the ultimate service contract?
  - H2 convey product improvements to consumers?
  - H2 improve product availability?
  - H2 plan the perfect presentation?

- Still others focus on process-related issues:
  - H2 create a team vision?
  - IWWM we move projects ahead?
  - H2 have a team develop a production schedule?
  - H2 be more productive?
  - HM I develop my own creativity?

- Yet others focus on climate or context issues:
  - HM we make meetings more productive?
  - H2 organize my division to be more creative?

o IWWM I remove sexism from my workplace?
o H2 get organizations to work well together?
o H2 make time for developing ideas?

- The rest focus on general issues:
  o IWWM I improve interaction with management?
  o H2 measure impact on sales volume?
  o HM I invent names for new products?
  o H2 develop an ongoing training program?
  o HM I improve my relationships with other people in my life?

Generating in Framing Problems

The purpose of generating in Framing Problems is to help identify a wide array or spectrum of possible problem statements, as illustrated in Figure 3.16. Problem statements are not possible solutions for a problem, but questions that open the door for your search for ideas that might become solutions or actions. The reason you identify problem statements is to prepare to generate options that will help you move your current realities closer to

Figure 3.16 The Framing Problems Stage

SOURCE: Copyright © 2009. The Creative Problem Solving Group, Inc. Reprinted with permission.

your image of the future state. There is little reason to generate problem statements if you do not plan to search actively and deliberately for new ways to deal with the problem.

Problem statements can be generated using any of the tools described in the CPS toolbox. We will describe one tool called the "Ladder of Abstraction" that is particularly helpful in Framing Problems. It will often help you to find a comfortable, stimulating way to state your problem.

Ladder of Abstraction

Sometimes people have difficulty searching for ideas because they have narrowed or limited their understanding and statement of the problem so much that they don't have any "room" for novel ideas or perspectives. In that case, it helps to restate the problem in a broader, more open form. On other occasions, people discover that a problem statement is so broad that their search for ideas flounders and lacks the specific direction they need to help move forward. The Ladder of Abstraction tool helps them consider problem statements at various levels to locate the most useful statement for the task.

Many different problem statements can be generated by asking two questions, "How?" and "Why?" By asking these questions and turning the responses into new problem statements, you can move up and down in levels of abstraction, as illustrated in Figure 3.17.

By moving up the Ladder of Abstraction, we mean posing the problem in a broader, more inclusive way. By moving down the ladder, we mean seeking a narrower, more specific question. For example, asking the question "Why?" promotes movement up the

Figure 3.17 The Ladder of Abstraction

ladder, where answers are more general and abstract. In Figure 3.18 (our Vernon Case Study), the initial problem statement was "In what ways might the guards control Vernon?"

Figure 3.18 An Example of the Ladder of Abstraction From the Vernon Case Study

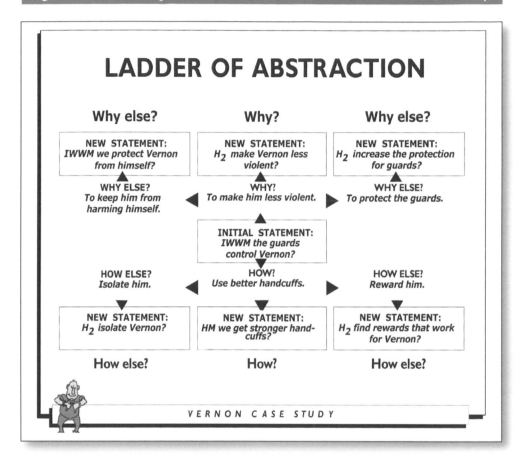

By asking the question, "Why do the guards want to control Vernon?" you might get the response, "To make him less violent." This response can be turned into a new problem statement: "How to make Vernon less violent?" If you ask, "Why do you want to make Vernon less violent?" one response might be, "To improve the quality of prison life." This response can also be turned into a new problem statement such as, "In what ways might we improve the quality of life in prison?" Each time you ask the question, "Why?" the resulting problem statements are broader and more abstract.

On the other hand, each time you ask the question, "How?" the answers lead you to new problem statements that become more specific and concrete. For example, asking "How might the guards control Vernon?" might result in the response, "Use better handcuffs." This response can be turned into a new problem statement: "How might we create stronger handcuffs?" This process can move you down the ladder to identify very specific and concrete problem statements.

The Ladder of Abstraction not only lets you move up and down levels, it also lets you move across similar abstraction levels. By asking "Why else?" and "How else?" you can identify several possible alternative statements at the same level of abstraction. Each of these responses can be turned into a new problem statement. In Figure 3.18, the problem statements above the initial statement tend to be more abstract and the problem statements below the initial statement tend to be more concrete and specific.

Focusing When Framing Problems

The purpose of focusing in Framing Problems is to help categorize, select, evaluate, refine, or screen specific pathways to pursue when solving a problem. When generating many, varied, and unusual problem statements, it is common to have some that seem more appropriate than others, and some that are repetitive or that overlap with other problem statements. Any of the focusing tools in the CPS toolbox in Chapter 2 can be used during Framing Problems. However, the specific tool we will review here is *Highlighting*. (This tool incorporates and extends the Selecting Hits tool.)

Highlighting

Sometimes, after Selecting Hits, you will find it helpful to categorize the options or to compress the number of options into a more manageable number. You might recognize several themes within the hits, and in this case, you might use Highlighting as your next step, as illustrated in Figure 3.19 and summarized in Figure 3.20.

Figure 3.19   An Illustration of Highlighting in Action

SOURCE: Copyright © 2009. The Creative Problem Solving Group, Inc. Reprinted with permission.

Figure 3.20   The General Steps of Highlighting

- Find the hits
- Find the relationships among the hits
- Find the hot spots
- Restate the hot spots

After you have identified the hits, look for common elements or relationships among several of the hits. Are some of them clearly linked by a common element or theme? Group them together.

Find the hot spots. After examining the hits for similarities and placing the related hits together, the next step in using the Highlighting tool is to identify the hot spots or name the relationship they share.

Restate the hot spots. Now that you have identified the dominant theme of each cluster, restate the hot spots as problem statements (if you were using this tool in another stage, you would restate the hot spot in relation to the options appropriate for that stage—opportunity statements, key cluster of data, ideas, promising solution, or possible direction for taking action). Often several themes can emerge within each category, which you might prioritize or weave together into a new or broader cluster.

When you have completed your work with the Selecting Hits and Highlighting tools, review the restatements or clusters you have formed and decide on the relative priority of each. This will help you in the focusing phase of Framing Problems, by guiding you in selecting an option (or combining more than one of the options) on which you will focus your problem-solving energy and efforts. You will use the results of your application of the Selecting Hits and Highlighting tools to choose or construct a problem statement that does the best job of posing the question for which you need and want many, varied, and novel ideas. It is possible to work several problem statements, if necessary (and if you have ample time and energy), so you might not necessarily close this stage by stating only a single problem statement.

Figure 3.21 provides a list of problem statements generated using brainstorming for the Vernon Case Study. The problem statements in bold represent the hits.

Figure 3.21   Examples of Problem Statements From the Vernon Case Study

Problem Statements

- IWWM the handcuffs be stronger?
- IWWM the nurses drug Vernon?
- HM Phil Seelig have Vernon shipped elsewhere?
- **IWWM we get Vernon released from prison?**
- IWWM Vernon's mom help Vernon?
- H2 keep Vernon in the building?
- HM the guards protect the nurses?
- **HM the warden control Vernon's behavior?**
- H2 develop a deterrent that works for Vernon?
- H2 rehabilitate Vernon?
- **H2 use another form of restraining?**
- **IWWM we improve construction of the handcuffs?**
- IWWM we involve Vernon in rehabilitation?
- **IWWM we develop alternative ways of transporting Vernon?**
- IWWM we train Vernon to become a guard?
- **H2 improve rehabilitation programs?**
- IWWM we improve the prison system?

VERNON CASE STUDY

Figure 3.22 gives an example of using the Highlighting tool to compress the problem statements generated for the Vernon Case Study.

Figure 3.22 An Example of Highlighting From the Vernon Case Study

HIGHLIGHTING

Hits

1. HM the warden control Vernon's behavior?
2. H2 use another form of restraining?
3. IWWM we improve the construction of the handcuffs?
4. IWWM we develop alternative ways of transporting Vernon?
5. H2 improve rehabilitation programs?
6. H2 develop a deterrent that works for Vernon?
7. IWWM we get Vernon released from prison?

Relationships between the Hits

CLUSTER 1

2. H2 use another form of restraining?
3. IWWM we improve the construction of the handcuffs?
4. IWWM we develop alternative ways of transporting Vernon?

CLUSTER 2

1. HM the warden control Vernon's behavior?
5. H2 improve rehabilitation programs?

Hot Spots

Cluster 1: Harm-free transportation

Cluster 2: Behavior modification

Restatement of Hot Spots

Cluster 1: In what ways might we transport Vernon?

Cluster 2: How to get Vernon involved in his own rehabilitation?

 VERNON CASE STUDY

Figure 3.23 summarizes the examples from the Vernon Case Study for all three stages in this component.

Figure 3.23   A Summary of Understanding the Challenge From the Vernon Case Study

Understanding the Challenge
Component Summary

Opportunity Statement

WIBNI the correction officers could perform their work in a safe manner?

Key Data

- Prison officials ordered that Vernon wear handcuffs whenever leaving his cell
- Vernon breaks handcuffs
- Vernon has assaulted guards and nurses
- He's big, strong, and violent
- Understand Vernon's motivations
- Guards won't go near him any longer

Problem Statement

How to get Vernon involved in his own rehabilitation?

 VERNON CASE STUDY

The Rest of the Story

What were the outcomes in the case of the software development company division facing impending doom from competition? We developed and implemented a 3-day workshop with the senior management team of the facility. The main focus of the workshop was to help them determine how to approach the impending dangers of patent expiration and increasing competition. Their decision was very interesting. Rather than creating new products in the same product area, and engaging in a direct battle with the competition, they decided to create an alternative vision of the future, one that moved them into different areas of business.

Through extensive prework with the group, we clarified their understanding of their current realities. We spent the first day and a half of the workshop creating a new vision for the business, using the Constructing Opportunities stage of CPS. This was an excellent place to begin because the group did not see the impending danger of competition as an opportunity. They perceived it as a major threat. As one person in the group put it, "People are going to lose their jobs if we don't do something about this." They ended up creating multiple business units to provide new products and services that built on their existing competencies.

Once they attained a clear agreement about their desired image of the future, we worked with the group to identify the core problems they might face in making the vision come true. Later, the group used the core problem statements they developed to generate ideas and plans to make the desired future into a reality. Today, the facility is doing extremely well, and two of the new business lines they created are very profitable. They were able to save most of the jobs and subsequently hired additional people to manage the new business lines.

Putting This Chapter to Work

This chapter has focused on ways to obtain clarity through generating and focusing opportunities, data, and problem statements. You were introduced to a number of specific tools as well as some helpful language to guide your thinking when moving toward clarity for your CPS efforts.

Activities to Guide Reflection and Action

Work on one or more of the following activities to review your understanding of the material in this chapter and to practice applying the content in real situations. If you are using this book as part of a course or study group, you may wish to work individually, and then compare your responses, or to work collaboratively as a team.

1. Practice identifying opportunities. Start by generating a long list of potential outcomes and obstacles (using the appropriate CPS language). Then, when you have many, varied, and unusual alternatives, apply the three "I's" of ownership to see which one might be suitable for you to approach.

2. Think about a situation in your work or personal life that required clarity—particularly about the current reality (data). Identify the role that emotions and feelings played in helping obtain a more complete understanding of the situation. Remember, we have all been taught to separate fact from opinion. Sometimes, opinions really count!

3. Take a look at your daily newspaper or an interesting news story from an online source. After giving the story a quick read, see if you can identify a major opportunity statement that captures the thrust of the story. Then generate a list of problem statements that the story suggests. Practice using the Ladder of Abstraction when you are generating the problem statements so that you end up with many, varied, and unusual problem statements. Many situations contain numerous perspectives from a problem definition point of view.

Generating Ideas

The best way to have a good idea is to have lots of ideas.

—Linus Pauling

The purpose of Chapter 4 is to examine the Creative Problem Solving (CPS) component Generating Ideas and its use in identifying many, varied, and unusual possibilities for any question or problem statement. After studying the Generating Ideas component, you will be able to do the following:

1. Define and give examples of fluency, flexibility, originality, and elaboration and explain their use in CPS.

2. Describe and apply several specific tools for generating many options, formulating different or varied possibilities, and developing novel or unusual options.

3. Identify and select ideas or clusters of ideas that are new, intriguing, and promising for further refinement and development.

4. Apply specific tools for Generating Ideas when working on your own problems and questions.

A group of educators from a suburban school district needed to generate ideas for helping elementary school students learn and apply a variety of creative-thinking and problem-solving tools. The district had a very positive and progressive image in the community; its students performed well on achievement measures, and the schools were successful in relation to many other traditional indicators of educational quality.

However, many of the district's administrators and teachers felt that some important aspects of teaching and learning were still missing from the picture. They expressed the concern that their students were not really learning the important skills and tools of creative and critical thinking that paved the way for more complex kinds of problem solving and decision making. They believed that those tools are important "new basics" that will be important for all students to know as they prepare for life and work in a complex, rapidly changing world. In some ways, the schools' successes on some criteria made it difficult to convince a number of people that anything should be changed at all or that any important skills were being inadequately dealt with in the district's classrooms. They were concerned that many classroom teachers weren't certain that anything was missing and that since "they weren't aware of what they didn't know," efforts to encourage them to learn new tools and to incorporate them into their daily teaching would meet with considerable resistance.

During a group meeting, we addressed the question, "In what ways might we bring creative- and critical-thinking tools into every classroom?" After reviewing the key information, the mixed feelings, and paradoxes in the situation, the group began Generating Ideas. After a few minutes, the group's energy and flow of ideas began to wane considerably. One of the group members said,

> You know, these are all ideas that have been tried and tried, and tried again. Our staff has seen them all at one time or another. Sometimes, the familiar ideas don't have any impact at all, and at other times, they work for a little while and then fade away when the novelty wears off.

Another person, looking at a beverage container on which there was a drawing of a superhero cartoon character, said, "Right! You know, what we need to get is a Masked Marauder who comes running, unannounced, into any classroom, and gets everyone fired up to be creative thinkers, and then dashes off without anyone knowing who it really was!" Everyone laughed, and we decided it was time to take a break!

How do you come up with ideas that extend beyond the ordinary, commonplace, or familiar possibilities? How do you stretch your thinking, and construct possibilities that really are novel and useful? What happens when someone makes a "flippant" and "far out" suggestion and no one can resist laughing? This chapter deals with these kinds of questions. We will examine the components and stages of the CPS framework that will help you generate many, varied, and unusual ideas and extend your search so that you will explore ideas that are both novel and useful.

Generating Ideas is the component that has most often (and for the longest time) been associated with CPS in informal discussions or descriptions of the process. People often perceive this component as an enjoyable, playful process. It is also an important component which can, and should, be taken seriously; it is more than just "having fun." Generating Ideas, as its name implies, is concerned with the efforts made by an individual or group to think of many, new, and varied ideas for solving a problem or answering an open-ended question. The question might involve a problem that you choose to address, one that was "given to you" by someone else, or one that you created when working in another CPS component or stage (e.g., the Framing Problems stage). The Generating Ideas component often results in the "raw material" that can be used for developing and implementing new solutions.

This chapter will examine some misunderstandings commonly associated with idea generation. It will provide an overview of the Generating Ideas component in a nutshell. It will also examine the purpose, input, processing, and output of the stage, as well as the specialized language contained within. We will examine the dynamic balance between generating and focusing in the Generating Ideas stage and present several tools for generating and focusing on ideas.

Generating Ideas in a Nutshell

Generating Ideas begins with a problem statement or question that has been worded carefully, so it will invite many, varied, and/or unusual ideas. The graphic for Generating Ideas (see Figure 4.1) summarizes the important *input, processing,* and *output* considerations for this component.

Figure 4.1 Generating Ideas in a Nutshell

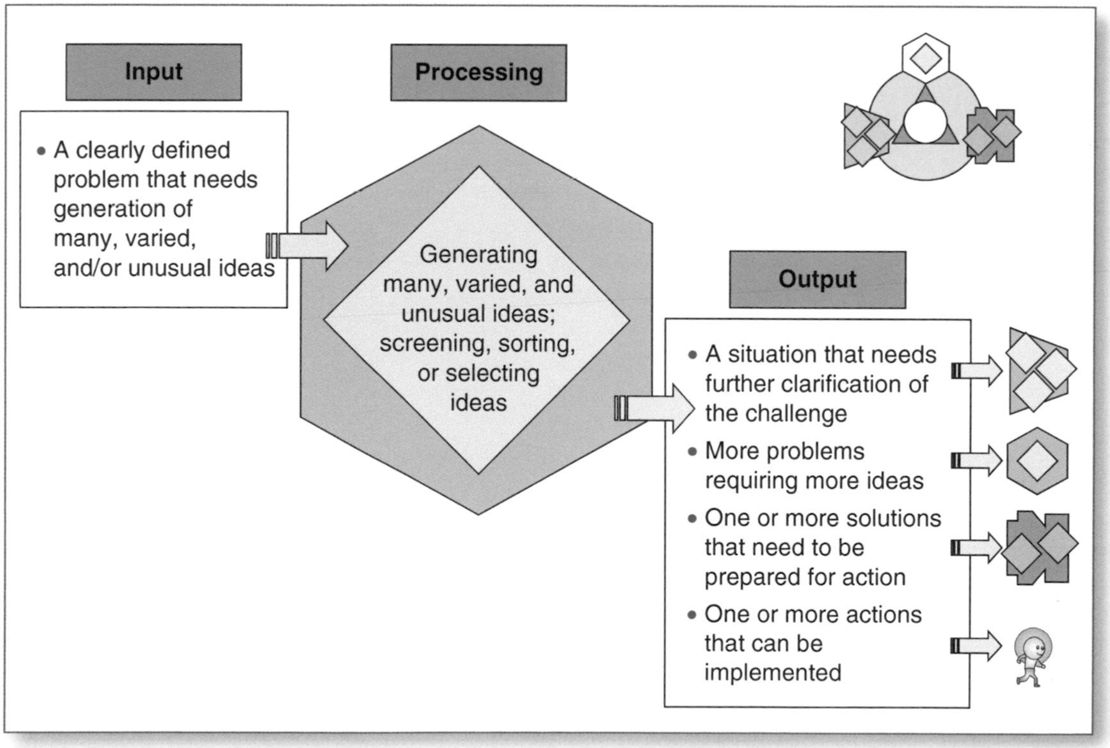
Input
• A clearly defined problem that needs generation of many, varied, and/or unusual ideas
Processing
Generating many, varied, and unusual ideas; screening, sorting, or selecting ideas
Output
• A situation that needs further clarification of the challenge
• More problems requiring more ideas
• One or more solutions that need to be prepared for action
• One or more actions that can be implemented

SOURCE: Copyright © 2009. The Creative Problem Solving Group, Inc. and The Center for Creative Learning, Inc. Reprinted with permission.

Input

The key question to pose in determining your need for the Generating Ideas component is "Do I (we) need many, varied, and unusual ideas to respond to a question that has already been formulated?" If you need and want new ideas, and you have a clearly worded and open-ended problem statement that invites creative thinking, this component would be an appropriate choice.

Processing

The Generating Ideas component is unique among the three process components, since it includes just one stage. In this component and stage, there is both a generating phase and a focusing phase, but the strongest emphasis is on the generating side. When Generating Ideas, you will use a number of tools to help produce new ideas. Applying the principle of deferred judgment and the guidelines for generating options, you will "stretch" your mind in an effort to respond to the problem statement. You will seek quantity, and you will also make deliberate efforts to generate ideas that draw on new perspectives or points of view, to challenge any assumptions and break away from habit-bound thinking, and to think of ideas that will be unique or unusual. Next, you will use one or more focusing tools to screen, strengthen, sort, or select promising possibilities.

Output

The output of the Generating Ideas component and stage involves creating possibilities that are promising, intriguing, or inviting for you. Your output will usually follow one of four pathways. You might decide that you need further clarification or redefinition of the problem and turn to the Understanding the Challenge component. Or you might decide that you really need additional idea generation, perhaps considering a related subproblem, for example, or pursuing a certain direction that emerged in the initial idea-generation efforts. You might recognize the need to build or refine some of the options that have been produced, or the need to analyze or evaluate the ideas more carefully, or the need to build acceptance and an implementation plan, which might lead you to work with the Preparing for Action component. Finally, you might end up with ideas that are specific and ready for action, so you will exit from the CPS process and move directly to implementing them.

The "stems" we will introduce in this chapter, to highlight the specific language for Generating Ideas, are presented in Table 4.1. These stems provide starting points or "triggers" for generating and focusing in this component and stage.

What Is the Generating Ideas Component and Stage?

The major focus of the Generating Ideas component and stage is to produce many options, varied possibilities, and novel, or new, ideas for solving a problem or effecting a change. In CPS terminology, an "idea" is a beginning concept or preliminary thought—an option or a possibility. It is a tentative image you have about how you might respond to an open-ended question or problem statement that invites you to think of many, varied, or unusual possibilities. We have often heard or observed two reactions from

Table 4.1 The Language That Guides Your Thinking in Generating Ideas

Generating Ideas	
Generate	Focus
Think of as many ideas as you can imagine for . . .	**Identify those ideas that stand out or seem most interesting . . .**
To generate a large quantity of ideas	To screen and sort ideas
Think of all the different kinds of ideas you can for . . .	**Select some ideas you might want to consider further . . .**
To generate a variety of ideas	To select promising ideas
Generate really unusual ideas for . . .	**Point out a few intriguing ideas . . .**
To generate unusual ideas	To identify novel ideas

participants after idea-generating sessions; they might seem at first glance to be para-doxical or contradictory, but they are actually quite consistent. First, most people find that participating in idea-generation activities is enjoyable, stimulating, or even exhila-rating. (It is not accidental that the people in Figure 4.2 are smiling!)

Figure 4.2 The Generating Ideas Stage

Second, most people also say after an active idea-generation session,

I'm exhausted! I feel drained; I had no idea that mental work could be so difficult and tiring! It was really great when we were working away at producing ideas, and so I didn't even notice how much effort and energy I was using—until we stopped.

Points to Remember About Idea Generation

Unfortunately, some observers have noticed only that idea generation is usually stimulating, energizing, and enjoyable and have overlooked the effort that it entails. As a result, several misunderstandings have become all too common. These are some key things to remember to help hold a productive view of idea generation.

• *CPS and brainstorming are not the same:* CPS is a method with several components and stages; it calls for a high level of involvement and extended effort. Brainstorming is a tool—but only one tool among many—that can be useful in any CPS stage. The terms are certainly not synonymous.

• *Brainstorming is a specific and well-defined tool—not a generic word:* Many people use the term *brainstorm* when they really mean any number of different things—meet, discuss, "have a bull session," get together and talk informally, or sometimes even debate or argue! It is important to understand that brainstorming is a tool and that there are specific guidelines and procedures for using it effectively.

• *There is much more to productive problem solving than brainstorming:* Too often, we hear people say that they're going to solve a problem by brainstorming, by themselves or with a group, or that they have meetings (and meetings, and more meetings . . .) in which all they do is brainstorm. If they are not able to devote time and effort, individually or in a group, to choosing and using a variety of tools and to focus their thinking as well to generate an ever-expanding list of ideas, they are not likely to be very productive problem solvers. Sometimes, people use most of their time to brainstorm and then rush to a hasty decision when time runs short (as we discussed in Chapter 2).

• *There is extensive research supporting the effectiveness of brainstorming:* It is unfortunate that many people have the mistaken idea that research supports the conclusion that brainstorming is not productive. If you review the literature thoroughly, you will discover that this conclusion is quite inaccurate and that there is much evidence to support the effectiveness of brainstorming as a tool (Isaksen, 1998; Isaksen & Gaulin, 2005). The literature actually confirms many specific criteria and procedures that must be known and applied for brainstorming to be effective. Many of the studies with negative results actually demonstrate very effectively the consequences of ignoring those criteria or procedures.

Finally, when it comes to idea generation, there is an apparent paradox between "fun" and "work." Some people believe that if it looks too much like fun, it can't really be intellectually worthwhile. There sometimes seems to be a certain kind of masochism in the notion that if an activity isn't dull, serious, boring, or even painful, it cannot have much intellectual merit. We are willing to let those who hold that view serve as the participants in their own sessions. Although we do not subscribe to the view that thinking must be dull, stodgy, or pedantic, we are equally dissatisfied with those who equate creativity with undisciplined "running off at the mind." In the name of creativity, there are too many peddlers of the "fun and games" view. CPS is definitely not associated with those approaches. Creative thinking demands both freedom and openness on the one hand and solid effort or sustained work on the other.

Although this component involves only one CPS stage, its tasks and activities are as important as any other components in the framework. It involves a substantial amount of energy and effort. Good ideas with high potential for success are not matters of luck; they are the result of a great deal of deliberate work in the Generating Ideas component and stage.

The Generating Phase

As we have noted, the unique characteristic of Generating Ideas is (as its name indicates) its emphasis on *generating*. We will present and illustrate several tools and also provide some practical guidelines for deciding when to use which tool and for combining tools.

Qualities to Consider When Generating Options

When you are generating options, keep four principal qualities in mind. They are not mutually exclusive, and all of them might be considered "creative" in one way or another. At certain times, in certain settings, or for particular tasks, however, it might be important to emphasize one quality more than the others. To avoid the situation depicted in Figure 4.3, consider all four qualities. Building on many years of inquiry by E. Paul Torrance, J. P. Guilford, and other pioneers in creativity research, we refer to these four qualities as *fluency, flexibility, originality,* and *elaboration.* These four qualities are important in the generating phase of any of the CPS stages.

- *Fluency*
  - The ability to generate many options.
  - The focus is on a large quantity.

- *Flexibility*
  - The ability to generate many different categories of options.
  - The focus is on having different types or kinds of options (varied perspectives or different viewpoints).

- *Originality*
  - The ability to generate novel associations.
  - The focus is on generating unusual or unique options.

- *Elaboration*
  - The ability to add detail to options and to make them richer, fuller, more complete, or more interesting.
  - The focus is on "fleshing out" or *expanding an option.*

Figure 4.3   There Are Many Qualities of Ideas to Consider

SOURCE: Copyright © 2009. The Creative Problem Solving Group, Inc. Reprinted with permission.

Using Generating Tools

In Chapter 2, we listed several tools for generating options that might be used in any of the CPS components or stages. In this section, we will share examples of several of those tools, illustrating how they can be useful in the Generating Ideas component and stage. Since we are in the Generating Ideas component, we will talk about their use for generating ideas. However, they can be used in other stages for generating other options, such as opportunity statements (Constructing Opportunities stage), problem statements (Framing Problems stage), or criteria statements (Developing Solutions stage), and, of course, they can also lead directly to action statements.

The specific tools for generating that we will examine here are as follows:

- Brainstorming With Post-its®
- Brainwriting
- SCAMPER (substitute, combine, adapt, modify, magnify, minify, put to other uses, eliminate, rearrange, reverse; based on Alex Osborn's Checklist of Idea-Spurring Questions)

- Forced Fitting
- Visually Identifying Relationships
- Imagery Trek
- Attribute Listing
- Morphological Matrix

Brainstorming With Post-its®

When using the Brainstorming tool, many options can come to mind very quickly, whether you're working by yourself or as part of a group. This can become an obstacle. When you're working in a group, and only one person is writing, it's easy to miss some possibilities. People in the group might forget some of their ideas when they're waiting for an opportunity to be heard. The effect might actually be to slow down the "flow" of possibilities if group members find that they're always waiting for their options to be recorded. When you're working alone, ideas can sometimes occur to you so quickly that it can be difficult to write them all down, too. In either case, some valuable new possibilities could be lost.

There are a number of ways to deal with this. For example, people in a group might write down their ideas on some notepaper while waiting for the recorder and share them when the flow slows down. An assistant recorder might help you capture the ideas. Or you might also use a generation tool that allows the group members to function independently.

Brainstorming With Post-its, as shown in Figure 4.4, involves the use of large (about 3 inches by 5 inches) Post-it notes. People write their ideas down, capturing one idea per Post-it note. They say their idea out loud and then place it on the flip-chart paper. Saying it out loud makes it possible for others to consider possible connections or to build on the idea; placing the Post-it note on the sheet captures the idea for later review and keeps it in view for the group. When you're working by yourself, using the notes can also help you capture ideas quickly and efficiently.

Some advantages of this tool include the following:

- *Speeding up the flow*

  Participants in a group do not have to wait for the facilitator to record each option before sharing another. Instead of having only one recorder for the group, each participant becomes a recorder. Working alone, you can complete the notes quickly, too.

- *Positive effect on fluency*

  The easier flow of options often leads to the production of a larger set of possibilities.

- *Improved sorting and focusing*

  Since each option is on its own Post-it, it can be moved around, categorized, and evaluated more efficiently. Although you can place the options in the order that they are generated, they can also be categorized as they are collected.

Figure 4.4 An Illustration of Brainstorming With Post-its® in Action

SOURCE: Copyright © 2009. The Creative Problem Solving Group, Inc. Reprinted with permission.

In a group, this tool allows everyone to hear, and thus, potentially, to build on each other's alternatives. We find that the amount of "hitchhiking" or building on the ideas of others is sometimes lower with this tool than it is with traditional brainstorming. Figure 4.5 provides an example of the tool using the Vernon Case Study.

Brainwriting

One common concern in many idea-generation sessions is that it is always possible for a few individuals (especially those who are more extroverted or verbal in their personality or style) to take over the group or dominate the group's efforts. Sometimes, they may not even be aware that certain members of the group are holding back or are not contributing their thoughts. Some members of the group might be content to let the more vocal members carry the ball. Others might be intimidated by the more vocal participants or might lack the confidence to express their thoughts. Another related concern is that some people report that the rapid pace and quick flow of oral ideas simply outruns their ability to frame and express their thoughts; the group's activity

Figure 4.5 An Example of Brainstorming With Post-its® From the Vernon Case Study

BRAINSTORMING WITH POST-ITS®

How to get Vernon involved in his own rehabilitation?

Threaten him	Isolate him	Encourage weight loss	Find out what he likes to do	Find out what bothers him
Let him escape	Shoot him	Drug him	Hire guards bigger than him	Shorten stay
Advance trial date	Seek out his relatives for advice	Seek out his friends for advice	Make friends with him	Be his buddy
Take advantage of his strength	Have him test security devices	Put him in charge of other inmates	Give him a lobotomy	Send him flowers
Put other inmates in charge of him	Seek help from the World Wrestling Federation (WWF)	Challenge the WWF to control Vernon	Hire guards from the WWF	Offer Vernon a contract with the WWF
Get him an audition at Universal Studios	Send his picture to Faces International	Offer him more food if he cooperates	Offer him less food if he cooperates	Reward him if he behaves
Ask him why he misbehaves	Punish him for misbehaving	Teach him a trade *	Trade him to another prison *	Find a beauty for the beast
Show him King Kong movies	Trade him to a football team *	Get him involved in sports *	Encourage him to channel his strength in a positive direction	Make him weak
Make him thin	Make him touch his chin	Don't make him do anything	Ask him to cooperate	Keep him shackled at all times
Transport him after four hours on a Stair-climber	Help him set goals	Assign someone to work closely with him	Allow him to achieve goals	Help Vernon to attain self-esteem
Help him attain self-actualization	Keep him happy	Find out what motivates him	Find out what aggravates him	Find out what agitates him
Make him wrestle alligators	Find out what he's afraid of	Have Vernon design his own rehabilitation program	Give him responsibilities	Keep him motivated

VERNON CASE STUDY

flows too rapidly for them to take their time and be ready to present their idea. To deal with these concerns, many group facilitators and leaders searched for ways to provide privacy and adequate "thinking space" for individuals in any group. A specific tool emerged, called Brainwriting (see Figure 4.6).

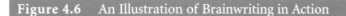

Figure 4.6   An Illustration of Brainwriting in Action

SOURCE: Copyright © 2009. The Creative Problem Solving Group, Inc. Reprinted with permission.

Brainwriting can be particularly useful to change the pace of a group idea-generation session, to provide privacy for participants, to enable individuals to contribute to the idea-generation efforts in a comfortable, self-paced manner, and to support the participants' varied needs for reflection time. Brainwriting can provide individuals with extra time for reflection and incubation of ideas while still maintaining a flow of possibilities.

In using the Brainwriting tool, each participant begins with a sheet of paper that has been divided into several blocks of space in which to write (usually 12 blocks per sheet). Each person writes three options on his or her sheet and then places the sheet in the center of the group. Participants exchange the sheets, reading what has already been written and then adding three new ideas to the sheet before exchanging it again for another sheet from those available in the center of the group. The exchange of the sheets, back and forth throughout the group, continues until all 12 blocks on every sheet have been filled with new ideas from the group.

Figure 4.7 provides an example of the Brainwriting tool using the Vernon Case Study. Notice that the ideas generated in the columns on the Brainwriting form build on previously written ideas, as the group members apply the tool.

Figure 4.7   An Example of Brainwriting From the Vernon Case Study

BRAINWRITING

Statement: <u>How to get Vernon involved in his own rehabilitation?</u>

ROW	OPTION A	OPTION B	OPTION C
1	*Ask Vernon how he would run the prison if he were in charge*	*Have Vernon assist in a rehabilitation program for another prisoner or prison*	*Have Vernon design a better security system*
2	*Give Vernon responsibility for other prisoners*	*Find Vernon some friends*	*Get Vernon a job in product development*
3	*Involve Vernon in an outreach program*	*Set up a match-maker service*	*Get Vernon a job outside the prison*

VERNON CASE STUDY

This tool allows for privacy or anonymity of contributions and the self-pacing of ideas presented to the group. There are also some potential limitations to consider. It often leads to less hitchhiking or piggybacking with other people's ideas. People sometimes miss the active interaction among participants, and they do not always see or keep in mind other possibilities that are being generated as they work with the tool.

SCAMPER

Osborn (1953) proposed a series of idea-spurring questions to help stimulate the flow of new ideas. These questions serve as "triggers" or "jumping-off points" for other new ideas. It is necessary neither to use all the questions nor to apply them in any fixed or prescribed sequence. Every question might be helpful for any task or setting, but any of the questions might be the source of a new idea or an inspiration that hadn't occurred before!

Eberle (1971, 1997) began with Osborn's list of questions and reorganized them to form a simple mnemonic device (or memory aid) consisting of key words and questions for each letter of the word *SCAMPER,* as depicted in Figure 4.8.

Figure 4.8   An Illustration of SCAMPER in Action

SOURCE: Copyright © 2009. The Creative Problem Solving Group, Inc. Reprinted with permission.

The words and phrases for each letter are as follows:

- *Substitute?* Who else? What else? Other ingredients? Other material? Other process? Other power? Other place? Other approach? Other tone of voice?
- *Combine?* How about a blend? An alloy? An assortment? An ensemble? Combine units? Combine purposes? Combine appeals? Combine ideas?
- *Adapt?* What else is like this? What other idea does this suggest? Does the past offer a parallel? What could I copy? Whom could I emulate?
- *Modify? Magnify?* What to add? *Minify?* What to subtract? New twist? Change meaning, color, motion, sound, order, form, shape? Greater frequency? Stronger? Longer? Omit? Streamline? Split up?

- *Put to other uses?* Could its form, weight, or structure suggest another use? New ways to use? Other uses if modified? Change the context?
- *Eliminate?* Suppose we leave this out? Fewer parts? Condensed? Lower? Shorter? Lighter? Understate? How can we make less more? What can we do without?
- *Rearrange?* Turn it upside down? How about opposites?
- *Reverse?* Reverse roles? Turn tables? Interchange components? Other sequence? Change pace? Change schedule? Transpose cause and effect?

You can use the questions in the SCAMPER list in any order, sequence, or combination. Use the list as a "menu" of questions from which to choose to stimulate the flow of ideas. Figure 4.9 demonstrates the SCAMPER tool, using the Vernon Case Study.

Using the SCAMPER tool can be especially helpful to you in stimulating flexibility or changes in viewpoint or perspective or in stimulating a search for possibilities that take an option in a new or different direction that you hadn't previously considered. When used with a group, the tool often stimulates the participants' energy and enthusiasm in the search for new possibilities. The possible limitations of this tool include the tendency for you to emphasize too literally or narrowly the specific words for each letter of the acronym or for you to focus too much on using each term in a rigid, fixed sequence. The tool is intended to stimulate exploration and playful searching for new directions, not to be a very narrow prescription of steps or activities.

Figure 4.9 An Example of SCAMPER From the Vernon Case Study

SCAMPER

Statement:	How to control Vernon more effectively?
Substitute?	Use other kinds of restraints (e.g., electronic or audio—high pitch sound, laser or light beam)
Combine?	Use tranquilizers and visual images
Adapt?	Change his diet so he's listless and docile. Use behavior modification to make him a leader
Modify? Minify? Magnify?	Magnify—get guards who make Vernon look small and wimpy Minify—use a small object to control him (Mace, stun gun)
Put to other uses?	Make Vernon the wrestling coach. Get him to start a Sumo team
Eliminate?	The prison—put him on a desert island, with shark-infested water—airlift supplies
Rearrange? Reverse?	Make him the guard within a special security block; keep changing his hours and schedule until he gets confused

VERNON CASE STUDY

Forced Fitting

Have you ever noticed that new ideas sometimes come to you when you are looking at one thing and suddenly see something else? The object you looked at probably had nothing at all to do with your problem, but, perhaps very suddenly, looking at it led you to think of a new or very original idea for the problem. The *Forced Fitting* tool (see Figure 4.10) is designed to evoke the same reaction, on demand rather than by accident or luck.

Forced Fitting can be used in a number of different variations, but its essence involves looking at objects (or models of objects) that have been selected randomly (and have no deliberate, explicit link or relationship to the question or problem statement on which you are working). Then, you seek new possibilities or options relating to the problem or question that were stimulated or prompted by the random objects given. A common story has it that the idea of "velcro" came from observing the way a burr or thistle attached itself to the cloth of a hiker's trousers. As a recent commercial product example, consider the company that produced a lamp that can be set to turn on and gradually become brighter at a preset time (a forced fitting of "alarm clock" with the basic lamp design).

Figure 4.10   An Illustration of Forced Fitting in Action

SOURCE: Copyright © 2009. The Creative Problem Solving Group, Inc. Reprinted with permission.

Forced Fitting helps stimulate new and original thinking without interrupting the existing flow of your ideas. In some situations, this might be all that's necessary to stimulate fresh new possibilities. In other situations, it may be necessary to break away from the existing flow to generate ideas that are very different from those currently being generated.

Visually Identifying Relationships

You might use any or all your senses to take your mind away from the problem at hand and to use unrelated images or observations as starting points or "springboards" for creating novel ideas. Rich new possibilities often emerge when you put ideas or images together that are not usually related to each other. *Visually Identifying Relationships* (see Figure 4.11) can help you discover some new and valuable possibilities by taking time for incubation—a deliberate process of "removing yourself" from a task to gain new perspectives.

Or consider the example of a truck manufacturer who illustrated the sturdiness and power, combined with the maneuverability, of its new model by using a rhinoceros on roller skates to portray them visually in print media advertising.

Figure 4.11   An Illustration of Visually Identifying Relationships in Action

SOURCE: Copyright © 2009. The Creative Problem Solving Group, Inc. Reprinted with permission.

Use up to four different pictures as stimuli to present when you are using this tool. You might use posters, prints that can be passed around and observed, or you might simply ask the group to look around and make a note of visual images that strike them within the immediate environment. Then, ask the group members to identify and share creative connections—new options for dealing with the problem or question that were triggered for them by any one of the visual images or a combination of the images. The best connections often come from interesting, unusual, or paradoxical stimuli that are not immediately recognizable by the participants (and will not immediately be linked to a certain product or response).

While the Visually Identifying Relationships tool usually involves using visual stimuli that are readily available, it can easily be modified by asking people to create their own visual images or by using materials that would draw on other sensory modes to stimulate new possibilities or connections. Figure 4.12 demonstrates this tool using the Vernon Case Study.

Figure 4.12 An Example of Visually Identifying Relationships From the Vernon Case Study

Visually Identifying Relationships

STATEMENT: How to get Vernon involved in his own rehabilitation?

List of Observations From:

STIMULUS #1: A poster of fall leaves

Leaves everywhere

Variety of color

Feel like swimming

Wet

CONNECTIONS:

Give Vernon a lot of activities to do

Find out what "colors make Vernon happy"

Build the prisoners an indoor swimming pool

Involve Vernon in teaching people how to swim

STIMULUS #2: Children in a school room

Concentrating

Never liked those small desks

Needs more light

Some kids really look like they want to leave

CONNECTIONS:

Offer board games and cards

Have Vernon build furniture

Install a poker table in the recreation room

Let Vernon escape

VERNON CASE STUDY

Imagery Trek

The *Imagery Trek* tool invites you to create new connections by taking a mental (or physical) journey in which you first move away from the task or problem at hand and then return, searching for ways to relate your images and impressions from that journey to new possibilities or options for dealing with the problem. Similar tools have been described as "visual confrontation" or "excursion" tools. These tools stimulate highly original or novel possibilities by creating distance—moving away from the problem (and your assumptions and beliefs about it) to see or construct new possibilities. As depicted in Figure 4.13, start by making a list of 10 to 20 words. Look for words that suggest positive images for you and that might be used as either a noun or

Figure 4.13 An Illustration of Imagery Trek in Action

a verb. Taking one word at a time, think about the images the word gives you. Take a "mental journey," in which you follow where that image leads you. Then, generate novel connections—possible ways in which that image might relate to the problem statement or question on which you are working. Try to refine and develop the images.

The potential advantages of using the Forced Fitting tool, the Visually Identifying Relationships tool, or the Imagery Trek tool are similar. Using any of these tools can create opportunities for mental stretching, helping you generate highly novel or unexpected options and helping you elaborate or refine ideas by including many rich and interesting details. The three tools differ in the stimuli they employ: objects (Forced Fitting tool), visual images (Visually Identifying Relationships tool), or images constructed in a mental journey (Imagery Trek tool). The potential disadvantage of any of these tools is that some people (especially individuals who place very high value on options that can immediately be recognized as practical, sensible, or realistic possibilities) may resist the tools and may consider them frivolous or silly. Using these tools may, in fact, lead to many ideas that are so unusual or challenging to people's experience that they may require substantial refinement or development to become workable options.

Attribute Listing

Attribute Listing is a tool in which you break an object, problem, or task down into its parts or elements and then generate ways to change, modify, or address the different elements. To use the Attribute Listing tool to generate ideas, begin by asking, "What are the main elements or parts (the attributes) of this problem or question?" If you were working on a product improvement task, such as finding many, varied, or unusual ways to improve an iPod, you might ask, "What are the main elements, or attributes, of an iPod?"

The responses might include "the sound, the memory, the power source, the headphone, the screen, the functionality, and the case of the iPod." You might identify as few as 3 or 4 key attributes or as many as 8 to 10. Next, take each attribute, one at a time, and try to generate new ideas by thinking only about that attribute. For example, thinking about the memory of the iPod might suggest more storage, multiple hard disks, or the capability to read even more different file types. Thinking about the case of the iPod might suggest making it water-resistant or unbreakable. Finally, consider combining some of the attributes or ideas you have generated to stimulate even more new possibilities.

Using the Attribute Listing tool helps you search for new possibilities in an organized, structured, or analytical way, and the tool can be particularly useful for improvement or incremental enhancement of existing products or procedures. It is not likely to stimulate highly original ideas that move the task or problem in a strikingly new or different direction.

Morphological Matrix

The *Morphological Matrix* (which comes from the word *morphology,* referring to the study of form or structure) is a generating tool that can be used to produce a large number of ideas very quickly and to create some possibilities that are guaranteed to be unusual. It is also very easy to use.

For any question or problem statement, begin by identifying some of the major parts or variables involved. These are called "parameters" of the problem or challenge and are represented in Figure 4.14 as Dough, Sauce, Topping, and Shape. There might be many parameters, but to keep the number of possibilities workable, we usually focus on three or four major parameters. A parameter is a major part or element of the problem that might take many forms or have many values. In story writing, for example, we might identify four important parameters: the main character, the place, a goal, and an obstacle. Each of these might have many forms or values. Many people (or things) might serve as the main character; the story might take place in any of a vast number of different places, and so on. To use this tool, you will create a matrix (or a grid or chart) of the parameters of your problem and then list many new ideas for each one independently (i.e., without attempting to "match" items in one column with the next). If you have 4 parameters (columns), with 10 rows in each column, there are 10,000 possible combinations, drawing one

Figure 4.14   An Illustration of the Morphological Matrix in Action

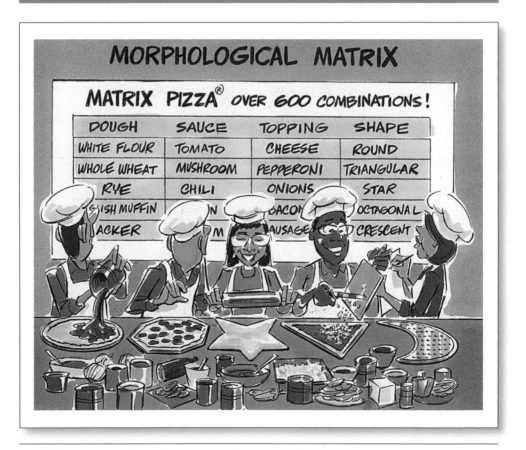

possibility at random from each of the four columns. Among these, there will surely be some original and fascinating possibilities.

Choosing Appropriate Tools

Having a suite of tools is one thing but knowing when to use any of them is another. Although we want to provide you with a rich array of tools to use in CPS, we also want you to know how to select and use only those tools that you need for a particular task at hand. Toward that end, we can build on the research of Gryskiewicz (1980, 1987, 1988). His research indicated that it is possible to select specific creative-thinking tools to promote particular outcomes. He distinguished four categories of idea generation. Although Gryskiewicz discussed "idea generation," his analysis can be applied in any of the CPS components. The four categories he proposed were as follows:

- Category 1: *Direct*—Ideas generated answer the problem statement directly.
- Category 2: *Supplementary*—Ideas generated involve a new use or application of the traditional ideas or "build" on them.
- Category 3: *Modification*—Ideas generated involve a structural (or more significant) change from the traditional ideas.
- Category 4: *Tangential*—Ideas involve entirely different uses or applications than those from other categories; a real "shift" in perspective.

Gryskiewicz (1980, 1987) proposed that the categories ranged from more developmental needs (options that fit easily into the existing structures or ways of operating), in Category 1, to more exploratory needs, in Category 4 (options that emphasize strikingly new and different directions). More developmental ideas emphasize doing what you are already doing but doing it better, whereas more exploratory possibilities open up significantly different definitions of the challenge than have been considered before.

Drawing on the ideas presented by Gryskiewicz (1980, 1987) and other analyses of the purposes of various tools, we formulated a model to guide you in choosing tools to apply in varying situations. This model is presented in Figure 4.15. The search for more developmental options is important when you are concerned with gradual, incremental change, in which your goal is to improve existing structures or operations. On the other hand, when you are concerned with creating entirely new structures or systems, and your goal is to stimulate change at the very foundations of the structure or operation, you may need to apply tools that will lead to more exploratory options.

We have found that some tools lend themselves more readily or easily to generating more comfortable, incremental, or developmental options, and others lend themselves better to generating more radical breakthrough or exploratory possibilities. When you need more developmental outcomes such as those in Gryskiewicz's Category 1 or 2, tools such as Attribute Listing or the Morphological Matrix (on the left in the figure) will be useful. They involve breaking the question or challenge into parts or subparts, which can then be explored or combined very systematically. Brainstorming and its variations (such as Brainwriting or Brainstorming With

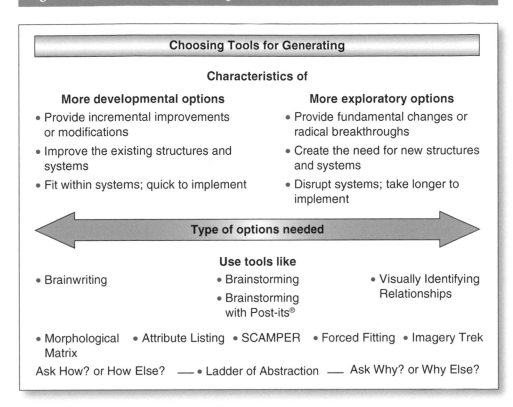

Figure 4.15 A Model for Guiding Your Generation Efforts

Post-its) are also moderately developmental, in that they permit ideas to stay close to existing paradigms or comfortable parameters for the problem. These tools lead to options that you will recognize easily as being relevant, workable, and useful in refining or enhancing an existing structure. The SCAMPER tool can also provide a structured way to improve ideas systematically and deliberately.

Tools such as Forced Fitting, Visually Identifying Relationships, or Imagery Trek (on the right in the figure) deliberately challenge individuals or groups to move even farther in the direction of unusual ideas or in the exploratory restructuring of the problem. They usually lead to a greater stretch or movement away from the original view or construction of the challenge and thus may be more exploratory in focus and more useful for searches involving Gryskiewicz's Categories 3 and 4. These tools often lead to the production of options that disrupt the current systems and require greater effort and resources, and a longer time to implement successfully.

Focusing in Generating Ideas

Frequently, productive applications of the Generating Ideas stage and a number of tools can result in hundreds of options to consider. We often see examples of idea-generating efforts that have led to several flip-chart pages full of ideas. It is important for you to remember, however, that sheer quantity is not enough. You must also be able to assess whether any of those ideas are promising, intriguing, or important enough to consider and develop as promising results or solutions. When you are concerned with focusing your thinking, or choosing among the options you have generated, you might review and use any of the focusing tools presented in Chapter 3 or 5. There are several tools from which to choose.

Given the primary emphasis on generating possibilities in this component and stage, your work in the focusing phase might be described as "light focusing." It is not concerned with absolute, final decisions or attaining closure about solutions to the problem or responses to your question. During the focusing phase of Generating Ideas, then, your most important goal is to identify one, several, or many possibilities that are *promising, intriguing, or inviting* to you. They may or may not be ideas that, at this time, you know how to implement, and you may not even be certain that they will be able to be implemented—but you are sufficiently attracted by their promise or potential to look at them more closely.

The Selecting Hits and Highlighting tools presented in Chapter 3 are effective for screening and selecting interesting, useful, or intriguing options from a more extensive list of possibilities. These tools are particularly useful in the focusing phase of Generating Ideas because your goal is to preserve or sustain the originality and uniqueness of the options you generated. More extensive, rigorous evaluation at this point is likely to result in weeding out or stifling the more novel or unusual options. To ensure that you don't eliminate your most unusual or original possibilities in this "light focusing," consider using the following variation of the *Selecting Hits* tool. Use a certain symbol (or a specific color press-on dot) to "flag" the ideas you have generated that are intriguing to you specifically because they are new, different, or unusual— because they really do stretch your thinking or pave the way for a challenging new way to look at the problem or question. Force yourself to look beyond the most obvious hits that will be easy to apply, and search for the ones that will be the most challenging. Sometimes these are "high-risk/high-gain" options that will produce outstanding results if you can develop them effectively (and if you don't trash them without ever considering them seriously).

Another approach to "light focusing" when Generating Ideas is to sort your options into categories. For example, you might use internal criteria to sort options informally into categories such as musts versus wants, short term versus long term, useful versus novel, simple versus complex, and fits existing system versus demands new systems. You might sort the entire list of ideas you have generated, or if there are too many to handle effectively, then you might concentrate on sorting just the most intriguing hits or hot spots. Figure 4.16 illustrates the light focusing that occurs in Generating Ideas, using the Vernon Case Study.

The Generating Ideas component can provide you with many (fluency), varied (flexibility), or unusual (originality) ideas or it can make your ideas richer, more detailed, or more interesting (elaboration).

Figure 4.17 provides an example of a Generating Ideas component summary using the Vernon Case Study. It represents the kind of output often produced using this component.

Figure 4.16   An Example of Sorting Options From the Vernon Case Study

SORTING OPTIONS
LONG TERM

- Find out what "colors make Vernon happy"
- Install a poker table in the recreation room

- Build prisoners an indoor swimming pool
- Have Vernon build furniture
- Install wall-to-wall carpeting in each cell
- Reward Vernon with a phone if he cooperates

FITS EXISTING SYSTEM ——————— **DEMANDS NEW SYSTEM**

- Give Vernon a lot of activities to do
- Offer board games and cards
- Pay Vernon to work
- Allow Vernon to have a huge feast in reward for good behavior

- Allow Vernon to escape
- Allow Vernon to have a pet
- Give out trophies for good behavior
- Allow Vernon to select his own food menu

SHORT TERM

VERNON CASE STUDY

Figure 4.17   A Summary of Generating Ideas From the Vernon Case Study

GENERATING IDEAS
Component Summary

Statement of the Problem and Key Data

How to get Vernon involved in his own rehabilitation?

- Prison Officials ordered that Vernon wear handcuffs whenever leaving his cell
- Vernon breaks handcuffs
- Vernon has assaulted guards and nurses
- He's big, strong, and violent
- Understand Vernon's motivations
- Guards won't go near him any longer

Promising Ideas

- Get to know Vernon and attempt to befriend him
- Fight muscle with muscle – bring in added strength to control him (he is 375 lbs., 6'3", and gets violent)
- Channel his strength in a positive direction
- Make him a trustee – use his strength to control other inmates
- Keep him happy and at peace – avoid getting him angry
- Market his unusual size and strength – get him in contact with organizations that might have a use for his rare abilities

VERNON CASE STUDY

The Rest of the Story

When a group of educators from a suburban school district came back together after their break, several members of the group were literally bursting with enthusiasm and energy. They could hardly wait for everyone to return and get settled in the meeting room. One of them said, "You know, something really struck us about the 'Masked Marauder' idea while we were out on our break. At first, we thought it was just silly. But, the more we thought about it, we discovered some real potentials!"

They went on to describe how the Masked Marauder might not be an actual person, dashing from classroom to classroom or school to school—but might be a cartoon character, or a set of characters, who would model, demonstrate, and share specific creative- and critical-thinking tools. The cartoon characters could "move" from place to place in a very convenient way—on videotape. The rest of the group started to nod in agreement and build on the idea.

Eventually, the group decided to design a plan for a series of videotaped programs in which costumed characters and puppets would be used to present, in the form of engaging and humorous stories, a variety of specific tools. The tapes could readily be duplicated and shared with teachers, integrated easily into the classroom setting, and applied with an economical level of preparation and training for the staff.

The group prepared a funding proposal for writing, developing, implementing, and evaluating the cartoon character videotape series. Their proposal was funded (for more than $70,000) by an area foundation, which enabled the programs to be produced professionally and at a high level of quality. The tapes were completed and were well received and widely used within the schools. They served as the springboard for other professional development activities as an outgrowth of the teachers' curiosity and support and for several other curriculum development projects. The evaluation was conducted as part of a staff member's doctoral dissertation.

The idea of the Masked Marauder that started as "comic relief" and without any sense of being a plausible or relevant possibility paid valuable dividends to that school district. When we search for varied and unusual ideas and extend our efforts to build them into promising new possibilities, excellent results can occur.

Putting This Chapter to Work

Our goals in this chapter were to help you understand the key concepts of fluency, flexibility, originality, and elaboration, to explain their use in CPS, and to enable you to describe and apply several specific tools for generating options.

Activities to Guide Reflection and Action

To review your understanding of the material in this chapter and to guide you in preparing to apply its content in real situations, it will help you to work on one or more of the following activities. You may wish to work individually or, if you are part of a course or team, collaboratively on the activities.

1. Whether or not they are explicitly aware of the tools in this chapter and their names, individuals and groups are often engaged in carrying them out in everyday situations. Observe a variety of common situations or experiences, and compile a list of "everyday applications" of each of the tools.

2. Many people or groups use the term *brainstorming* carelessly and inappropriately. Identify some actual group experiences in which you have observed those challenges, and identify how you would have recommended specific changes in the group's behavior to promote more effective thinking.

3. Identify at least two specific situations in your own personal or professional setting in which you might use any of the tools described in this chapter to attain greater flexibility or originality and to increase your productivity and success. Be prepared to explain why you believe that certain generating tools might be particularly helpful in those situations.

Preparing for Action

Few ideas are in themselves practical. It is for the want of active imagination in their application rather than their means of acquisition that they fail of success.

—John Arnold

The purpose of Chapter 5 is to examine the Preparing for Action component of Creative Problem Solving (CPS) and its functions in transforming ideas into action. As a result of studying the Preparing for Action component, you will be able to do the following:

1. Examine your promising possibilities closely and thoroughly.
2. Select and use appropriate tools to select, analyze, evaluate, develop, or refine options that hold promise for becoming workable solutions.
3. Formulate possible solutions into a workable plan of action.

The component includes two stages, Developing Solutions and Building Acceptance. The specific objectives on which you will work for each stage are listed below.

Developing Solutions. Through your study of this chapter, you will be able to do the following:

1. Explain the purposes of the Developing Solutions stage.
2. Define criteria and their use.
3. Identify sources and categories of criteria.
4. Generate a variety of criteria for a specific task.
5. Select the most appropriate and important criteria for use with a specific task.
6. Explain and use several alternative tools to evaluate and develop options.

(Continued)

(Continued)

7. Explain and give examples of three different uses of criteria (to screen, select, or support ideas).

8. Distinguish criteria that are essential for evaluating options from those that are primarily useful for polishing or refining options.

9. Apply evaluation and development tools on several possible solutions for a task of your own.

Building Acceptance. Through your study of this chapter, you will be able to do the following:

1. Identify and consider many possible sources of assistance or resistance for implementing potential solutions.

2. Develop a list of possible actions or responses that might be considered for key sources of assistance or resistance.

3. Identify at least 10 reasons why people might resist the change you want to create and strategies to overcome them.

4. Identify ways to prevent obstacles from arising or to overcome them if they do occur.

5. Formulate a detailed plan of action, including specific steps to be taken (short-, medium-, and long-range actions, as well as obtaining feedback and revising the plan).

The head of strategy for a major division of a large global chemical company was engaged in an organizational recapitalization effort. The project involved spending millions of dollars to develop a way to increase their speed and capacity to produce and deliver a special paper-like product that was in very high demand. Their eventual goal was to increase the market share of the product. They wanted our help in making sure that they were getting the best use of the resources they were investing. In particular, they wanted help to be sure that the way they were investing the resources would provide for future growth, particularly the ability to produce new and improved products.

We worked with the group to develop some very new and interesting possibilities for new applications of the product. However, as you may know from your own experience, having a good idea is not always enough to get it implemented. What do you need to do in order to get highly novel ideas implemented? What can you do to ensure that others will accept the changes you are trying to make? This is the focus of this chapter, Preparing for Action.

Although each CPS component has a unique emphasis, they each share a common underlying concern: finding varied ways of creating and supporting change. By change, we mean the act or process of making a product, process, event, or interaction different or better. Each CPS component helps you deal with a particular aspect of change. In the Understanding the Challenge component, you establish, clarify, and direct your problem-solving efforts. Change is more easily and effectively managed when you know where you want to go, what you have to start with, and a particular pathway on which to embark. There is an old saying, "If you do not know where you're going, any road will get you there." In the Generating Ideas component, your efforts to manage change shift toward generating ideas—moving from having a few promising options to having a rich variety of new and promising alternatives. Powerful change arises from having many, varied, and original choices from which to choose.

In this chapter, we will explore the Preparing for Action component. Its primary emphasis is on transforming ideas into action. The two stages of this component provide tools that help you manage the change process more effectively and transform your promising ideas into real action steps. We will describe how you can use these stages to manage change successfully. We will help you understand the input, processing, and output for taking action creatively. We will describe and illustrate practical tools you can apply in Developing Solutions and Building Acceptance.

Preparing for Action in a Nutshell

You will use the Preparing for Action component (see Figure 5.1) to deal with situations that require you to transform your promising ideas into action. The tools in each stage of this component will help you choose and strengthen promising solutions and plan to implement those solutions efficiently and effectively.

Figure 5.1 Preparing for Action in a Nutshell

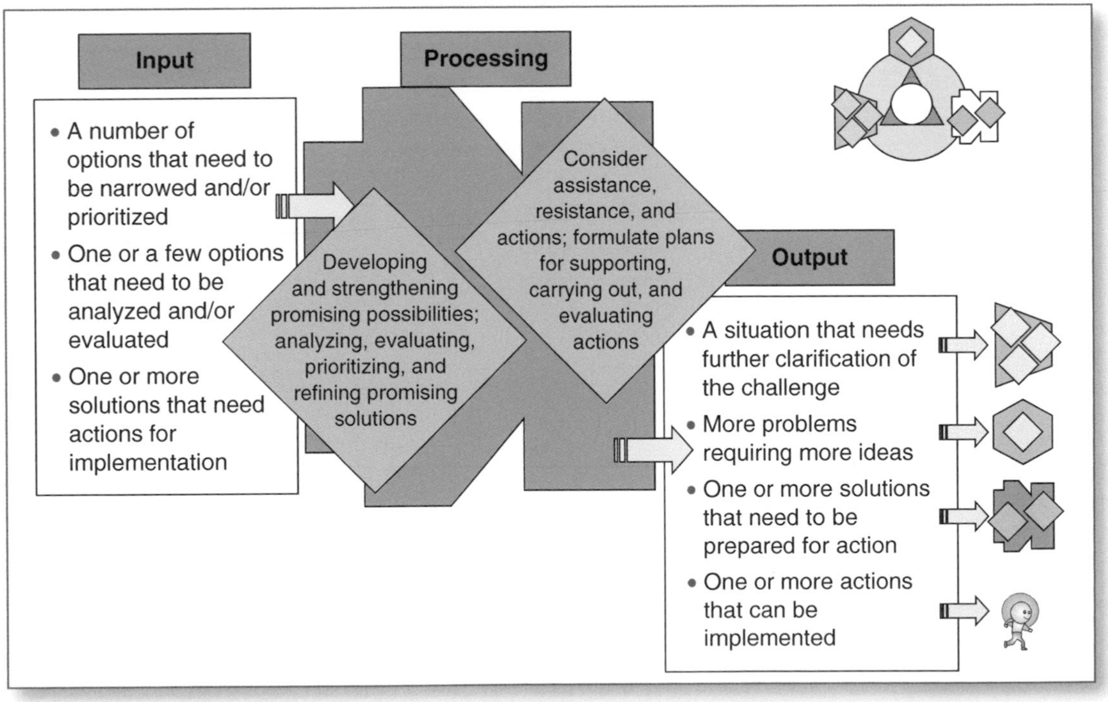

Input
- A number of options that need to be narrowed and/or prioritized
- One or a few options that need to be analyzed and/or evaluated
- One or more solutions that need actions for implementation

Processing
- Developing and strengthening promising possibilities; analyzing, evaluating, prioritizing, and refining promising solutions
- Consider assistance, resistance, and actions; formulate plans for supporting, carrying out, and evaluating actions

Output
- A situation that needs further clarification of the challenge
- More problems requiring more ideas
- One or more solutions that need to be prepared for action
- One or more actions that can be implemented

Input

You may find the Preparing for Action component helpful whenever you need to make decisions, develop or strengthen options, identify forces that have impact on your implementation efforts, or develop a specific plan for gaining acceptance and use.

Processing

This component contains two CPS stages, Developing Solutions and Building Acceptance. In Developing Solutions (represented by the diamond on the lower left of Figure 5.1), the focus is on analyzing, evaluating, and strengthening your promising options. This may require you to identify key criteria (standards, indicators, or "yardsticks") for evaluating and improving your solutions, making them more valuable and useful.

Building Acceptance (represented by the diamond on the upper right in Figure 5.1) focuses on generating and identifying key sources of assistance and resistance in the situation. These are factors that might help or hinder your efforts and your eventual success. Building Acceptance also focuses on developing and sequencing action steps for implementing your solutions.

Output

The kind of processing that takes place in Preparing for Action influences the kind of outputs from this component. For example, as a result of developing a plan of action, you may have identified some new problems for which you need to spend time in the Generating Ideas component. You may have identified additional promising solutions that need analysis and development and choose to spend additional time in Preparing for Action. Developing your plan may have revealed an entirely new area of opportunity that requires focus and clarity and may benefit from using the Understanding the Challenge component. Finally, you may be satisfied with your plan and proceed directly to putting your steps into action.

The "stems" we will introduce in this chapter, to highlight the specific language for Preparing for Action, are presented in Table 5.1. These stems provide starting points or "triggers" for generating and focusing in this component and its stages.

Table 5.1 The Language That Guides Your Thinking in Preparing for Action

Developing Solutions	Building Acceptance
Will it . . . ? Will they . . . ? (WI . . . ?) To generate criteria	Who? What? Where? When? Why? To generate sources of assistance and resistance
If I had to choose only one of these, which would it be? To operate the PCA (Paired Comparison Analysis)	What I see myself doing is . . . (WISMDI . . .)

Developing Solutions	Building Acceptance
	What we see ourselves doing is . . . (WWSODI . . .) To identify action steps
If I (option), to what extent will it . . . ? To operate the Evaluation Matrix	Who will do what by when? To develop a plan of action

What Is the Developing Solutions Stage?

The role of Developing Solutions in transforming ideas into action is to help turn your interesting ideas, thoughts, or images into workable solutions. By solution, we mean an option or alternative that resolves a problem, answers a question, or meets a challenge. Ideas might be thought of as the "raw materials" for solutions. Ideas represent options or possibilities that are promising and appealing to you but need to be expanded, developed, or "fleshed out" to become workable solutions. Developing ideas into solutions involves screening and analyzing options, making decisions about alternatives, and strengthening tentative solutions (see Figure 5.2).

Figure 5.2   The Developing Solutions Stage

Developing Solutions as a CPS stage is unique in its primary emphasis on focusing. Both generating and focusing occur in each stage within the Understanding the Challenge, Generating Ideas, and Preparing for Action components. In some stages, such as Generating Ideas, there is often greater emphasis on "stretching," diverging, or generating possibilities. In Developing Solutions, applying tools for selecting, analyzing, and refining solutions plays a greater role in your work. Several factors influence how you will focus and build workable solutions. These include quantity of options, level of ownership, quality of the options, and task demands.

Quantity of Options. The number of options you examine influences the use of focusing tools. When you use generating tools, it is very likely that you have a large number of options to consider for focusing. It would be ineffective to merely *slam on the brakes* and select the one or two winners from a group of more than a 100 options. For this reason, it is more appropriate to choose your approach to focusing more carefully. For example, when you have generated a large number of options, you may need to spend some time categorizing or sorting them. If this results in many possible options, you may find it useful to compress or prioritize them. If you end up with a few promising options, you may want to spend your energy developing and strengthening them. We will share a model to help you specifically target your use of CPS-focusing tools based on the number of options under consideration.

Level of Ownership. Your focusing choices and actions will also be influenced by how widely distributed or spread out the actual ownership is for the challenge or concern. If no one really owns the task, then random choice or voting can be used without the nonproductive side effects. Devoting much time or energy to making deliberate and high-quality choices would be wasteful. If you are the sole client or owner of the task, you can make an individual decision about your focusing (with some input from others if needed). When you share the ownership of the task with others, you will generally need to invest more energy in obtaining input from others, developing a consensus, or working on agreement regarding your approach to focusing. Group decision making is often more complex and challenging than making a decision as an individual. If you have ever been part of a group that needs to make a shared decision or come to agreement, you will know what we mean. Level of ownership will also influence your choice and application of focusing tools.

Quality of Options. The quality of the available options can influence the approach you take to focusing. Generally, the more novel your options are, the more you will need to be affirmative or developmental in your approach. Using focusing tools deliberately and affirmatively helps stimulate building and "fleshing out" new options. You may also find yourself in a situation where none of the options appear to be workable or usable. Rather than applying focusing in Developing Solutions, you may find it more beneficial to:

- Reexamine your ownership of the problem and solution.
- Develop more clarity about the problem for which your options were generated.

- Investigate whether you are missing a critical piece of data about the context.
- Generate more ideas.

Task Demands. The task on which you are working will often have a great influence on the kind of focusing you will need to pursue. Some tasks will require a variety of "others" to be committed to action. These kinds of tasks will require more involvement in the focusing activity and more deliberate use of the focusing tools. Generally, the more the task requires the involvement or support of "stakeholders," the more your focusing efforts need to be explicit and deliberate. Also, the particular type of task can influence the kind of focusing you pursue. Focusing can emphasize sorting or categorizing, selecting or choosing, compressing or narrowing, prioritizing or analyzing and developing. Different tools might be chosen for each of these approaches to focusing.

Generating in Developing Solutions

There is an apparent paradox in Developing Solutions that often stimulates some interesting comments. In a stage where the primary emphasis is on evaluating and deciding about the most promising options, how can the emphasis also be on generating? For example, some situations require you to be clear and explicit about your criteria. For these kinds of situations, it is often helpful to first generate a list of criteria to help you focus and develop your options. Then, you can select those that are the most important.

This apparent mix of generating and focusing is actually a productive example of the dynamic and harmonious balance that exists between generative and evaluative thinking (already discussed in Chapter 2). Like other stages of CPS, Developing Solutions has both a generating and a focusing phase. Generating is designed to help you produce criteria so that you may effectively analyze your options. Having a list of many varied and unusual criteria from which to choose will improve the likelihood of your efforts to be more deliberately developmental.

Generating in Developing Solutions can also involve generating advantages, limitations, unique qualities, and ways to overcome limitations of an option while applying the ALUo tool (which was discussed in Chapter 2). In this stage, you will find many opportunities to use ALUo. This tool is primarily used when you want or need to strengthen and develop an option. Although its primary purpose is to help you focus, you will use generative thinking as well.

To make decisions, analyze options, or develop solutions that produce desired results, we often use *criteria*. Criteria are standards, rules, tests, or means on which judgments or decisions can be based. They provide "yardsticks" to help guide your selection, evaluation, and development of solutions (see Figure 5.3). Criteria are useful for situations in which you need to screen, sort, or categorize a large number of options; select promising options from a variety of alternatives; identify, choose, prioritize, or compress options; or support, develop, or improve your most promising options.

One of the key issues in Developing Solutions is how clear and explicit your criteria need to be to screen, select, and support your tentative solutions effectively. We distinguish between two kinds of criteria (see Figure 5.4). Implicit or informal criteria are unspoken and internal criteria you use without specific awareness or attention. They are

Figure 5.3   An Illustration of Criteria in Action

SOURCE: Copyright © 2009. The Creative Problem Solving Group, Inc. Reprinted with permission.

Figure 5.4   Criteria Can Be Both Explicit and Implicit

IMPLICIT (Informal)	EXPLICIT (Formal)
Internally and unconsciously known	Identifiable and communicable
Sources	**Sources**
• Personality	• Data
• Preference	• Situation
• Perspective	• Constraint
• Prejudice	• Experience
• Perception	• Future image

influenced by your personality, preferences, and experience, as well as by your prejudices and perceptions. Explicit or formal criteria are those that can be specifically identified and explained. They come from sources of data or constraints imposed by a situation, as well as from your own personal experiences and images of desired future states. You choose them deliberately to meet the requirements of the situation.

We all make many decisions casually, informally, or spontaneously, without the need to invoke complicated, structured analyses or procedures. For example, we rarely conduct a formal evaluation using explicit criteria to select our daily clothing. There are other occasions when it is necessary to have explicit criteria on which to base a decision.

Generating Criteria

Generating many and varied criteria helps ensure that you have considered the most appropriate criteria for focusing your solutions. To generate criteria, we use the stem Will it . . . ? (or Will they . . . ?). To demonstrate the generation and use of criteria, we will use an example of buying a house. To generate criteria for buying a house, you might say, "Will it (the house) have four bedrooms?" or "Will it be affordable on our income?" (See Figure 5.5 for a more extensive list of criteria used to buy a house.)

Figure 5.5   Sample Criteria for Buying a House

• **Have four bedrooms?**	• Be affordable?
• Have a two-car garage?	• **Reduce my commute?**
• Have a basement?	• Have a good floor plan?
• **Be in good shape?**	• Be pretty?
• Be well constructed?	• Be well located?
• Have adequate insulation?	• Be somewhat private?
• Be easy to maintain?	• Be expandable?
• **Have access to good schools?**	• Be the right size?
• Have access to shopping?	• Have the right land?
• Have decent plumbing?	• Have good lighting?
• Have a yard with easy upkeep?	• Have adequate storage?
• Have nice neighbors?	• Have a good furnace?
• Have good resale value?	• Be taxed fairly?
• **Have more than one bathroom?**	• Have 220 service?
• Be accessible to recreation?	• Have a decent roof?
• Have modern wiring?	• Be convenient to get to?

The criteria you might generate for buying a house will probably differ from those you would use to select a college or graduate school to attend. For many kinds of problems, a number of general categories often emerge that can help you generate criteria. For example, in many kinds of problems—such as buying a house or selecting a school—you might need to consider factors such as cost and location. We use the acronym CARTS to describe the categories we see most often (see Figure 5.6). You may find it helpful to use CARTS as a checklist for generating criteria to help ensure that you have considered a variety of criteria.

Figure 5.6   Common Categories of Criteria

> **CARTS: Categories of Criteria**
>
> **C**osts – expenses associated with an option
>
> **A**cceptance – level of acceptability or resistance options may face
>
> **R**esources – kind, amount, and availability of necessary materials, skills, supplies, or equipment
>
> **T**ime – amount or availability of time
>
> **S**pace – kind, amount, or availability of space needed for a given situation

Focusing in Developing Solutions

Focusing in Developing Solutions will be influenced by a variety of factors. The task you work on may require you to simply apply implicit criteria as you make decisions about your options. For example, you can use criteria to implicitly sort options into categories such as Musts versus Wants, Short Term versus Long Term, Useful versus Novel, Simple versus Complex, and Fits Existing System versus Demands New Systems. It is not necessary in all situations to develop a list of explicit criteria by generating in Developing Solutions.

In other situations, you may need to generate and focus on key criteria and apply those to screen, select, and support your promising options. In these cases, focusing in Developing Solutions may include applying the Selecting Hits tool described in Chapter 3 to identify key criteria. Once identified, you will apply the criteria to your options. (See Figure 5.5 for an example of Selecting Hits used to identify key criteria. The criteria in bold represent the hits.) Make sure the criteria you choose are appropriate for your situation, easily understood, communicable, specific, and measurable. Also, be certain to keep the same meaning for each criterion throughout its specific application.

Other situations may require a systematic and structured approach to analyzing, developing, and refining your options. We have developed a variety of tools for situations where you need a deliberate, conscious, and powerful approach to analyzing, evaluating, and developing options. The challenge in those situations becomes knowing which tool(s) to apply for your specific needs.

Choosing Tools for Focusing

To help you make this choice, we developed a model to assist you in targeting your evaluation and development activities. The Choosing Tools for Focusing model (see Figure 5.7) is designed to help you choose tools based on the quantity of options you need to organize, evaluate, analyze, prioritize, or develop. The tools are arranged in the model according to the number of options for which they are most appropriately used. As the model suggests, Selecting Hits and Highlighting (used for clustering and compressing options into meaningful categories), Musts/Wants (used for quick sorting of options), and SML (Short, Medium, Long—used to sort options based on a timeline) are most appropriately used to organize a large number of options.

For situations in which you have one or a few options, all of which are possible, but which will benefit from further analysis and development, the ALUo (Advantages, Limitations and Unique Qualities, and Overcoming Limitations) tool presented in Chapter 2 is most appropriate. It takes quality time and energy to conduct a comprehensive evaluation and development of an option using ALUo, though, so it may not be cost-effective to conduct an ALUo on 10 or 20 items.

The model also contains tools that help you evaluate, analyze, or prioritize a moderate number of options under consideration. Criteria, which we examined earlier in this chapter, will help you analyze a moderate number of options against explicit standards. However, there may be times when you need to make a more systematic application of those criteria to evaluate a moderate number of promising options. In this case, the Evaluation Matrix tool would be most appropriate to use. If you need to prioritize a moderate number of options, then the Paired Comparison Analysis (PCA) will be most appropriate as it helps you rank order your options based on their relative

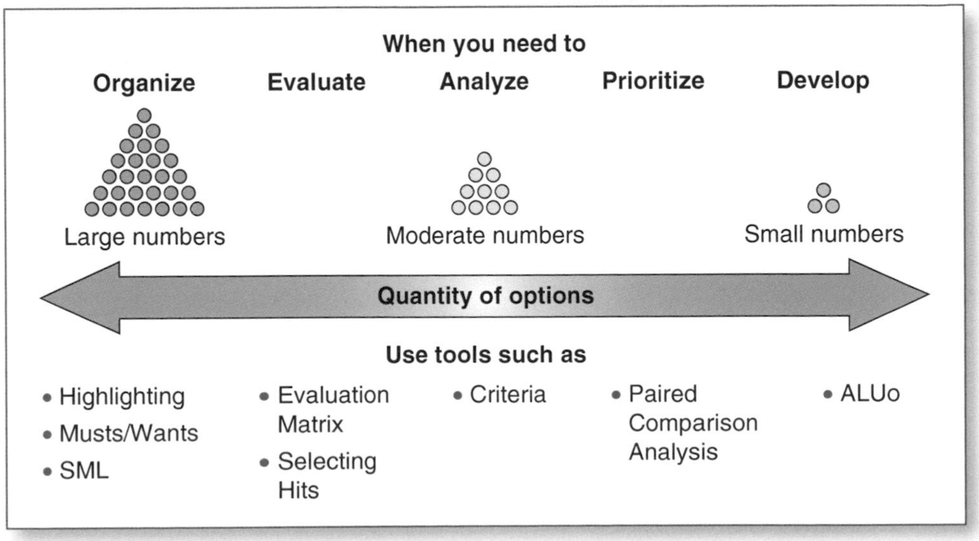

Figure 5.7   A Model to Help You Select the Appropriate Focusing Tool

importance. We will examine the Evaluation Matrix and PCA next in this chapter. The SML tool will be examined in the Building Acceptance section of this chapter.

The Evaluation Matrix

The Evaluation Matrix provides a structure for evaluating your options systematically against your criteria (see Figure 5.8). It can be used during the focusing phase of any CPS stage—whenever you have options that need to be evaluated against criteria. For example, although we will examine the use of the tool for Developing Solutions, it can also be used to evaluate statements of opportunity (in Constructing Opportunities), problem statements (in Framing Problems), and action steps (in Building Acceptance). The results of the matrix will help you better understand, develop, and strengthen your promising options. To apply the matrix, follow these directions.

Figure 5.8   An Illustration of the Evaluation Matrix in Action

Prepare the matrix. Identify the options you want to evaluate and place them down the left side of the matrix. In the example of buying a house found in Figure 5.9, we identified the options as addresses and placed them in the matrix. We identified the key criteria used to evaluate the options and placed them along the top of the matrix. At this point, the order in which you write the options or criteria is not important. It is helpful

Figure 5.9 Use the Evaluation Matrix to Buy a House

Options	Schools	Bathrooms	Four bedrooms	Commute	Condition			Scale
								5 - Excellent
								4
5700 Oak Lane	1	1	0	0	2			3
495 Elm	3	3	2	5	4			2
53 S. Main	5	5	5	4	5			1
1095 Dodge	5	5	5	3	4			0 - Poor

Criteria

to word the options and criteria in such a way as to make the matrix easier to complete. Phrase the criteria and options using the following sentence structure: If (option), to what extent will it (criteria)? In our example, the sentence would read as follows: If I buy 5700 Oak Lane, to what extent will it have good schools?

Complete the matrix. To complete the matrix, begin by first choosing an appropriate rating system (e.g., 0 = *Poor*, 5 = *Excellent*, etc.) to use in evaluating the options against the criteria. Next, evaluate each option against each criterion using the sentence, If . . . to what extent will it . . . ? We use the scale to evaluate how well or to what extent the particular option meets the criteria. For example, in our house example shown in Figure 5.9, 5700 Oak Lane is rated as a "1" on schools because the schools are not of the quality desired. The option 495 Elm is rated as a "3" because the schools meet this criterion to a moderate degree. The option 1095 Dodge received a "5" because the house was located in a district known for having high-quality school programs.

In this matrix, it is important to go down the (vertical) columns, rather than across the (horizontal) rows. If you were to select your favorite option and work across all the criteria, you might score this option higher because of a halo effect. By using one criterion at a time to evaluate all the options, you will decrease the chance of inflating the evaluation for your favorite options.

Interpret the results. To get the most out of the Evaluation Matrix, be careful not to rely only on summing the numbers or using them just to identify the "best" or "worst" options. Use the matrix to identify where your options are strong and where they might be weak. Where options receive high scores (using the number scale in our example), it suggests that those options do well against the criteria. Where scores are low, it suggests that the options might need to be developed or strengthened. This can be done by identifying why the option does not do well against the criteria: phrase the reason into a question beginning with the stems "How to . . ." or "How might . . ." and then generate suggestions to develop or strengthen the option. If using a numerical scale does not work well for your situation, then identify and use an alternative scale. See Figure 5.10 for an example of using a nonnumeric scale with the Vernon Case Study.

Figure 5.10 An Example of the Evaluation Matrix From the Vernon Case Study

Evaluation Matrix

Criteria

Options	Be acceptable to Vernon	Be easy to implement	Reduce potential harm	Bring fast results	Be acceptable to staff
1. Know and befriend Vernon	Positive	Neutral	Positive	Positive	Negative
2. Bring in added strength	Neutral	Neutral	Positive	Positive	Positive
3. Reduce his time in prison	Positive	Positive	Positive	Positive	Positive
4. Channel strength in a positive direction	Positive	Neutral	Positive	Neutral	Positive
5. Make him a trustee	Positive	Neutral	Positive	Positive	Positive
6. Keep him happy and avoid getting him angry	Positive	Positive	Positive	Positive	Positive
7. Market his unusual ability	Neutral	Neutral	Positive	Positive	Neutral

Rating scale

Positive
Neutral
Negative

VERNON CASE STUDY

Paired Comparison Analysis

Some tasks may require you to make careful choices and decisions about your options based on their relative priority or ranking. For example, you may be thinking about which problem(s) statement(s) associated with a certain task need to be addressed first, or which solutions are more important to consider for analysis, development, and implementation. For situations that require ranking or prioritizing, the PCA is an appropriate tool (see Figure 5.11). Although the PCA can be used to rank or prioritize options of any kind, we will demonstrate its use on choosing criteria.

The PCA helps you set a priority by comparing all your options against each other, one pair at a time, and making decisions about their importance in relationship to each

Figure 5.11   An Illustration of the Paired Comparison Analysis in Action

SOURCE: Copyright © 2009. The Creative Problem Solving Group, Inc. Reprinted with permission.

other. If you could have only one of the two, which would you choose? These decisions force you to identify the relative sense of priority between the options. By comparing all the options against each other, you can develop an overall sense of priority the options have in relationship to each other. You can use the PCA individually to develop a sense of personal priority, or in a group to develop or test consensus.

To help ensure effective application of the PCA, be certain that the options are parallel and distinct. Options are *parallel* when they are at the same level of abstraction and when they are consistently worded in a positive or negative direction. When you make the choice between the two options, your choice should be between two items that are both positive and desirable, not between one you want and one you do not. Options could include problem statements, ideas, criteria, actions, and so on. For example, the criteria in Figure 5.12 are parallel. The two criteria "Will it have four bedrooms?" and "Will it have a basement?" are in parallel form if both are desired characteristics of the future home. In the example shown in Figure 5.13, "Will it be unaffordable?" and "Will it have a fireplace?" are not parallel. One is stated in a negative and the other is stated in a positive direction.

Your options must also be *distinct* from each other. You must be able to hold each option separately in your mind as you compare them with each other. For an option

Figure 5.12 Examples of Criteria That Are Parallel and Distinct

Parallel and distinct

Examples of parallel criteria:
Will it . . .

- Have four bedrooms?
- Have a basement?

Examples of distinct criteria:
Will it . . .

- Be within 30 minutes of my work?
- Have 2.5 bathrooms?

Figure 5.13 Examples of Criteria That Are Not Parallel and Distinct

Not parallel and distinct

Examples of nonparallel criteria:
Will it . . .

- Be unaffordable?
- Have a fireplace?

Examples of nondistinct criteria:
Will it . . .

- Be well constructed?
- Meet all building codes?

to be distinct, it must be recognized as being different or nonredundant. In the example shown in Figure 5.12, "Will it be within 30 minutes of my work?" and "Will it have 2.5 bathrooms?" are distinct in that they are completely independent aspects of the desired future home. In the example shown in Figure 5.13, "Will it be well constructed?" and "Will it meet all building codes?" are not distinct. You would hope that these two criteria are closely related.

Be careful not to try and pack too many different options into one, more general or inclusive, option as it will be hard to make clear choices when some options are larger or more comprehensive than others. For example, the criterion "Will it have everything we want in a home?" includes other criteria such as "Will it have a large backyard?" "Will it have a front porch?" and "Will it be in a nice neighborhood?" If these were prioritized, it would be difficult to hold them apart in your mind. As a result, "Will it have everything we want in a home?" will probably turn out to be the highest priority.

Put your options in the PCA. To complete the PCA, write the parallel and distinct options down the left side of the PCA form to the left of the letters "A" through "I." See Figure 5.14 for an example. One criterion should be placed next to each letter on the grid. You might want to abbreviate the options to fit them in the form. These criteria in the example came from the initial list presented in Figure 5.5. Those presented in the PCA are the key criteria converged on using the Selecting Hits tool. In our example, the criterion "affordable" is next to "A," "four bedrooms" is next to "B," and so on. (Although this example shows nine criteria being prioritized, it is not necessary to have nine options to use a PCA.)

Compare each pair of options. To start the PCA, compare options "A" and "B" and decide which one is the most important. Write the letter of the more important option in the top left-hand box. Next, determine how much more important the option is over the other using the scale: 1 = *slightly more important,* 2 = *moderately more important,* and

3 = *much more important.* If "A" is much more important than "B," you would place a value of 3 above the letter "A" you wrote in the box. In our example (Figure 5.14), you will notice that of the two options A = affordable and B = four bedrooms, affordable is moderately more important.

Figure 5.14 An Example of the Paired Comparison Analysis

		B.	C.	D.	E.	F.	G.	H.	I.	Sum of Scores
Affordable	A.	A^2	C^2	D^2	E^1	F^1	G^1	H^3	I^1	A = 2
Four bedrooms	B.		B^1	D^1	B^2	B^1	B^3	H^1	B^1	B = 8
Reduce commute	C.			D^3	C^2	F^1	C^1	H^1	C^2	C = 7
Good schools	D.				D^3	D^1	D^2	D^1	D^1	D = 14
Adequate storage	E.					F^1	G^1	H^3	I^1	E = 1
Good condition	F.						F^2	H^1	F^1	F = 6
Easy maintenance	G.							H^3	I^1	G = 2
More bathrooms	H.								H^2	H = 14
Good resale	I.									I = 3

Scale
1 = **Slightly** more important
2 = **Moderately** more important
3 = **Much** more important

To complete the PCA, work along the top row to compare "A" against all other options. For example, the left-most box on the top row is the comparison of criterion "A" (affordable) and criterion "B" (four bedrooms), the second box is "A" (affordable) and "C" (reduce commute), and so on. When finished, work along the second row comparing "B" with all other options. Continue this process until each option has been compared with each other.

Sum the scores. To examine the relative priority of the options, find all the boxes in which each letter was chosen, add up their appropriate exponents, and place the total next to each letter on the right side of the PCA. For example, in our example in Figure 5.14, the letter "B" appeared five times in the grid with the sum of its exponents being eight. Be sure to look to the column above the letter and the row to the right of the letter when adding the sum of the numbers.

Interpret the results. To interpret the results of the PCA, examine the sums next to each letter. The numbers provide you with a relative sense of priority among the options. The options with the higher numbers represent higher-priority items. In our house example, the two criteria of the highest priority are D (good schools) and H (more bathrooms).

In using the PCA, remember the following guidelines:

- The PCA will help you understand the priority of only those options you placed within the grid. An important criterion left out may change the relative rankings or priority of the options you examined.

- Results from the PCA do not indicate importance of any option; use the PCA when all the options are important but need to be ranked or prioritized for use.

- Use the numbers as a way to help clarify your understanding of the relative importance of the options, not to signify the "winners" and "losers." For example, if you have two options that are two points apart from each other, it would be difficult (and not very useful) to argue that one is the "winner" and the other is in "second place."

The PCA takes time and energy to complete. Use it for those situations in which the benefits from applying it outweigh the costs. We have developed a Web-based tool called The Prioritizer™ to make the application of PCA easier. Contact CPSB (Creative Problem Solving Group, Inc.) if you are interested in learning more.

Summarizing the Developing Solutions Stage

In summary, the purpose of the Developing Solutions stage is to help you strengthen and develop promising options. It organizes tools for evaluating and developing tentative solutions for a given problem-solving situation. Although the stage has both a generating and a focusing phase, the major emphasis of the stage is on focusing. Generating in Developing Solutions includes generating criteria and overcoming limitations to develop solutions. Focusing in Developing Solutions includes conducting deliberate, "conscious" examination by analyzing, evaluating, developing, and refining your options. The tools we examined in the stage were the PCA for prioritizing options and the Evaluation Matrix for evaluating options against criteria. The outcome of using Developing Solutions is one or more promising solutions that you have evaluated and strengthened.

What Is the Building Acceptance Stage?

So far, what you have learned about CPS can help you obtain acceptance by ensuring that you are working on the most appropriate challenge or problem; generating many, varied, and unusual ideas; or developing and strengthening your tentative solution. The Building Acceptance stage deals with taking your solution into the world. It includes understanding the context and people to take action and implement your solution. It is about making change and taking initiative for action.

Changing your present situation can often be very complicated and challenging. To make change happen, you must deliberately plan your actions, implement them, and then monitor the effects to ensure that the change is producing the desired effects (see Figure 5.15). You have probably witnessed or experienced situations in which an idea or solution that seemed to be very promising did not have great success or impact. For example, think back to the last time you implemented a solution that required people to work in new, different, or unfamiliar ways. What kinds of reactions did you get from others? Were they positive and supportive ("Nice idea" or "I wish I had thought of it!")? Or were they critical and focused on limitations ("This will never work!" or "We already tried that and it didn't work!")?

Figure 5.15 A Deliberate Plan of Action Helps Ensure Effective Implementation

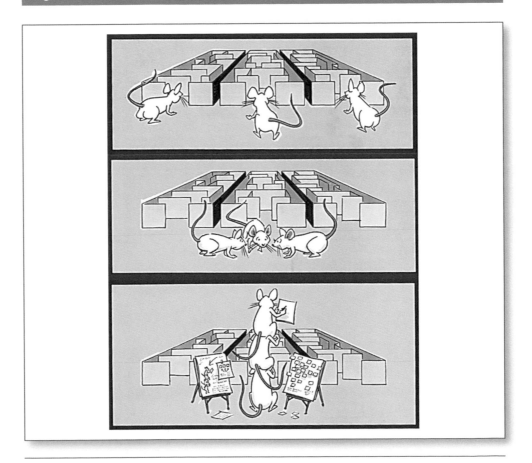

SOURCE: Copyright © 2009. The Creative Problem Solving Group, Inc. Reprinted with permission.

Transforming ideas into action can often look like the situation represented in Figure 5.16. When you attempt to make change happen, you will often need to coordinate your actions with those of others. When you attempt to coordinate actions, you will often need to obtain agreement through engaging in communications and involvement. Ideas often die from lack of follow-through, lack of commitment, or not receiving the support needed. These situations remind us very clearly that there can be a great difference between good solutions and those solutions that are accepted by others.

Figure 5.16 Finding Acceptance Is Crucial to Successful Implementation

SOURCE: Copyright © 2009. The Creative Problem Solving Group, Inc. Reprinted with permission.

Building Acceptance addresses a special set of critical concerns in transforming ideas into action. While Developing Solutions focuses on transforming ideas into solutions, Building Acceptance focuses on transforming promising solutions into action—moving from the present situation toward the desired future state. Building Acceptance challenges you to look at promising solutions through the eyes of others, examining the solutions in new ways that will lead to successful action (see Figure 5.17).

Since the emphasis of Building Acceptance is on preparing the people and the context to accept the change implied by the new solution, you will often begin by

Figure 5.17 The Building Acceptance Stage

identifying and understanding the forces that will assist or resist your efforts. You will identify the assisters, using them to help make success possible. They might contribute in a variety of ways, lending their skills, talents, and experience to your action plan. They might also help in dealing with the sources of resistance, to prevent or overcome obstacles, or even to engage them as assisters. In other situations, your Building Acceptance efforts might require only that you develop a specific plan of action to increase the likelihood of managing the change process successfully.

Many factors can influence how, and how successfully, you manage change. The kind of change you desire will influence your approach. Change that is highly novel or unusual may require more extensive evaluation, development, and refinement than change that is more improvement focused or designed to make something better. Step change or "radical breakthroughs" may also require you to devote more effort and energy to selling or marketing your desired changes than continuous improvement or incremental change.

Level of Involvement. The number of people who must be involved in the change initiative will also affect your planning efforts. Changes that involve groups of people will require more energy and time when focusing or making decisions. As the number of people involved in implementation increases, your plan of action will need to be more comprehensive, explicit, and communicable, and it will require more collaboration and cooperative effort. It may also need to be more flexible because of the increased possibility of an unpredicted factor or circumstance (i.e., someone getting sick or a change in job status) that requires alteration or modification of the plan.

Degree of Complexity. The complexity of the change will also influence your planning efforts. Change that is simple and clear-cut may require consideration of few factors and simpler decision-making needs and pathways. However, highly complex change, requiring attention to many ideas, will involve more steps and more effort, particularly during decision making and evaluation activities. Therefore, a more systematic and deliberate approach to focusing will be necessary. Complex change will also require you to consider a web of interrelated actions and activities that need to be implemented simultaneously.

A Formula for Change. It often takes special attention and commitment on the part of an individual or group to help make change a reality. They invest the time, energy, and commitment necessary to make sure that a desired change takes place. It is generally their personal energy, passion, and commitment to the change that help them succeed, even against seemingly impossible odds. One way of making sense of the many things you must consider to obtain acceptance for new ideas is to consider the formula for change identified in Figure 5.18.

Figure 5.18   Our Formula for Change

$$C = f_e(D, V_1, V_2, P)$$

The Choice and Commitment to change is a function of Dissatisfaction with current reality, a Vision of the future, Values that will endure, and a Process for getting there, reflecting the empowerment to effect change.

As a change agent, your choice and commitment to making change (C) will be influenced by your level of dissatisfaction with current reality (D), and by the clarity of the vision you hold for the future (V_1), as well as the constancy and quality of the values you hold (V_2). It will also be influenced by your process plan (P) for transforming your current reality into the future image.

When all these elements are present, change is more likely to happen. However, the likelihood of change occurring when an individual or group has one element in the formula missing is small. For example, we find some people have beautiful visions for the future but no understanding of their context, their values, or the reality around them. As a result, they do not know how to identify, access, or manage the necessary resources to make their vision a reality. Others have a solid understanding of the current reality but have no image or vision for what could be. As a result, they make daily choices that do not move them forward in any new direction. Still others have a vision and an understanding of their current reality but no process or plan for transforming their current reality into their vision. As a result, they often get frustrated because they do not know how to proceed. As Joel Barker (1990) suggested, "Vision without action is merely a dream. Action without vision is just passing time. Vision with action can change the world" (p. 7).

Change agents often face different levels of resistance from those who will be influenced by proposed changes. Resistance can come from personal orientations (e.g., blocks and barriers, preferences or styles of creativity, previous habits and experiences) or situational outlooks (e.g., perceptions of immediacy, level of importance, climate) of those involved. Kanter (1983) identified the 10 general reasons people resist change and suggested strategies to overcome them (see Table 5.2).

Table 5.2 Kanter's Reasons for Resisting Change

Reason	Strategy
Loss of control	Give people a choice, some involvement in decisions
Too much uncertainty	Share information as soon as possible
Surprise	Plant seeds of possible change
The difference effect	Make the change seem as familiar as possible
Need for familiar surroundings	Keep as much the same as possible
Can I do it?	Education and training
Ripple effect	Understanding people's values
More work	Inform employees' families of the change
Past resentments	Maintain high quality work life
Sometimes the threat is real	Chance to let go of past, find opportunity for future

The purpose of the Building Acceptance stage of CPS is to help ensure that you can overcome resistance and use sources of assistance as you take actions to implement your solutions.

Generating in Building Acceptance

You can use generating in three ways when Building Acceptance. In some situations, you may need to generate sources of assistance and resistance to identify forces in your context that influence the effective implementation of your solutions. In other situations, you may understand your context and simply need to identify the specific actions you might take to make the changes happen. In these cases, you generate potential action steps. Other situations may require you to modify the solutions that you evaluated during Developing Solutions to increase the likelihood of their acceptance. In this case, you might need to generate ways to overcome limitations. Let's look more closely at these three generating activities in Building Acceptance.

Generating Sources of Assistance and Resistance

In preparing for acceptance, we find it helpful to generate *sources of assistance and resistance* (see Table 5.3). Sources of assistance and resistance are those forces in the context that might positively or negatively influence the implementation of your solutions.

Table 5.3 Identifying Sources of Assistance and Resistance to Plan for Acceptance

	Sources of Assistance	Sources of Resistance
WHO	Helpful people?	Who may limit effectiveness of your plan?
WHAT	Helpful things, objects, or activities?	Things that may impede your progress?
WHEN	Preferred or useful locations or events?	Locations which may be inappropriate?
WHERE	Appropriate times or situations?	Are there particularly inappropriate times?
WHY	Effective reasons?	Reasons for not accepting your plan?

Generate possible assisters. Searching for sources of assistance involves trying to determine what forces in the context you can draw on for help in implementing your action plan. The people on whom you will depend for support are important assisters. Who else, in addition to you, will support the promising solutions? Remember that people are not the only assisters. Anything that will help improve your chances of successful action could be an assister. What are the essential resources or things you will need to implement the solution? When is the best time to carry out your plan? You can ask yourself Who? What? When? Where? and Why? to consider other sources of assistance as illustrated in Table 5.3. You can also use any of the other generating tools to come up with many, varied, and unusual assisters.

Generate possible resisters. Be wary of the trap of convincing yourself that "nothing could possibly go wrong." Very few solutions are ever foolproof. The newer and more original they are, the greater the chances that something can go wrong, and that it will! The effective problem solver (that's you) accepts this dose of reality and takes precautions accordingly. Resisters are people, places, things, times, or actions that might go wrong, create difficulties, or operate against your desired changes. Once again, consider asking yourself, "Who? What? Where? When? and Why?" Who are the critics or opponents? Who might have something to lose if the solutions work or something to gain if they do not? What important things or resources might be missing, unavailable when you need them, lost or overlooked? (For an example of generating assisters and resisters, see Figures 5.19 and 5.20.)

Figure 5.19 An Example of Assisters and Resisters (Who? What?) From the Vernon Case Study

Planning for acceptance

Promising option(s):
- Get to know Vernon and attempt to befriend him
- Keep Vernon happy – avoid getting him angry

Sources of assistance	Sources of resistance
WHO Helpful people? Vernon Prison Vernon's relatives Vernon's friends Other inmates Correction officials	Who may limit effectiveness of your plan? Jose Aponte and other prison guards Other inmates Vernon
WHAT Helpful things, objects, or activities? Recreation activities Rewards Food Priviledges Personal items Luxuries	Things that may impede your progress? Justice system Handcuffs Daily rountines Vernon's weight and size Vernon's temper Need to transport Vernon

VERNON CASE STUDY

Figure 5.20 An Example of Assisters and Resisters (Where? When? Why?) From the Vernon Case Study

Planning for acceptance

WHERE Preferred or useful locations or events?	Locations which may be inappropriate?
Recreation room	Yard
Counselor's office	Mess hall
Visiting area	Detention cell
Yard	Showers
	Bathroom
WHEN Appropriate times or situations?	Are there particularly inappropriate times?
Transporting him	At night
Counseling session	When transporting him
Recreation hours	Showering
	When sleeping
	First thing in the morning
WHY Effective reasons?	Reasons for not accepting your plan?
Reduce harm	Somebody could get hurt
Rehabilitate him	It would not make a difference
Protect nurses and guards	Vernon may not be nice
To move him through the system efficiently	Take too long
	Other inmates may take offense

VERNON CASE STUDY

It is not necessary to use the questions in any particular order or sequence. As with any generating activity, be sure to use the guidelines to generate many, varied, and unusual assisters and resisters. The most successful way to approach the generation is to stretch to consider answers that are beyond the obvious ones. It may be surprising for you to discover the number of people who might be able to help implement the solutions or the number of other assisters there might be. You might also be surprised that some people (or other resources) might be both assisters and resisters. If you find that the same item appears as both an assister and a resister, then consider it a key planning factor.

Generating Potential Action Steps

Can you recall times when you or someone else you know had to do some unusual things to get a solution implemented successfully? There is as much a need for creativity in Preparing for Action as there is in the other CPS components. Generating in Building Acceptance also involves generating potential action steps, or the activities, behaviors, or operations you consider to transform your solution into reality. Using the guidelines for generating options, generate potential action steps by answering the question, What actions might I (we) take to implement my (our) solution(s)? or How might I (we) accomplish this solution?

Consider generating possibilities for changing your current reality. Generate as many varied and unusual options as you can to create a rich set of options from which to choose. Figure 5.21 provides an example of generating potential action steps for the Vernon Case Study by answering the question, "How?"

Figure 5.21 An Example of Action Steps From the Vernon Case Study

Action steps

Generate specific actions to address key planning issues identified in Sources of Assistance & Resistance

HOW Needed actions?	Actions or activities that may be operating against solution(s)?
Contact Vernon's relatives	Vernon's situation and criminal record may inhibit staff
Schedule a talk with Vernon	
Coordinate our efforts	The guards' perceptions of Vernon may create negative situation
Provide him with responsibility	
Channel his strength	Prison life is not supportive
Show Vernon respect	Trial may be a source of anger

VERNON CASE STUDY

When generating potential action steps, be sure to stretch yourself to look for novel or unusual ways to take action. Challenge yourself to look beyond obvious or common approaches to implementing your solutions. When you are working individually on an action plan, try asking someone else about actions you might take. An outsider's perspectives might add new and valuable insights.

Identifying and Overcoming Limitations

Another common activity in the generating phase of Building Acceptance involves identifying and then overcoming key limitations of your solutions. This activity is particularly important when you need to follow up on limitations that were initially discovered in Developing Solutions, such as in the results of an ALUo or Evaluation Matrix. To identify and overcome limitations from an ALUo, use the Selecting Hits tool to identify the key limitations and generate ways by which they can be overcome. If you used a matrix to discover some limitations, identify the critical issue(s) and phrase them as questions (or problem statements) beginning with "How to . . ." Then, using the guidelines for generating options, generate many, varied, and unusual ways to overcome each limitation.

Focusing in Building Acceptance

After generating in Building Acceptance, you will have identified a variety of assisters and resisters, potential actions or ways to develop and strengthen solutions, and/or possible ways to overcome key limitations in the solution. As you focus in Building Acceptance, direct your attention and efforts to moving from your current reality toward your desired future state. You will work on this by focusing your energy on your critical forces and actions. This can be done using the Selecting Hits tool. When identifying your critical forces, pay particular attention to those sources that appear as both assisters and resisters. They may be key leverage points for your implementation efforts.

Sequencing Action Steps

Focusing in Building Acceptance will help you concentrate your energy and coordinate your efforts by identifying and sequencing actions you are committed to taking. During the generating phase of Building Acceptance, many tools helped you identify and list possible action steps that you (or others) might take. Now, your task is to ask the more difficult questions: "Which steps am I (or are we) really going to take?" and "Why, When, Where, and How will those steps need to be taken?"

In sequencing your action steps, your goal is to organize the actions into short-, medium-, and long-term items. This is a perfect application of the SML (short, medium, long) tool depicted in Figure 5.22. This tool is used to sort options with respect to a timeline and helps you identify the order in which options should be considered. Prior to sorting your actions, clarify two things. First, determine what you mean by short-, medium-, and long-term. For example, short-term to a research and development scientist may be 1 to 2 years. For a teacher, short-term might be by the end of the term (a few months). Second, determine whether the actions will be started or finished within the specific time frame.

Figure 5.22 An Illustration of SML (Short, Medium, Long) in Action

SOURCE: Copyright © 2009. The Creative Problem Solving Group, Inc. Reprinted with permission.

For example, will you begin an action in the medium term, or will you complete the action by medium term? Both these things need to be clarified before using the SML tool so that you are consistent in how you are deciding what goes into each part of the SML.

Sort your actions using the stem "What I see myself doing is. . . ." This stem can be used for each of the categories. For example, "What I see myself doing in one week is. . . ." Figure 5.23 provides an example of SML using the Vernon Case Study.

To jump-start your implementation efforts, be sure to include some short-term actions that can be taken in the next 24 hours. These can be things such as making a phone call, purchasing a project planner, speaking with a family member, and so on. There is some research on the effects of partially completed tasks that suggests they haunt you more than the ones you put away without doing anything on until later. Generally speaking, later seldom comes.

Figure 5.23 An Example of SML (Short, Medium, Long) From the Vernon Case Study

SML

Short-, medium-, and long-range actions

1. Identify short-term actions needed to help successful implementation.

Short-term actions are those to be taken by *Friday (One week)*

SHORT-TERM ACTIONS

Schedule counseling session, talk to Vernon
Phone calls to handcuff manufacturer, Universal Studios, etc.
Contact district attorney
Meet with inmate trustees
Charge the personnel dept. with searching for new guards
Meet with Phil Seelig

---

2. Identify medium-term actions needed to ensure successful implementation.

Medium-term actions need to be implemented by *Friday (Two weeks)*   <u>One week from</u>

MEDIUM-TERM ACTIONS

Have agents and entertainment professionals interview Vernon
Contact Vernon's friends, relatives, and girlfriends
Encourage physical recreation activities
Empower Vernon as a trustee
Have a contingency plan to bring in immediate strength
"Pull strings" necessary to advance trial date
Network with other prisons for advice
Increase time in cell if necessary
Attempt to get a guard to gain Vernon's confidence

---

3. Identify actions needed to be taken in the long term.

Long-term actions need to be taken by *Three weeks*

LONG-TERM ACTIONS

Initiate need for better restraining devices
Hire big, strong guards
Ask Vernon to help counsel other inmates
Keep staff advised of Vernon's progress
Publicize the success story

 VERNON CASE STUDY

Planning for Implementation

From our experience with groups over many years, we will offer an observation about implementation: Groups who leave a session or training course with a specific plan of action have a greater likelihood of implementing their solutions successfully than those who merely go away with enthusiasm and good intentions.

The extent and detail necessary when you are Preparing for Action depends on several factors, including the task and the action steps themselves, the nature of the key assisters and resisters, the time frame, and the location and degree of involvement in the solution. In some instances, a general set of short-, medium-, and long-term action steps may be quite sufficient. In other cases, much more extensive and detailed implementation planning may be necessary.

Planning for implementation involves identifying and recording the specific details for the key actions you, or others, will need to take (see Figure 5.24). It

---

Figure 5.24 An Example of an Implementation Plan From the Vernon Case Study

Planning for implementation

Action Talk with Vernon	**Who**	Tom McTernan, Counselor
	Start	Mon. 10 am **Finish** 12 pm
	Where	In Tom's office
	Why	Get to know and understand Vernon – likes, dislikes, etc.
Measure of Success A surface understanding of Vernon's motivation	**How**	Attempt to do it one-on-one with no restraints

Action Conduct a staff meeting	**Who**	Myself, Warden X
	Start	Tue. 9 am **Finish** 11:30 am
	Where	Conference room C
Measure of Success Staff walking away empowered to take action	**Why**	Delegate responsibilities regarding Vernon
	How	I will direct the meeting

Action Charge the personnel department with searching for new guards	**Who**	Rich Maiola, Correction Official
	Start	Monday **Finish** Friday
	Where	Applicant files, other prisons and correctional facilities
Measure of success Obtaining a list of candidates	**Why**	To bring in added strength
	How	Memo

VERNON CASE STUDY

addresses questions such as who is going to do what to, with, or for whom by when? How will you know the action taken was successful? and Where will the action take place? It also includes identifying important reasons for the action as a reminder of the goal or purpose. For those cases in which you may need more extensive and detailed planning, you may wish to consider using a specific project-planning method.

Implementation Checklist

Having a written plan will not always be enough to ensure effective and successful implementation. However, it can often help you avoid the challenges symbolized in Figure 5.25. Research has identified several factors to help increase the power of your implementation plan. For example, Rogers (1995) identified five factors to increase the effectiveness of your planning and implementation (see Figure 5.26). He suggests that if your plan shows the relative advantage of your solutions over previous approaches and their compatibility or consistency with existing values, experiences, or needs, the likelihood of them being implemented increases. Also, as you make the plan easy to understand and use (less complex), make it observable, and give people a chance to try parts of it, the greater the chance of successful implementation.

Figure 5.25   Looking Good on Paper Is Not Always Enough

SOURCE: Copyright © 2009. The Creative Problem Solving Group, Inc. Reprinted with permission.

Figure 5.26 A Checklist to Help Increase Chances of Implementation

**Rogers (1995) identified five factors that are
likely to increase the rate of adoption of innovation**

- **Relative advantage** – Being better than previous idea
- **Compatibility** – Consistent with values, experiences, and needs
- **Complexity** – Being difficult to understand and use
- **Trialability** – May be experimented with on a limited basis
- **Observability** – Results are visible to others

We used these five categories to develop a checklist to help you examine the effectiveness of your plan and to identify places where it might be strong or need improvement or modification.

Relative Advantage. Being better than the previous solution: How well does my plan show how much better off people will be when they adopt the plan?

- Why is this plan better than what has been done before?
- What advantages or benefits might there be to accepting the plan?
- Who will gain from the implementation of the plan?
- How will I (or others) be rewarded by adopting the plan?
- How might I emphasize the plan's benefits to all?

Compatibility. Consistent with values, experiences, and needs: How well does my plan demonstrate that it is compatible with current values, past experiences, and needs?

- Is the plan consistent with current practice?
- Does the plan meet the needs of a particular group?
- Does it offer better ways to reach our common goals?
- Who will naturally support and agree with the plan?
- Can it be favorably named, packaged, or presented?

Complexity. Being difficult to understand and use: How well does my plan provide for easy communication, comprehension, and use?

- Is the plan easy for others to understand?
- Can it be explained clearly to many different people?
- Will the plan be easily communicated?

- How might the plan be made more simple or easy to understand?
- Is the plan easy to use or follow?

Trialability. May be experimented with on a limited basis: How well does my plan allow for trialability?

- Can the plan be tried out or tested?
- Can uncertainty be reduced?
- Can we begin with a few parts of the plan?
- How might others be encouraged to try out the plan?
- Can the plan be modified by you or others?

Observability. Results are visible to others: How well does my plan provide results that are easily observed and visible to others?

- Is the plan easy for others to find or obtain?
- Can the plan be made more visible to others?
- How might I make the plan easier for others to see?
- Will others be able to see the effects of the plan?
- Are there good reasons for not making the entire plan visible?

Other Questions. The following are some general questions that will help your planning and implementation efforts.

- What other resources will I need, and how might I get them?
- What obstacles exist and how might we prevent or overcome them?
- What new challenges might be created and dealt with?
- How might I encourage commitment to the plan?
- What feedback about the plan is needed?

Obtaining Feedback on Your Plan

Effective problem solvers realize that implementing change successfully often requires continuous monitoring and feedback. Moving from your current situation toward your desired situation will probably not happen overnight, nor proceed exactly as planned. Many unforeseen obstacles or opportunities can arise during implementation.

To help manage the change process effectively, identify several key points during the implementation process that might provide you with feedback on your progress. These may be key people to contact, times to gather information, locations to measure impact, or other indicators of progress. Figure 5.27 is an illustration of how to get feedback on your implementation plan using the Vernon Case Study.

Figure 5.27 Obtaining Feedback on the Plan From the Vernon Case Study

Obtaining feedback on the plan

Identify checkpoints and sources of feedback regarding your plan in order to ensure that it is working well and that you can identify specific ways to improve it in the future.

- Who might you check with?

  Guards   Counselor   Vernon

  Nurses   Correction Official

- What will you want to know? (How will you know it is successful? What questions will you ask?)

  Has there been an improvement in Vernon's behavior?

  Has anyone from the entertainment industry contacted Vernon?

- When would be the best time(s) to check?

  Every day

  Review end of the week

- What locations might be important to consider?

  Know what happens when Vernon is transported from his cell
  Daily reports in my "in-box"

- What reasons can you offer for using these checkpoints?

  Timely response in case of emergency

  A shared understanding of our efforts

- Identify future challenges created by implementing your plan of action?

  How to maintain a controlled situation with Vernon as a trustee?

  How to avoid perceived favoritism?

- How might I be sure to acquire the feedback?

  Receive reports

  Speak with Vernon myself

 VERNON CASE STUDY

In summary, Building Acceptance is designed to help you manage the transformation of your current situation into a new and desired state. The stage provides a lens with which you can examine both the context within which change is needed and the solution(s) that will be used to create the change. This enables you to develop a plan for effectively implementing your solutions and managing the transformation of the context.

The Rest of the Story

A large global chemical company wanted entirely new applications for its special paper. We designed a 3-day workshop to create new market/application opportunities that would significantly increase the market share for the paper product. It turned out that our challenge was not only to help them identify new applications but also to help them be successful in entering these new markets with unique product applications.

Therefore, we designed the session with particular emphasis on the working climate and the likelihood of its impact on the success or failure of their implementation (we will discuss more about climate in Chapter 8). This work on climate provided the team with data about their organization and its readiness to accept changes created by this project. The data were used to help them identify their pockets of positive energy (assisters) that would support their efforts and pockets of energy that might impede their progress (resisters). The information also helped them develop informed plans that increased the likelihood of successful implementation.

Plans are good. But was anything actually done with the result of their work? In this story, it was particularly interesting that an idea was created that changed the product so dramatically that it opened up a large number of different markets. The concept was highly novel and had immediate implications for the division. Before our meeting was finished, four of the people from the group were put on an airplane to one of the new facilities being built. Their job was to stop the construction crews from pouring concrete into the ground in order to redesign the building. They wanted it to include the capacity to produce this new characteristic of the special paper. You know you're finished Preparing for Action when you have what you need to get started. When the time is right, the changes will start to move naturally.

Putting This Chapter to Work

Our goals of this chapter were to help you understand the Preparing for Action component and the two stages it contains: Developing Solutions and Building Acceptance. We examined the language of the component along with tools that enable you to analyze, develop, and refine promising options and put effective plans in place for making productive changes happen.

Activities to Guide Reflection and Action

Work on the following activities to review your understanding of the material in this chapter and to practice applying it in real situations. If you are using this book as part of a course or study group, you may wish to work individually, and then compare your responses, or to work collaboratively as a team.

1. Identify a situation from your past in which you made an important decision. Consider whether you used primary (implicit) criteria or secondary (explicit) criteria. What were some of the key advantages and limitations of using that form of criteria in that particular situation? Surmise at what point you typically keep your criteria implicit and at what point you make them explicit when making decisions.

2. Consider a situation you are currently facing that requires you to make an important decision. Complete the following activities:

- Generate a list of 10 to 12 criteria you might use to help you with the decision.

- Identify the top 5 to 7 criteria you want to use to help you with your decision using the Selecting Hits tool described in Chapter 3.

- Prioritize your list of 5 to 7 criteria using the PCA tool described in this chapter.

- Identify any resulting insights you have about your criteria that will help you with your decision.

3. Think back in your life to two situations in which you took action to make a change happen. The first should be a situation that did not require you to involve anyone else in taking action or making the change. You knew what you needed to do and you could implement the necessary action successfully on your own. The second should be a situation where you knew what needed to be done, but it required you to involve other people to successfully make the change happen. Compare and contrast what you had to do to be successful in each situation. Single out any factors you needed to address to be successful in the second situation that did not emerge as issues in the first.

4. Consider the situation you identified in #2. Understanding that you have made your decision and it is necessary to consider how to get the decision implemented, complete the following activities:

- Generate a list of 10 to 12 potential sources of assistance that may help you be successful with taking action on your decision.

- Generate a list of 10 to 12 potential sources of resistance you may face when implementing your decision.

- Identify the top 3 to 5 sources of assistance and the top 3 to 5 sources of resistance using the Selecting Hits tool (from Chapter 3).

- Generate some actions you can take that will help you capitalize on the sources of assistance and overcome the sources of resistance as you implement your decision.

Planning Your Approach to CPS

To exist is to change, to change is to mature, to mature is to go on creating oneself, endlessly.

—Linus Pauling

The purpose of this chapter is to overview the Planning Your Approach component of Creative Problem Solving (CPS). The two basic issues for Planning Your Approach include Appraising Tasks, in which you assess and verify the appropriateness of CPS for a task, and Designing Process, in which you plan how to apply CPS effectively and efficiently. As a result of reading this chapter, you will be able to do the following:

1. Describe the Planning Your Approach component of CPS.

2. Explain why Planning Your Approach is a management component by comparing and contrasting it with the three other process components of CPS.

3. Identify the purpose of the Appraising Tasks stage and name the four main elements in Task Appraisal.

4. Make use of the key issues and questions contained in the People and Context dimension of Appraising Tasks.

5. Make use of the key issues and questions contained in the Process and Content dimension of Appraising Tasks.

6. Identify the purpose of the Designing Process stage of the Planning Your Approach component.

7. Explain the effects of content, people, and context on Designing Process.

Ahome for the aged was located in an urban center. The facility was affiliated with a particular religious tradition, and our first meeting with the executive director happened to be on a high religious holiday within this community's tradition, so we were served a special lunch. The director had heard about our work with creativity and change. He wanted to see if there was something we could do to help.

He explained to us that he had a very different vision of how things should be for the elderly, and for those needing assistance to get along, than what was currently going on in his own facility (and within other facilities he knew). During our lunch conversation, he shared a detailed image of the kind of environment he thought should be created, as well as the kind of organization he thought would be required to take care of people within this new kind of place. The place he described seemed more like a modern and open campus than a hospital. It would operate as a flat organization in which the staff closest to the residents would make the decisions about the residents' care.

It was an exciting meeting and we were particularly impressed with the director's vision and his image of a dramatic improvement in the way people would be living their golden years. As we walked away from our meeting, we asked ourselves, "Is this an initiative that we could and should do something about? Is this something for which CPS would be appropriate? If so, how should we go forward?"

This chapter will guide you in making decisions about the most appropriate and effective use of CPS. We will address two fundamental questions that will help you successfully apply the tools, guidelines, and components of CPS from Chapters 2 through 5. The first question is "How do you decide whether or not to use CPS?" The second is "How do you design the most effective use of CPS?"

CPS is a powerful framework for solving problems, responding to challenges, and taking advantage of opportunities. However, we do not see it as an all-purpose method for dealing with every problem or challenge in life. You must have some way to decide if CPS is an appropriate method to use for any given task. We call this decision-making activity "Appraising Tasks." This is the stage of the Planning Your Approach component in which you assess the needs, the people involved, and the situation, and then you qualify CPS as your method. *Qualify* means deciding whether or not CPS is appropriate for the task.

The second question deals with making specific choices about tailoring CPS to fit your needs, the people using it, and the situation in which it will be applied. Since there are two broad sets of guidelines, six stages, three process components, and a variety of different tools, you will need to make a number of choices to help you configure and adjust the actual approach you will take. We refer to this customizing as Designing Process.

Planning Your Approach in a Nutshell

Planning Your Approach (see Figure 6.1) is the newest component of CPS, and it is playing a powerful role in the way we organize and use the rest of the process. The structure of the process is designed for flexible learning and application, not for rigid

Figure 6.1 Planning Your Approach in a Nutshell

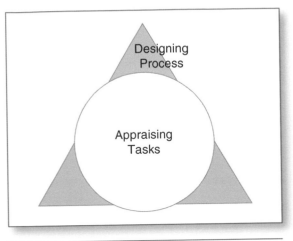

Designing
Process

Appraising
Tasks

SOURCE: Copyright © 2009. The Creative Problem Solving Group, Inc. and The Center for Creative Learning, Inc. Reprinted with permission.

or thoughtless use. It is not designed or presented as the only way to think creatively. The spirit of the process is one of service to your needs. In service to these needs, the structure of the process allows for and encourages your own flexible control.

CPS is one of the only methods that deliberately considers the key aspects of people, content, and context as a part of the problem-solving system. The closest thing we could find comes from the Kepner-Tregoe method (Kepner & Tregoe, 1981; Spitzer & Evans, 1997). Kepner-Tregoe (KT) is widely used and contains a deliberate stage called "situation appraisal." This stage includes efforts to bring order and clarity to a complex situation and to determine priorities and actions to resolve each concern. Situation appraisal helps determine if other patterns of thinking may be required. It is the only one of the four thinking processes within KT that does not actually resolve a specific concern. Its aim is to clarify and assess the concerns and then to move on to one or more of the three remaining critical-thinking aspects of problem analysis, decision analysis, and potential problem-opportunity analysis.

Most other methods are provided to you as a recipe. You usually follow predetermined steps and procedures and end up with a particular result. CPS encourages you to think carefully about what you want from the process and to consider the people involved and the situation surrounding your task. In a way, CPS functions as a system, including the people, context, method, and content. As parts of a system, these four elements are interdependent and contribute to each other. Since CPS offers you a complete system, it is possible for you to design your unique way through the process. This is why we need a component such as Planning Your Approach.

Planning Your Approach is a management component of CPS that helps you be mindful about your efforts as you actually work to resolve the challenge or reach out for the opportunity. We refer to it as a "management component" because it means overseeing, directing, and monitoring your own efforts. It is something you always keep in mind as you are using the other components of CPS.

Planning Your Approach helps you manage your process efforts and actions. You can engage in Planning Your Approach as deliberate preparation before you apply CPS. It should also function consistently "behind the scenes" to help you guide the way you are working on process. Its primary purpose is to guide your choice and use of the other components, stages, and tools.

This component is like an operating system that always runs in the background while you are using your computer. The management component allows the "applications" to run. If your situation calls for you to write a report, you may choose applying Microsoft Word as your application. If it calls for crunching some numbers, you may choose to apply Microsoft Excel. Perhaps your situation calls for you to make a presentation. In this case, you may choose Microsoft PowerPoint. Sometimes you may want to insert a table in your document, so you may need to use both Word and Excel. As your operating system, Planning Your Approach allows you to continuously monitor and manage what you are doing and thinking about. Psychologists and educators describe this as metacognitive processing.

In the other components of CPS, you produce specific outcomes that relate directly to the real-life content of the task on which you are working. Your work within the three process components of Understanding the Challenge, Generating Ideas, and Preparing for Action has a specific strategic purpose contributing to solving your problem, effecting a change, or reaching your goal. At some point, you are finished with the work you have been doing or the tools you have been using in any component or stage. The management component helps you structure and organize your approach to the content. The continuous monitoring allows you to confirm that your efforts are on track, or to redirect your attention and effort as needed; it helps you control the direction and flow of your energy and attention.

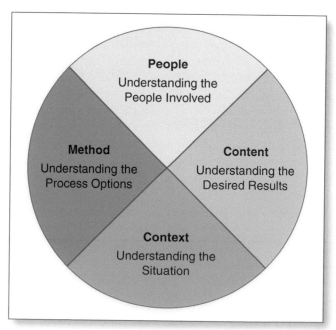

Figure 6.2   The Four Elements of Appraising Tasks

There are two stages in Planning Your Approach. The first, Appraising Tasks, involves learning about the needs, people, and context, and then qualifying the use of CPS (see Figure 6.2). Qualifying CPS is about ensuring that it is a good fit or match for the requirements of the task. It results in a decision about whether or not to use CPS as you take on the challenge or opportunity. Appraising Tasks involves making an evaluation of the work or a systematic estimate of the scope of the challenge or opportunity. What you learn about the task from the point of view of the people involved, the situation or context, and the needs and desired results will influence what you do in the other stage of Planning Your Approach.

In Designing Process, you take advantage of the learning and insights you have gained during Appraising Tasks and then optimize your use of CPS. In the Draw Your Natural Process exercise in Chapter 2, you probably noticed that the actual process you used for that specific situation depended on a number of factors. That's also true for the story at the beginning of this chapter. When Planning Your Approach, you will have to consider many factors. Table 6.1 identifies nine of the important factors associated with Planning Your Approach.

Some of these factors may be more or less important in different contexts, but effective application of CPS always requires understanding many of them. The key elements of the Appraising Tasks and Designing Process stages arise from these factors. It is quite possible that people involved with the task will have different perspectives on

Table 6.1   There Are Many Factors to Consider When Planning Your Approach

Importance	To what extent is this task a high priority for you and for others?
Kind and degree of ownership	Is this a task about which people care, for which they have enthusiasm, and in which thay are interested? Do they have the authority and opportunity to take action? Are they willing to use their imaginations to think up new possibilities?
Ambiguity	To what extent is the task "messy," ill-defined, or lacking in structure?
Complexity	Is the task simple and distinct, or complex and made up of many different elements?
Novelty	To what extent are you seeking new possibilities that will break new ground, or be surprising departures from reality? Are you seeking options that are familiar, easy to implement, or considered safe?
Timeline	Does this task require immediate attention and action or can you work on it over a longer period of time? Will the task require a single (one-time) effort, or will it require many different efforts?
History	To what extent does the task depend on understanding the background information? What have you already tried to accomplish?
Involvement of others	Should someone work on this task alone, with a few others, or with many others?
Vision of desired future	To what extent might people view the task as an obstacle or threat to be overcome, a gap to be closed, or an opportunity to be achieved?

each of the factors. One of the goals of Planning Your Approach is to obtain consensus about the important issues, especially when a group is involved.

The following sections will provide you a general overview of Appraising Tasks and Designing Process. We will describe both stages of Planning Your Approach in more detail in the subsequent chapters.

What Is Appraising Tasks?

To plan your approach to CPS effectively, you will need a basic understanding of the task to be accomplished. Appraising Tasks allows you to inquire and reflect on what actually needs to be done. The main issue is considering what you would like to know or learn about before you actually design your approach to the process. *Appraising* means taking stock of, or sizing up, the task. This appraisal allows you to determine the suitability, worth, and potential effectiveness of applying CPS. The results you obtain may lead you to decide that CPS is not an appropriate method for the task at hand.

A *task* is any piece of work, an effort to be undertaken, or a project to be done. Tasks come in many sizes. Some are very large and complex, such as transforming the way an organization engages in product development or raising the standards of performance for learners within an entire state. Others are smaller and more specific, such as obtaining new ideas for marketing an existing product or finding new and improved methods to teach economics to elementary school students. We use the stems "I wish . . ." or "We need to . . ." to distinguish a task statement.

Appraising Tasks provides a deliberate structure for thinking about problem solving for tasks requiring the use of creativity. Making deliberate judgments about whether or not to apply CPS helps us ensure that the method is being applied appropriately.

Although Appraising Tasks is essential in our current view of CPS, it could also be valuable and productive for managing other change methods (Isaksen & Tidd, 2006). This stage provides a deliberate opportunity to qualify the use of CPS as well as to examine and understand better the people involved in the change, the context surrounding it, and the desired outcome or needed result (see Figure 6.2). By considering this entire system, you are in a better position to make estimates and decisions regarding the factors outlined in Table 6.1.

You may appraise tasks on topics and issues you are facing on your own or as a facilitator working with a client or a group of clients or when you are facing a larger change initiative. You can also learn about the people and the situation in an effort to qualify the use of CPS. Those who are responsible for implementing the change will also benefit from Appraising Tasks.

The People and Context Dimension

Most problem-solving methods focus mainly on their special tools and on the methods themselves. It is almost as though the method has become the solution or answer. Our approach to CPS includes deliberately considering the people and the place and adjusting the method to ensure an appropriate fit.

People. Appraising Tasks involves understanding the people who might be involved. This includes a focus on ensuring that there is sufficient ownership to use CPS effectively. Ownership means that there is someone who will take the results forward, that there is interest and energy in the task, and that there is room to engage the imagination. Having sufficient ownership for the task is a go or no-go decision and is the central issue when considering the people aspect of Appraising Tasks. We find that one of the key reasons any method is unsuccessful is that there is no one responsible for and interested in following through on the results.

Understanding the influence and characteristics of people also includes the ideas of diversity and task expertise. Diversity encompasses the different characteristics, styles, and backgrounds people possess and is essential for some applications of CPS. Other tasks require that those involved have a high level of knowledge, information, and experience in the subject matter or specific domain of the task. You can read more about the aspect of people when Appraising Tasks in Chapter 7.

Context. Another aspect of Appraising Tasks includes examining the context. The central question for this area of Appraising Tasks is "How ready, willing, and able is the situation for creativity and the change it implies?" This question includes an examination of the climate, culture, and history within which the task is embedded. It also includes a look into the strategic priorities, leadership, and energy present in the context, as well as the time, attention, and resources available in the context.

Sometimes you have the right people, but the environment, climate, or timing is simply not right for the effort to be successful. You can read more about the role context plays when applying CPS in Chapter 8.

The Content-Method Dimension

This dimension of Appraising Tasks deals with being clear about the desired results. This dimension is about getting the results you want or need and following a deliberate pathway or process to obtain them. Although your choices would also be influenced by both the people and the context, this dimension involves the mindful matching of your approach to the specific needs of the task. This requires you to be able to distinguish the process from the content.

Content. Comprehending the desired outcome provides you with information about the actual desired results and the needs within the task. The content of the task must be appropriate for a creative kind of problem solving. This means that the task must involve a need for newness, novelty, and an original response. It also means that you understand the size of the impact you want to have, as well as where the best place is to start or exert leverage in order to make a difference. The central content question is "What is it you need to achieve?" You can read more about the aspect of content when Appraising Tasks in Chapter 9.

Method. Appraising Tasks provides for deliberate qualification for your use of CPS. There are many different methods for change. Our approach to CPS is but one. As we discussed in Chapter 1, CPS is best applied when you face the need for new solutions or when your situation is ambiguous or complex. Our approach requires a need for novelty, clarity of ownership, and an appropriate climate for change. Although CPS is an open and flexible framework, it is better suited for some tasks over others. Therefore, the central questions for this aspect of Appraising Tasks are "What do I need to know about CPS to consider it for use on the task?" and "What does my knowledge of other method choices add to my decision about using CPS?"

To help you answer these questions and make an informed decision about CPS, it will help you to know the specific purpose and unique features of CPS. You will want to know how confident you can be that CPS will help you to be productive on the particular kind of task and that using CPS is worth the costs to get the benefits. See Chapter 10 for more information on the method aspect of Planning Your Approach.

The four elements of people, context, content, and method comprise the core system and need to be considered when productively using CPS to manage change. We call these four elements a "system" because what goes on in one element influences what happens in the other elements. They function like a musical quartet. In the quartet, each musical instrument can make beautiful music by itself. However, to listen to the full experience of the quartet, you must hear all four instruments playing together.

The same holds true with the four elements of the core system (people, context, content, and method). To fully understand what it takes to productively manage change, you need to listen to, understand, and act on what is taking place in each of the elements. For example, it would be difficult to understand what the desired results are for a task without thinking about the people asking for them or the context in which they will be created. It would be difficult to truly understand the people involved without understanding the context in which they live or work. It would be difficult to make a good decision about the use of a method without understanding the desired results or the people involved in creating them.

You can examine each of the four elements on its own. However, to fully understand the task, you need to consider each element in relationship to the other elements. The Appraising Tasks stage of Planning Your Approach is designed to help you do exactly that.

What Is Designing Process?

When you have a task that is appropriate for CPS, you need to figure out *how* to take your journey through the process of working on the task. We call this "Designing Process," and it is illustrated in Figure 6.3. Its purpose is to determine how to best proceed with the specific operational application of CPS. This requires an understanding of CPS, the people to be involved, and the situation within which you will be working. It also means designing the series of actions or operations you must take to meet the needs of your task.

Designing Process includes more than just project planning and the technical aspects surrounding the design of your approach. Engaging in Designing Process

Figure 6.3 Designing Process in a Nutshell

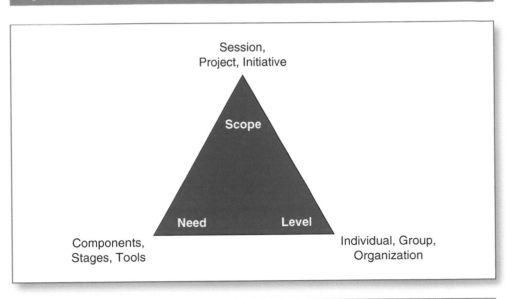

allows you to be mindful and reflective about the spirit of the approach as well as build motivation and commitment for participating in the process. It allows you to customize and personalize your application of CPS so that it will fit your particular need and circumstances. Based on the specific needs, you will be able to configure your particular pathway through the general framework to optimize the investment of time, talent, and energy you will make. This will have an impact on the level and scale of your CPS application. The Designing Process stage involves using inputs from the people, context, content, and method elements of the task to customize your approach to CPS.

Required Results From the Process

Information about the required results for the task will help guide your decision making regarding the scope of CPS application necessary to accomplish the desired task outcomes. The size of the task determines the level of interaction, the kind of method to be applied, and what may happen in the context as you apply the method. Some tasks may need only a single workshop, meeting, or session. Larger or more complex tasks may demand a series of sessions, meetings, or workshops that are managed as a project or long-term change initiative.

The nature of the task may also dictate the character of the process you use to address the task. For example, some tasks might be best approached by coaching, mentoring, or some approach other than CPS.

Needed Elements of the Method

Part of Designing Process is determining the best parts of CPS to use in focusing your efforts on the task. It involves making the CPS process manageable and delivering results in a way that optimizes the benefit and impact from your effort. It means that you need to have a deliberate plan for what you will do and how it will be accomplished. At this point, you need to decide what component you should work within. You will make strategic decisions about the tools you will apply, the stages that best fit the design, and the overall components that will best serve your needs. See Chapter 10 for more information on the method aspect of Planning Your Approach.

Desired Involvement and Interaction

People are key to implementing all change efforts. In fact, organizations don't change; people do. To successfully approach the task, you may need to involve or interact with others. You may do this for a number of different reasons. In any case, Designing Process includes being planful about how you involve others in your use of CPS. At one level, you may choose to work on a task on your own. The topic may be too personal or too private or it may simply not benefit from involving others. The involvement or interaction with others for these tasks may be small or nonexistent. At another level, you might benefit from involving others in your use of CPS for a task. You may have a task where you need input from others based on their common or deep knowledge, experience, and skill associated with the task or related subject area. Or you may need a diverse array of perspectives (i.e., people from different cultural, gender, age, or functional backgrounds). Your task may be more concerned with implementation and acceptance or engagement. For these tasks, you may involve others based on issues of politics, representation, and influence rather than because of expertise.

At a third level, some tasks will be so large that they require a high level of involvement and participation in your use of CPS. These tasks often depend on having a high degree of acceptance of the outcomes or on including a diverse array of perspectives from a variety of groups. For example, many long-term strategic projects in organizations may require you to involve people from different departments, functions, or cultures in the change process. These often require many different kinds of interactions, including one-on-one meetings, small-group sessions, and large-group meetings. During a longer-term initiative, additional methods such as research, regular planning meetings, and other approaches to project management may take place independently from CPS.

If you plan to involve others in your use of CPS with a group or at an organizational level, additional planning may be helpful and necessary. For example, when using a group, it will be necessary to prepare people involved for taking on specific roles and responsibilities. They will need to know how they are expected to participate, their scope of responsibilities, and the desired outcomes of their contributions.

Decisions about involving others during these planning activities will influence the concrete and specific plans for applying CPS. Involving different people may demand particular kinds of interaction. For example, most meetings occur in the same place at the same time. The movement and need to use other forms of interaction is growing. An implication is that your process planning may include organizing your meetings at the same time but at different places (videoconferencing, teleconferencing, etc.), different places at different times (Web sites, bulletin boards, written and print media, etc.), or at the same place but at a different time (message systems, databases, visible displays, learning centers, etc.). These approaches may require specific technology or other material resources.

Constraints From the Context

Different situations in the organization may require a certain degree of visible structure and support. For example, certain organizations (Polaroid, Du Pont, Kodak, Exxon, and Lucent) have found it useful to have a distinct center for creativity. These central structures offer information, training, facilitation, and application services across functions and traditional product categories. Others have relied on a broad skills-transfer initiative or a "SWAT team" approach. Often, this had been led through the human resource function due to its focus on building competencies. The constraints from the context may influence the amount and kind of time, attention, and resources that will be available (people, staff, use of external consultants, time, money, technology, etc.). Still other organizations prefer a more informal or low-key approach (i.e., the creeping quiet virus approach).

Certain situations, due to the climate, culture, or history, may require that results be shown early in the process. Some organizations may demand quick wins from any change program. Others may take a long-term perspective and allow for investments in other aspects of the process. In either case, you can learn how quickly results must be delivered and shape your approach accordingly. If the leadership guiding the change process is asking for a fundamental, big, and innovative change, and the situation is calling for quick, simple, and inexpensive results, you're in for a challenging piece of work!

Another constraint that may affect Designing Process is how many projects have already been launched. You may find that some places suffer from initiative overload. People in these places have too many existing projects and can barely make progress on what's already "on their platter."

The Rest of the Story

We decided to help the executive director of the home change his organization. We held a meeting that included the director's reports and provided a creativity briefing to illustrate the CPS method and a few of its tools. Following that meeting, they decided to move forward with CPS as a main set of tools in their arsenal for change.

The first step in the process was to train key leadership in CPS as a common language and set of tools for managing this change effort. Then the key leadership designed a transition plan to completely transform their organization. We then trained the next two levels of management in CPS. Part of the power in this part of the design was that we used the transition plan and design for the new organizational structure (created by the senior management team) as the main tasks the two management levels addressed during the workshops. It resulted in high levels of buy-in and acceptance of the plan, as well as a greater understanding of what it would take to successfully implement the plan.

Five years later, the home is entirely and significantly transformed. The organization is now located about 15 miles from its original site with a completely different kind of environment. What was a cramped work environment located in the city is now a wide-open campus environment located in the countryside. This campus contains entirely new buildings designed to the unique and specific criteria of the management team. The management teams themselves custom-designed the buildings using the CPS language and tools.

When you walk through the buildings, there is an incredibly different feeling of openness and cleanliness, with a buzz of healthy activity and interaction. The physical place has an entirely different climate, as is shown in a modern, state-of-the-art facility, health club, shops, and lots of choices and levels of service available to residents. The space is designed to support decentralized decision making. People who were managers in the earlier system are now considered CEOs of their own units. The main responsibility of the director is now to help protect against doing things the old way.

What helped us be successful was that we considered the entire system (people, context, content, and method) in planning the initiative. We also engaged in continuous Planning Your Approach with the management team throughout the initiative. This was particularly important during the first few meetings as we developed a better understanding of the people involved, the context they were in, and their need for making change. It was also helpful that we engaged the management team in building the process design we used for the initiative—rather than telling them what they needed to do. This resulted in greater commitment to the initiative, as well as quicker and more effective implementation.

The new campus has been a success in so many ways. For example, they have been recognized at a statewide level for their excellent work in improving the quality of life for many families. One of the more interesting measures of success, however, is that they have a significantly lower number of residents with bedsores (Babij, 1999). They continue their investment in training the next wave of management in CPS and keeping their new organizational culture alive and growing.

What were the specific issues we focused on to understand the executive director's task? What kind of questions did we ask him to get the information we needed? The next four chapters will provide you with more detail on the two dimensions of People and Context and Method and Content that we used to be successful with the urban facility.

Putting This Chapter to Work

This chapter has been focused on Planning Your Approach to CPS. We identified two main stages to help you guide or manage your approach to CPS. The first was Appraising Tasks to consider the people and place as well as the method to address your needs. The second stage was Designing Process to create the most appropriate pathway through CPS.

Activities to Guide Reflection and Action

Work on one or more of the following activities to review your understanding of the material in this chapter and to practice applying the content in real situations. If you are using this book as part of a course or study group, you may wish to work individually, and then compare your responses, or to work collaboratively as a team.

1. Identify a situation from your past that required a new response or solution. It could also be one that was rather ambiguous or complex. Once you have this task in mind, try addressing each of the four main elements of Appraising Tasks to see what you can learn. Be sure to address the areas of the people involved, the context surrounding the task, and the desired outcome, as well as the method you used to address the task. Check to be sure that you have insights and all the key information from all four areas.

2. Select an interesting news story from the newspaper or an online source. See if you can identify answers to the key Appraising Tasks areas. If not, try phrasing a question that might help you fill the gaps.

3. Make a list of possible tasks that would benefit from applying CPS. For each item, see if you can identify which component and stage of CPS might be most appropriate. Then identify if the task would be best approached by someone working alone or by a group.

7

People as Creative Problem Solvers

Imagination is the secret reservoir of the riches of the human race.

—Maude L. Frandsen

The purposes of this chapter are to help you understand the importance of personal characteristics and factors in Planning Your Approach to Creative Problem Solving (CPS) and the role of diversity, ownership, and task expertise in the Appraising Tasks stage. As a result of your reading and study of this chapter, you should be able to do the following:

1. Describe the importance of understanding personal characteristics and style preferences when Planning Your Approach to CPS for individuals, teams, or organizations.

2. Identify several cognitive and personality characteristics related to creativity and explain their implications for preparing for CPS and for applying CPS effectively (individually or with teams, groups, or organizations).

3. Identify and explain the important elements of diversity, ownership, and task expertise, and describe their significance and use in any CPS component or stage.

4. Describe at least three ways of applying your knowledge of people to the opportunities and challenges on which you work in your own setting.

A group of managers and technical people in the advertising industry wanted to be trained in the use of creative-thinking and problem-solving tools. We were a bit hesitant at first, thinking, "Here we are—being asked to train people in an advertising agency, reputed to be a highly creative profession, in the use of creative-thinking and problem-solving skills!"

We addressed the issues of creativity and diversity during a 1-day workshop. We also practiced some of the creative-thinking tools on a task that was real to the agency. It involved helping the organization become more nimble. Although they were already very successful, they wanted to improve their ability to respond to needs, act more quickly on customer requests, and turn the organization around quickly and efficiently to pursue new opportunities.

During our day together, we learned much about people in advertising. As in many other organizations, there were some very strong boundaries between people in different functions. However, one boundary was particularly interesting in this organization. They call those people who deal with the design and art side of the business the "creatives." They create the actual advertisements for customers. The people who deal with the client relationship side of the business (e.g., finances, client management) are called the "suits." The "suits" often perceive the "creatives" as an uncontrollable group of flaky people, while the "creatives" perceive the "suits" as non-creative drones. For all intents and purposes, they often see each other as a necessary evil. Needless to say, there was quite a bit of tension between the two groups, and it was having a negative impact on the agency's capacity to be nimble.

We tell this story to demonstrate how your personal characteristics can have a sizable impact on your creative problem-solving behavior, whether you are working alone or with others in teams or groups. Without doubt, you have had experiences in which new projects leaped forward when certain people initiated and promoted them. Those people probably demonstrated a knack for explaining a new idea in ways that got everyone else excited. They had boundless energy or dogged persistence for moving their projects forward. They dreamed about the future and drew others into their vision, knowing exactly what to do to guide an idea through all the channels and over all the hurdles.

On the other hand, you have probably also had the opposite experience. You might have been working alone or as part of a group with an important goal or purpose in mind and some methods and tools to use in working toward that goal—only to discover that "things just didn't turn out right." Perhaps, you found that some people were stubborn or resistant, unwilling to look at the task in an open-minded way or determined to do things differently or to give greater priority to other tasks. Perhaps you were frustrated by poor communication, lack of communication, lack of support, or others' failure to follow up on their commitments and decisions. Perhaps some key people had not been consulted or brought on board, and as a result, they let the task die on their desks (or killed it before it even got started).

These experiences point out the importance of understanding the *people* with whom you will be working whenever you are dealing with change and innovation (translating creative ideas into new products, processes, or services). Using CPS cannot guarantee or ensure success; effective, powerful results will always be influenced by the people working on the tasks. In this chapter, we will discuss a number of personal characteristics and behaviors that can be observed when creativity is put into action by any person or group. We will examine the importance of people's ownership when you are planning or applying any CPS components, stages, or tools. *Ownership* refers to the responsibility, power, or authority that people have for any task. Ownership was defined in Chapter 3. Their ownership might arise in different ways, and varying degrees, from their knowledge, experience, professional or personal expertise, formal authority, or status in relation to the task.

This chapter will examine some of the unique personal characteristics and preferences people bring to any task. We will refer to this variety as *diversity*—the many and varied differences among people (in their characteristics, consistent patterns of behavior, styles, and preferences) that make it possible for creativity to be expressed in so many different ways and forms. Diversity also deals with your conscious and deliberate efforts to be aware of the potential impact of those differences on the effectiveness of CPS and therefore your commitment to recognize, respect, and respond to them. Understanding and responding to diversity also involves knowing how individuals bring their own creativity to bear on personal or group tasks, and how people interact and work creatively in groups.

This chapter will also examine *task expertise*, which addresses the specific background, information, experience, and preparation of the people involved in using CPS. Any task can be understood, defined, developed or constructed, structured, and accepted or rejected in different ways, by many people, at different times, and for varied reasons. Often, there is no single, "absolute," correct or best way to proceed, and so communication and decision making can be important issues to address for any task.

Ownership

Ownership is an essential aspect of the importance of *people* in planning your CPS approach or applying any creative approach to problem solving. *Ownership* involves the nature or extent, and the location, of personal involvement or investment in a task and the ability to promote or inhibit implementation or action. In more informal terms, ownership involves the power and inclination to make things happen. When you have clarity about ownership, whether you are working independently or in a group, you will know how to stimulate, support, nurture, or encourage positive steps. You (and others) understand why you are working on the task, and you feel confident and enthusiastic because you know there is likely to be follow-up and that the results of your work will be put to use. When ownership is missing, you (and others) will wonder why you are working on the task, why you should invest any time or effort in it, and you may easily come to feel frustrated, discouraged, uninvolved, or even cynical about the work.

Three main factors contribute to ownership (see Figure 7.1). They are *influence* (the ability to take action), *interest* (caring about the task, wanting to deal with it), and *imagination* (the need for and openness to novel or new possibilities or directions).

Figure 7.1   Three Main Factors That Constitute Ownership

Interest
Do you really *want* to work on this challenge?

Influence
Do you feel you have enough clout or leverage to *effect* the change?

Imagination
Do you need or wish to consider something *new*?

Influence

You have influence when you (individually, or with others in a group) actually have the authority or responsibility for implementing the results or outcomes of your work. It is clear that your proposed ideas or actions "really will go somewhere" as a result of your applications of CPS. In group settings, we often distinguish between two influential roles, the *client* (a person or people with immediate or direct responsibility or authority for action) and the *sponsor* (a person or group with ultimate authority or control over the task). Locating and verifying influence helps you plan and prepare effectively to apply CPS. Being clear about influence helps you define and respect decision-making responsibilities when you are applying CPS.

Interest

The second important factor we consider in establishing ownership is interest. It involves the extent to which you can assess and verify your commitment and willingness to engage in working on a task and your degree of emotional investment in the task. When you care about what you're working on, or have a high level of interest in and energy for the task, you will have a higher level of ownership, and it is more likely that in such a scenario you will engage willingly and with some enthusiasm in applying CPS.

It takes energy to be creative. If you are indifferent or negative about the task, you may respond in an offhand or superficial way, investing little personal energy or thought in the task or the process. The same issues and questions apply to other people when you are working as part of a group on any task. When you are applying CPS, a high or low level of interest will usually become readily apparent!

Imagination

This factor involves your need for novelty, or for new directions, ideas, solutions, or actions. The most appropriate applications of CPS involve a need for and interest in new perspectives that will also be useful. When it is clear that this need is present, you (and other people, if you're working in a group) will be eager to engage in applying CPS and will move forward as a result. Imagination implies an attitude of openness to newness. This indicates a high level of ownership. If the task does not call for new perspectives, you will be more likely to minimize your effort and commitment, and you will simply focus on "getting it wrapped up and out of the way."

Some Key Questions About Ownership

When you are considering ownership while Appraising Tasks, some questions to ask include the following:

1. What is the level of ownership and who has it?

2. To what extent does someone (or do some people) have the authority and responsibility for taking action?

3. To what extent do people actually care about, and have enthusiasm or passion for, the task?

4. To what extent does the task call for new perspectives or directions?

5. What is the nature of the clientship and who has it? Who is the sponsor, and what level of support will she or he provide?

Diversity

We consider it important to look at many variables that are constantly at work to influence any person's thoughts, feelings, and actions. These factors are what make you unique, and in turn they will have a powerful impact on your approach to CPS. In addition to helping you understand your own creativity, knowing about characteristics and preferences will also improve your appreciation of how other people prefer to handle similar situations in very different ways. For many tasks requiring a creative approach, there is value in considering and including a variety of points of view. The aim should be to include and involve the widest spectrum of diversity that you can manage effectively. When Appraising Tasks, thinking about the ways in which people differ leads us to ask, "Who are the key players, and how do they work together?" A partial list of the important ways people differ might include the following:

1. How competent or skillful you are with specific creativity-related methods and tools

2. Your motivation to work on certain challenges

3. The social and cultural setting in which you grew up and now live

4. The people who guided and inspired you throughout your life

5. Your age, gender, and interests

6. Your preferred styles of creativity, decision making, and problem solving

Torrance (1979) described creativity as the synthesis of abilities, skills, and motivation. These three categories, which are illustrated in Figure 7.2, might be used to organize or synthesize a much larger list of specific personal characteristics.

Figure 7.2 Torrance's Model for Predicting Creative Behavior

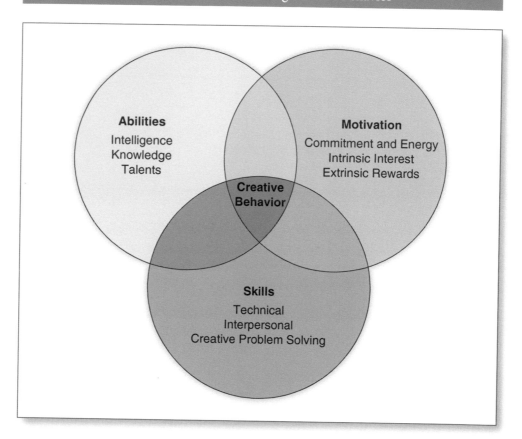

Creative abilities, or natural capacities and strengths, are present to some degree in all people. But creative behavior also draws on skills, or applications of tools and procedures that people have learned and practiced, and requires motivation, or the engagement and passion to accomplish a task or meet a goal.

Research on personality dynamics and dimensions related to creativity in the individual has been important since it contributed to our understanding of many personal factors that can make a difference in applying CPS. However, a newer approach has emerged, focusing on one's *style* of creativity. This approach emphasizes the importance of understanding differences in how each of us prefers to use our creativity or in how our creativity is best expressed.

As we began to look beyond describing people by referring to their level of creativity (e.g., highly creative, moderately creative, or uncreative), we began to consider another important question: "How are you creative?" Dealing with this question helped us view the role of the person in CPS in several new ways that extend our understanding of creativity and CPS in ways that would not have been possible had we examined only the issues of "level" of creativity.

The question of creativity style assumes that you have creativity. The more important concern is how you choose or prefer to demonstrate it. Considering style helps you understand how to become "your creative best." Personally, you can increase your awareness of your own style needs and preferences and attempt to be flexible when necessary about working in other ways. In group settings, knowing your own style and those of other group members will be helpful in reducing friction and in seeing things from other points of view. The goal is a better appreciation and constructive use of personal diversity. Let's examine how this works using one helpful approach to the problem-solving style. The contrasting views of level and style are illustrated in Figure 7.3.

Figure 7.3   The Contrasting Views of Level and Style

Level – How creative am I?

Style – How am I creative?

We have been involved in an extensive program of research and development in which we have studied theory, research, and practice to gain a richer, deeper, and more focused understanding of the nature and dynamics of problem-solving style (e.g., Isaksen, 2004; Isaksen & Geuens, 2007; Selby, Treffinger, & Isaksen, 2007a, 2007b; Selby, Treffinger, Isaksen, & Lauer, 2004; Treffinger, Selby, & Isaksen, 2008).

Problem-Solving Style

We define problem-solving styles as consistent individual differences in the ways people prefer to plan and carry out generating and focusing, to gain clarity, produce ideas, or prepare for action when solving problems or managing change (Selby, Treffinger, & Isaksen, 2002). Problem-solving styles are natural and neutral. They reflect the way you prefer to behave when solving problems and, as such, are stable and reflect how you can be your very best. Problem-solving styles are not rigid, fixed, and inflexible or excuses for not doing things well. They do not reflect your ability, expertise, or level of success in solving problems.

When creating, solving problems, and managing change, some people, working alone or in groups, seek to *improve* on ideas, products, processes, or services that already exist—polishing them, "adding new twists," making them better, or extending their applications in new directions. Other people prefer to direct their efforts to breaking totally new ground—"going where no one has gone before." Our recent research and development efforts have now resulted in the publication of a new instrument that will help us gain a richer and deeper understanding of these differences and, in a broader sense, the role that one's personal style preferences play in creativity and innovation. The instrument is VIEW: An Assessment of Problem Solving Style™ (Selby et al., 2007a, 2007b; Treffinger, Selby, Isaksen, & Crumel, 2007). VIEW represents and assesses three dimensions of style preferences that are unique and important in understanding and guiding the efforts of individuals and groups to manage their creative problem-solving or inventive efforts effectively. These are *Orientation to Change, Manner of Processing,* and *Ways of Deciding.*

Orientation to Change

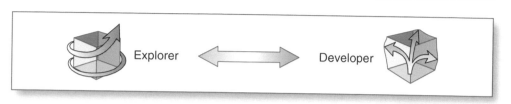

Figure 7.4 Orientation to Change

SOURCE: Selby et al. (2007b). Reprinted with permission.

This VIEW dimension provides an overall indication of the person's perceived preferences in two general styles for managing change and solving problems creatively. Orientation to Change includes two contrasting styles: the *Explorer* and the *Developer* (Figure 7.4). Although it is convenient to characterize each of these preferences using descriptors of people with extreme preferences, most people share some inclinations associated with each style. How a person emphasizes these approaches in her or his typical individual behavior across varying contexts, and over a sustained period of time, and the consistency or clarity of our preferences contribute to the location of the overall preference along the Explorer-Developer continuum.

The Explorer Style. Webster's definition of *explore* includes "to travel over new territory for adventure or discovery." A person with a preference for the Explorer style seeks to break new ground, thrives on venturing in uncharted directions, and follows interesting possibilities wherever they might lead. If developed and refined, however, your efforts to generate many unusual and original options might provide the foundation for productive new directions. You may find structure confining or limiting to your creative problem-solving efforts. You may tend to enjoy risk and uncertainty, plunge into a situation, and improvise your planning as the situation unfolds. You may prefer to follow your own unique pathway ("marching to the beat of your own drummer"), and you may choose not to conform to rules, procedures, or authority that you find arbitrary or that seem to stifle your creativity. You may hold new ideas loosely and let go of them early as attractive new possibilities emerge.

The Developer Style. Webster's definitions of *develop* include "setting forth or making clear by degrees or in detail . . . to move from the original position . . . to one providing more opportunity for effective use, [or] to come into being gradually." A person who prefers the Developer style considers the basic elements, ingredients, or ideas in a task or situation and organizes, synthesizes, refines, and enhances them, forming or shaping them into a more complete, functional, and useful condition or outcome. The term *Developer* indicates an individual who brings tasks to fulfillment. You are comfortable working in well-structured situations and acting with knowledge of and respect for existing expectations, rules, and procedures. You may hold your initial ideas tightly and find it difficult to let them go in favor of new possibilities.

Table 7.1 describes some of the unique contributions of the Explorer and Developer styles when applying CPS (drawing on Treffinger et al., 2007; Treffinger et al., 2008).

Table 7.1 Unique Contributions of the Explorer and Developer Styles When Applying CPS

Explorer Style	Developer Style
Prefer broad and abstract challenges and problems—highly abstract	Prefer tasks and challenges that are concrete and precisely defined
Readily generate many new and unusual ideas within and outside the existing paradigm	Readily generate a variety of ideas that are practical and useful within the existing paradigm
Prefer high-level approaches to implementation—relying on adapting spontaneously to emerging challenges	Prefer detailed and thorough approaches to implementation—relying on planful responses to challenges
May redefine the task for the client and formulate a process design that allows for improvisation	May dig deep for a detailed understanding of the task and develop a well-structured process design

SOURCE: Adapted by permission from Selby et al. (2007b).

Manner of Processing

The next dimension of VIEW, *Manner of Processing,* describes the person's preference for working *externally* (i.e., with other people throughout the process) or *internally* (i.e., thinking and working alone before sharing ideas with others) when managing change and solving problems (Figure 7.5). This dimension deals with preferences of how and when you use your own inner energy and resources, as well as the energy and resources of others. It includes your inclinations for different ways of handling information and when you prefer to share your thinking during problem solving and managing change.

Figure 7.5 Manner of Processing

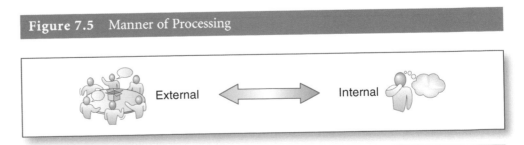

External ⟷ Internal

SOURCE: Selby et al. (2007b). Reprinted with permission.

The External Style. Individuals who exhibit a well-developed preference for an external style draw their energy from interaction with others, discussing possibilities and building from the ideas of others. They prefer physical engagement with the environment. When learning new and difficult material, those with an External style preference clarify their ideas and understandings through discussion. They find the input of authorities helpful as part of their active discussion. They are not bothered by noise in the study area, approach learning in several ways, and often find that physical mobility enhances their learning, thinking, and problem-solving skills. When solving problems, they seek a great deal of input from others before reaching closure. Externals tend to be seen by others as good team members and often appear full of energy. Preferring action to reflection, they may appear to rush into things before others are ready to proceed.

The Internal Style. Those with a well-developed Internal style look first reflectively to their own inner resources and draw energy from their reflection. They prefer to consider ideas on their own before sharing them with others. They embark on action only after giving it careful consideration. People with an Internal preference emphasize quiet reflection and processing of information at their own pace. They tend to become engrossed in inner events, ideas, and concepts. They prefer learning privately, working at least initially without the help of peers or authority figures. They may seem quiet and might be perceived by others as pensive or withdrawn.

Table 7.2 describes some of the unique contributions of the External and Internal styles when applying CPS (drawing on Treffinger et al., 2007; Treffinger et al., 2008).

Table 7.2 Unique Contributions of the External and Internal Styles When Applying CPS

External Style	Internal Style
Prefer to understand the challenge through direct and active engagement—involving open exchange with many others	Prefer a thoughtful and reflective understanding of the challenge through inward-directed analysis—seeking to think things through on their own
May readily engage in a lively exchange with others and naturally enjoy generating many and unusual ideas	May work at their own pace when generating ideas, enjoying opportunities to work alone through quiet contemplation
Prefer to take action as quickly as possible and involve many others along the way	Prefer to take action following the careful and complete development of a plan
Obtain clarity about the task through open dialogue and prefer a process design that will quickly result in action	Obtain clarity about the task following a dialogue that allows time for individual reflection for deeper understanding and detailed planning of process

SOURCE: Adapted by permission from Selby et al. (2007b).

Ways of Deciding

The final dimension of VIEW, *Ways of Deciding,* deals with your preferences for balancing and emphasizing task concerns (i.e., emphasizing logic, rationality, and appropriateness) and your personal or interpersonal needs (i.e., maintaining harmony and interpersonal relationships) when focusing your thinking and moving toward decisions and actions (Figure 7.6). When making decisions during problem solving, you may prefer the Person or Task style as your first or primary emphasis. Everyone can consider both approaches, but your style preferences describe the approach that you tend to emphasize initially or to which you may give great weight in decision making.

Figure 7.6 Ways of Deciding

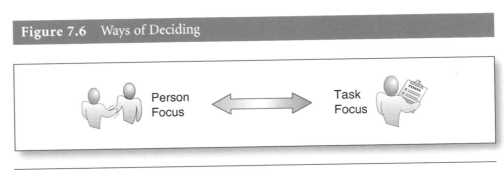

SOURCE: Selby et al. (2007b). Reprinted with permission.

The Person Style. If you prefer the Person style, you first consider the impact of choices and decisions on people's feelings and support and on the need for harmony and positive relationships. You prefer to be emotionally involved when setting priorities. You may often be seen as warm, friendly, and caring. You may be quick to become aware of, and respond to, the needs of others. Person-oriented deciders seek solutions or decisions for which there will be broad acceptance or "buy-in" by all concerned. They tend to emphasize a concern for others affected by the decision.

The Task Style. If you prefer the Task style, you may tend to look first at choices and decisions that are logical and sensible, and that can be justified objectively. You may prefer making judgments that are impersonal, based on well-reasoned conclusions. Individuals with a Task style of decision making seek mastery of content or information to help them arrive at the "best solution" or response or at a solution they can readily defend or justify. They may stress the need for staying cool and free from emotion while seeking clarity, precision, and logical order. Task-oriented deciders are focused primarily on getting results.

Table 7.3 describes some of the unique contributions of the Person and Task styles when applying CPS (drawing on Treffinger et al., 2007; Treffinger et al., 2008).

Table 7.3 Unique Contributions of the Person and Task Styles When Applying CPS

Person Style	Task Style
Prefer to seek an understanding of the challenge everyone can agree with and embrace—taking a caring and human angle	Prefer to seek an understanding of the challenge that will lead to the best results—taking an impersonal and logical angle
When generating ideas, may ensure that everyone is heard and appreciated and offer ideas aimed at meeting human needs and issues	When generating ideas, may focus on offering options they believe are the most promising and realistic aimed at getting high-quality results
Prefer pointing out the positive aspects of alternatives, enthusiastically supporting actions that help people—in a personalized manner	Prefer identifying flaws in potential alternatives and outlining effects and consequences of decisions—in a detached manner
When planning their approach, will seek a desired outcome that fully considers the impact on people and a process design to which everyone can agree	When planning their approach, will ask for a desired outcome based on an objective and rigorous examination and a process approach that proceeds logically toward obtaining results

SOURCE: Adapted by permission from Selby et al. (2007b).

Moderate Preferences

You may have a moderate style if your preferences for any of these dimensions of problem-solving style are unclear or not very strongly differentiated. Moderate style preferences can often place you in between those with stronger or more pronounced inclinations. This may provide the opportunity to act as a bridge—to open up channels of communication and provide improved understanding and use of different points of view.

Those with moderate preferences can often take a problem-solving approach that is more situationally sensitive—as their preference often depends on the demands of a specific context.

Remember that every individual possesses all the qualities we have outlined, although they will not all be developed, expressed, or preferred to the same degree. This leads us to the next section that addresses the challenge of working outside our natural style inclinations.

Working Outside Your Preferences

Many situations will call for us to behave in a manner that is outside our normal range of preferred behavior. These occasions call for us to stretch and learn new ways of thinking and behaving. Some refer to this as "coping." The ability to match our behavior to differing situational demands may be considered a sign of psychological maturity. Coping for long periods of time may also have its costs. It takes energy and motivation to sustain coping. Without having the needed energy, coping may cause stress and other potentially harmful effects. One alternative is to learn tools and techniques that make it easier to perform these different but desired behaviors. For example, if you have a natural preference for Generating Ideas, but find focusing these options to be challenging, you may benefit from learning and applying focusing tools.

Another alternative is to take advantage of the diverse styles that may be available to you. We call this "coverage." When a specific situation calls for a particular style of behavior that is not your own, you may be able to identify someone else who has that natural inclination. This is one of the key benefits of diversity.

Some Key Questions About Diversity

When you are considering diversity, some of the key questions to ask are as follows:

1. Do you have the right people (and mix of people) for the task on which you will be working?

2. Is there enough variety to ensure that many viewpoints and approaches will be represented?

3. Is there so much variety that it will be challenging to establish and maintain effective communication and collaboration?

4. How will you help people understand, appreciate, and make effective use of the diversity among participants?

5. If you are working alone, how will your personal characteristics and style preferences influence your thinking and decision making? How will you ensure that you don't overlook key issues and concerns that people with other preferences might raise?

To learn more about problem-solving style, visit the VIEW Web site at www .ViewStyle.net.

Task Expertise

Finally, when you are Appraising Tasks or applying any of the CPS components or stages, it is also important to consider the question of task expertise. *Task expertise* is the extent to which people bring appropriate knowledge, information, and experience to the job at hand. The expertise to which we're referring is specific to any particular task on which people are working at a certain time and in a specific context. We are not referring to task expertise as a global, generalized, or all-purpose view of ability or natural talent that transcends tasks or settings. Any person might have a high degree of expertise for one task but might be an absolute novice for another task. For example, a manager might bring a very extensive and valuable storehouse of information and personal experience to a task that involves production or technical skills but might be totally unqualified to deal with a challenge that involves human resources or financial planning.

There are also several "layers" of expertise in or surrounding any task. Some relevant knowledge and information concerns the specific task itself—knowing the task definition and specifications. However, it might also be important to consider a broader level of task expertise, in the form of knowledge about the discipline, domain, or field in which the task is located. Sometimes, it will also be important and valuable to take into account an even broader level of expertise, drawing from other domains that are only indirectly related to the specific task (and sometimes from unrelated domains, which might be the source for highly novel possibilities or connections to be formed). Creative success will involve breadth of knowledge or expertise for some tasks, while depth of expertise may be more important for other tasks.

Task expertise might involve the content of the task on which you are working and the knowledge and skills of the people in relation to their understanding of it. It might also involve applying CPS or a variety of specific talents and transferable skills (e.g., writing, illustration, design, or computer skills) that people bring to a certain task. This task expertise might come from within the group. In other situations, you may need to bring in or hire people with the appropriate and necessary task expertise to get the job done. This is often the approach when people hire consultants. The task expertise might only be needed for a short or determined period of time, and therefore, it may be appropriate to hire it in rather than learn and integrate it within the group or organization.

Finally, task expertise includes the extent to which people are aware of, have skills in, and are willing to carry out leadership practices or behaviors. Expertise in leadership involves credibility and integrity and practices such as creating a powerful future vision, inspiring others to join in holding that vision, enabling others to take action, modeling appropriate action, and celebrating the accomplishments of many team or group members (Kouzes & Posner, 2007). Effective leaders have expertise in directing the behavior of others, coaching individuals, participating actively in complex task efforts, and delegating effectively (Blanchard, 1985), or what Gryskiewicz (1999) described as "influencing a community of practice." For additional information on the importance of expertise in relation to creative leadership, consult Isaksen and Tidd (2006).

In many ways, then, the issues of task expertise apply to every member of a group and need to be considered when planning, preparing for, or applying CPS to a group setting. It is important to ensure that people share a common understanding of the key information about the task. Incomplete information, inconsistent understanding of key information among group members, ineffective communication, or the absence of essential skills within the group will hamper effective application of CPS and, more important, effective group performance on the task.

Some Key Questions About Task Expertise

In relation to task expertise, some of the key questions to consider include the following:

1. Do you (and others) have enough knowledge or expertise about the content of the task and about CPS to be able to work effectively on this task?

2. Do you understand the strengths and needs you (and others) will bring to the task?

3. To what extent do you have specific background and experience that will be relevant to the present task? Do you have enough information to deal competently with the task? Do you have so much experience that you might be closed minded or unresponsive to new possibilities or directions?

4. What kinds of information resources and support will be available?

5. What additional information might be important and helpful to obtain or access?

Using Information About People When Appraising Tasks

As you can see, *ownership, diversity,* and *task expertise* are interrelated in several ways when you are considering the "people" dimension of Appraising Tasks in the Planning Your Approach component and when you are applying any CPS component or stage. These questions and issues will have significant effects on your decision to apply CPS, or not to do so (in Appraising Tasks). They are also important for your planning and preparation (in the Designing Process stage) and for your choices and actions in any other component or stage.

You might discover that you need a different "mix" of people, in relation to style preferences and various elements of task expertise, to deal successfully with the various tasks. Some tasks may call for depth of knowledge and richness of expertise, others for very specialized expertise and skills. Considerable style diversity might be important and valuable when there is substantial commonality of expertise and experience to sustain a spirit of openness and exploration within the group (although the members of the group must also know how to manage style diversity comfortably). Other, more interdisciplinary (or cross-functional) tasks may require a group that is very diverse in expertise and background, to enable the group to share and value different perspectives as they work together on a task that affects many people, teams, or units (or an entire organization). It is also important to be very clear about ownership to help people work collaboratively. You will seek to help everyone understand that their expertise in an area does not necessarily make them the client for the task. In other settings, where diversity is high and the group's expertise is widely varied, you will seek to identify the client so the group knows that there is one!

Considering diversity, ownership, and task expertise helps you consider whether or not to apply CPS, and if you do proceed, it gives you valuable information to use in the Designing Process and in your CPS activities. As a result of your efforts to understand the people who will be involved as problem solvers, four broad options will be available for you when you are Appraising Tasks. These are:

Apply CPS

If you can define and clarify specific ownership for the task, if the "makeup and mix" of style preferences seems appropriate, and if you can verify that the task expertise among participants is appropriate, you have evidence that supports a decision to proceed in applying CPS.

Modify the Task

You might decide that you have an appropriate group with whom to work, in relation to ownership, diversity, and expertise, but you may have concerns about the nature or definition of the task. In this case, before proceeding to apply CPS, it may be important to review the task with the client or sponsor and to restructure or redefine the task to enable the group to work on it more effectively.

Find the Right People

You might decide that the task is appropriate and adequately defined but that there are concerns about the ownership, diversity, or expertise of the group membership. In this case, the best course of action will be to seek to restructure the group membership so that the people will be able to work effectively on the task.

Wait or Withdraw

If you determine that there are serious, or potentially serious, concerns about any (or several) of the three key factors, your wisest course of action might be to decide not to apply CPS under the present circumstances. You might consider ways to postpone working on the task until you can modify the group makeup, locate a sponsor, and clarify ownership or modify the definition of the task. There can also be times when you will be wise to consider other possible methods or even to decline working on the task. An important lesson, often difficult to learn, is that sometimes the wisest decision is not to proceed.

The Rest of the Story

Our hesitancy about working with the managers and technical people from the advertising agency wore off shortly after meeting the group. We worked together to understand diversity issues related to their natural preferences for using creativity, making decisions, and solving problems, and their implications for working alone or with others. The workshop helped them develop an appreciation for the contributions that people from different functions could make to solving problems in creative ways.

Of all the issues the group could have worked on during the workshop, they chose to address the division created among people and between functions as a result of using the terms *suits* and *creatives*. From being initially hesitant to talk about the issue openly, they eventually chose it as the core issue to address for helping make the organization more nimble. They realized that the language they were using sent the message that creativity belonged to one function and not the other. The group wanted to find a way to remove the use of the terms that promoted isolation, defensiveness, or strife, so as to improve their agency's capacity to be nimble.

It demonstrated to us the importance of diversity in helping people learn to work together in productive and constructive ways. When we provide people with information that will help them understand the value of diversity, and offer them the methods and tools that will help them get the best from that diversity, they discover and apply ways to recognize, use, and celebrate the contributions of others.

Putting This Chapter to Work

Our goals in this chapter were to help you understand the importance of people—individual characteristics and interpersonal relationships—when you are Planning Your Approach to CPS. We highlighted three important factors (diversity, ownership, and task expertise) that influence your effectiveness in planning for and applying CPS.

Activities to Guide Reflection and Action

Work on one or more of the following activities to review your understanding of the material in this chapter and to practice applying the content in real situations. If you are using this book as part of a course or study group, you may wish to work individually and then compare your responses or work collaboratively as a team.

1. Think about two actual groups of which you have been a participant or leader: one that was very exciting, effective, and productive, and the other, a group that was frustrating, constantly struggling, and eventually unproductive. Consider the elements of diversity, ownership, and task expertise discussed in this chapter. Identify the factors that you believe were most significant in distinguishing one group from the other.

2. As you reflect on your experiences in the two groups in #1, what factors might you have been able to change or handle differently so that the ineffective, dissatisfying group might have become more productive and rewarding?

3. For each of VIEW's three dimensions, describe how you might differentiate the instruction or training for participants with each style preference. (For example, how might you guide or instruct participants with an Explorer style preference differently from the way you would work with those who have a Developer style preference?)

4. Think about a situation in which you are responsible for managing or directing an individual or a team (e.g., a project group, a committee or task force on a particular topic or problem, a performance review or evaluation conference). Create a plan for taking diversity, ownership, and task expertise into account constructively in your planning for that responsibility.

The Context
for CPS

Nature . . . has not fitted people to any specific environment. . . . Among the multitude of animals which scamper, fly, burrow, and swim around us, humans are the only ones who are not locked into their environment. Their imagination, reason, emotional subtlety and toughness, make it possible for them not to accept the environment but to change it.

—Jacob Bronowski

The purpose of this chapter is to provide an overview of three important aspects of the Context element of Appraising Tasks: (1) readiness (culture, climate, and history), (2) willingness (strategic priority, change leadership, and energy), and (3) ability (time, attention, and resources) for applying Creative Problem Solving (CPS) for any task.

As a result of studying this chapter, you should be able to do the following:

1. Describe the importance of understanding the situation surrounding a task (including readiness, willingness, and ability) when Planning Your Approach to CPS.

2. List and explain nine important dimensions of an organization's climate and their impact on creativity.

3. Identify at least three ways in which knowledge of *readiness* (climate, culture, and history) will help people understand, nurture, and manage creativity and change.

4. Describe the importance of taking *willingness* (including strategic priorities, change leadership, and energy) into account when planning your CPS approach.

5. Describe the importance of taking *ability* (including time, attention, and resources) into account when planning your CPS approach.

6. Design a plan for applying your knowledge of Context to the opportunities and challenges on which you work in your own setting.

The managing director of a major symphony orchestra was engaged in an organizational transformation initiative. The initiative included creating a strategic architecture, which involved clarifying the organization's purpose, developing and setting in motion a new 5- to 7-year vision, and identifying its organizational values and mission elements.

One of the challenges the senior management team had was the readiness of the organization to support the changes they wanted to make. The team knew that the changes were big and that they would need the involvement and participation of everyone on the staff to make them happen. We needed to know whether the Context was ready to accept the changes associated with the vision. Some people seemed excited about the changes that might happen. However, some did not appear to perceive a need for change. Others did not think that they could use creativity to make the change happen. Others just didn't seem interested in making changes happen at all—even though they thought change was necessary.

We knew the organization was filled with bright and capable people. However, we did not know how ready the working environment would be to support change. What does it take for a working environment to be ready, willing, and able to support change? What are the characteristics of such an environment, and how is it established?

In Chapter 7, we looked at the importance of understanding and taking into account a number of personal characteristics and influences when planning your CPS approach. However, whenever CPS is applied by people, their efforts are surrounded by and immersed in a certain setting or situation—the "Context" for their CPS efforts. The effects of contextual factors might be positive, stimulating, and enabling of creativity and innovation, or they might be negative, inhibiting, or stifling. Furthermore, some aspects or parts of the Context may be supportive; others may not be ready.

Perhaps you have been fortunate to be part of a new project or plan that turned out to be just "the right thing at the right time," in a dynamic, vibrant organization that was waiting for the idea to come along and was ready to swing into action. You have probably also had experiences when a new and promising idea or direction died because it got lost in the labyrinth of policy, finance, or administration. Perhaps a critical person left a key position and the innovation lost its champion. Perhaps everyone's enthusiasm and energy waned as the result of foot-dragging and seemingly endless rounds of review, discussion, and more review. Perhaps a new initiative "lost its steam" or momentum because of changing conditions that realigned priorities, positions, and resource commitments.

These experiences all point out the importance of being wise, alert, and informed about the *context* or *situation* when you are dealing with creativity and change. Using CPS—or any other set of problem-solving tools—cannot guarantee or ensure success. Effective, powerful results will always be influenced by many factors that make up the organizational context in which work takes place.

The Environment Conducive to Creativity

We will begin by asking you to think of two working situations from your own experience. First, consider the "best-case" scenario from your work experience—a situation in which you were highly successful and in which you attained significant results or accomplishments. List a number of words or phrases describing that work environment. Second, consider the "worst-case" scenario—a situation in which your efforts led to little or no success and in which you (and others) felt little sense of accomplishment or pride. List a number of words or phrases describing that environment, too.

Next, compare and analyze your two lists of words or phrases. As you examine either list, consider these questions:

• What aspects of the work environment contributed, positively or negatively, to the task and to your work?

• What factors stimulated or enhanced your productivity and creative accomplishments?

• On the other hand, what factors were obstacles or barriers that stifled or inhibited your work and your results?

Compare your list of "stimulants" and "obstacles" with the factors shown in Table 8.1, which are drawn from research and from our experiences with many different groups. Does Table 8.1 include many of the items on your list? Does it remind you of some additional factors you might have overlooked in your list?

Table 8.1 Stimulants and Obstacles to a Creative Environment

Stimulants	Obstacles
Freedom and sense of control	Overly bureaucratic
Encouragement	Evaluation too harsh or premature; not constructive
Collaborative atmosphere	Insufficient resources
Challenge	Excessive time pressure
Appropriate recognition and rewards	Emphasis on status quo
Open to trying something different	Too much focus on internal politics
Ability to disagree about issues without personalizing them	Hidden agendas
Important, worthwhile, or meaningful projects or tasks to work on	

Isaksen, Lauer, Ekvall, and Britz (2001) proposed an integrative model of the organizational context called the *Model for Organizational Change*; it is presented in Figure 8.1.

Organizational climate, which is influenced by internal organizational and psychological processes as well as external factors, has effects on both individual and organizational performance. Organizational processes include group problem solving, decision making, communication, and coordination. Psychological processes include learning, individual problem-solving skills, creativity skills, and motivation. These factors exert a direct influence on the performance and accomplishments of individuals, work groups, and often, the entire organization (Amabile & Gryskiewicz, 1988;

Figure 8.1 Climate Is a Central Factor Within Organizations

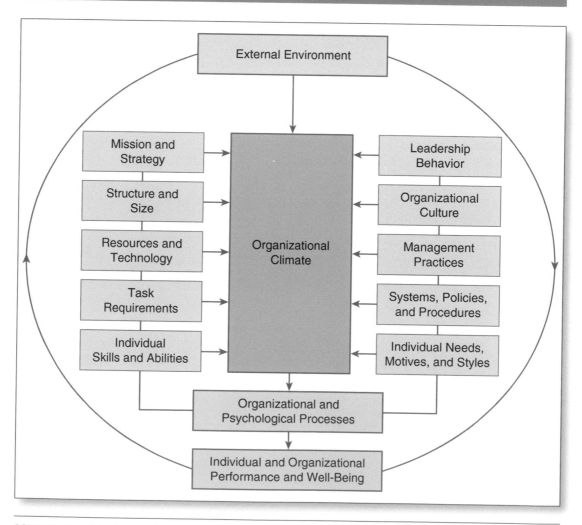

Prajogo & Ahmed, 2006; Service & Boockholdt, 1998; Witt & Beorkrem, 1989). The model outlines several examples of important organizational factors that affect climate, which, in turn, affect organizational productivity and performance.

As you can see, Context is a complex combination of many different factors. Some of these are quite specific and "localized," taking place in the ordinary transactions between and among peers, fellow workers, or supervisors on a daily basis. These are factors that stimulate or get you "fired up" when they are working for you or at other times might be nuisances, irritants, or even rather solid "brick walls." Do the individuals in your immediate environment provide a great deal of support, encouragement, praise, and reward for each other's efforts? Do people have the resources, equipment, and support they need to function creatively? You might find that you feel differently about some of these factors depending on when you're asked about them or on the specific task at hand. They change from time to time, and at least a few of them might well be factors you can influence or even control rather easily.

Others are much broader, more general dimensions of our real world; they are the large-scale "givens" of life for everyone. Does your organization have a long history of valuing and supporting creativity and change? Or instead, rewarding those who conform and play the games, while pushing (perhaps not too subtly) those who do not to look elsewhere or to linger unproductively in some minor role in the organization? Does society value and encourage creative efforts in your area of interest or talent? Is the world around you, literally or figuratively, at peace, or do stress, conflict, and fear prevail?

It is important to understand the context for creativity and change when Planning Your Approach using the Appraising Tasks stage. These efforts are important for several reasons.

Support for Creative Productivity. Understanding and valuing diversity, and the tension that often accompanies it, contributes to establishing a context that supports creativity and change. People's perception of the climate in their workplace is often a significant factor in determining their productivity.

Support for People's Efforts. Systems and structures that support renewal and growth must be developed if organizations are to remain vital. However, the structures and systems themselves will not be sufficient; people need to perceive that it is important, acceptable, and desirable to be involved in those systems.

Enhance Satisfaction. Deliberate efforts to construct and maintain a positive context influence the organization's success (and often its survival) and enhance the satisfaction of its members. Linking social systems with technical systems is essential if high levels of productivity and performance are to be achieved. Pasmore (1988) proposed that organizational design must meet the demands of the external environment as well as the internal social and technical systems:

> No matter how permanent they may seem, organizations are at best temporary solutions to ill-defined problems. They are responses to specific circumstances based upon imperfect information and unclear desires; they are alliances among people in the face of uncertainty. Most importantly, they are capable of being transformed at will. . . . (p. 4)

Respond to Change. Both the pace of change and the demands of competition are increasing for all organizations. People need to better understand the dynamics associated with dealing effectively with change to increase productivity and enhance competitive position in the marketplace. All this must be accomplished with an increasing level of complexity in how businesses operate.

Knowledge Management. Knowledge is exploding and becoming more and more specialized. We must be able to establish a constructive context so that knowledge can be used and shared efficiently and effectively.

Writers have used a variety of different terms in their efforts to understand and describe these factors. We might summarize them informally using three everyday terms. When you consider the context of a specific task for which you are contemplating using CPS, are you (and is the group or organization) *ready, willing,* and *able* to work on the task? Being ready means determining that the history, culture, and climate are conducive to creative efforts and outcomes or that you are prepared to deal with the challenges that are likely to arise. Willing suggests that the task has a high strategic priority and is recognized as important, worthwhile, and necessary to address. Being able means that the resources are in place or available to support the necessary work and to ensure follow-up and implementation.

Are You Ready for Change?

An organization's *culture* is long-standing, deeply rooted, and usually slow (sometimes very difficult) to change. It represents the way threads have been woven together to create a fabric. The organization's *climate* for creativity represents the set of patterns or procedures involved within the daily life of the organization, as those are experienced, understood, and interpreted by the people within the organization. As shown in Figure 8.2, there are clear distinctions between the culture and the climate of an organization.

We are not alone in making a clear distinction between culture and climate. Thomson (2000) indicated,

> Changing the culture of an organization by tackling it head on as a single facet of organizational life is really, really tough. To go deep into cultural change you have to be talking about beliefs and values, and these go to the very soul of the organization and its people. It is much easier to change the climate and language of the business. (p. 240)

Figure 8.2   The Distinction Between Organizational Culture and Climate

Culture	Climate
The values, beliefs, history, traditions, etc., reflecting the deeper foundations of the organization	Recurring patterns of behavior, attitudes, and feelings that characterize life in the organization
What the organization values	What organization members experience

What do we mean when we talk about "climate" for creativity? Think about *where* you were when you had your personal best or breakthrough idea for a particular challenge or opportunity in your experience. Describe several important aspects of that place or setting. (In the exercise earlier in this chapter, we asked you to think about many factors. For this exercise, just think about the place or setting where your creative breakthrough came to you.) Were you at your place of work, or were you elsewhere, doing other things (e.g., driving, sleeping, dreaming, shaving, bathing, exercising, resting)? We often ask this question to large groups; rarely have we heard that people's best ideas occurred during formal working hours at the office. When people explain why their best ideas occur elsewhere, they begin to describe an environment that is conducive to creativity.

Climate is a concept that was developed in the late 1930s by the social scientists Lewin, Lippitt, and White (1939). They used the term to describe the subjective "feeling," "air," or "atmosphere" they encountered in their studies of organizations. From their observations, they found that different organizations had distinctly different climates. They saw linkages between the climate and factors such as motivation, productivity, sick time, profits, and success. Ekvall (1983, 1987) described organizational climate as the attitudes, feelings, and behavior patterns that characterize life within the organization. He differentiated organizational climate from that of culture and individual psychological climate. Although influenced by a variety of factors (see Figure 8.3), Ekvall suggested, organizational climate may waver but is fairly stable over time.

Figure 8.3 The Many Factors That Affect Organizational Climate

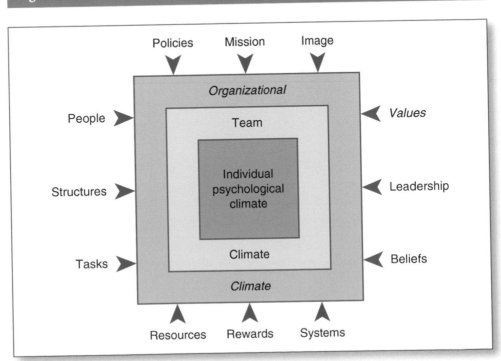

The literature abounds with guidelines for establishing an environment for creativity. VanGundy (1984) indicated that the factors that determine a group's creative environment can be placed into three categories: (1) the external environment, (2) the internal creative climate of individuals within a group, and (3) the quality of interpersonal relationships among the group members. Raudsepp (1988) listed 24 guidelines for establishing a creative environment. He subtitled these "two dozen ways to turn on your organization's light bulbs."

Both culture and climate information help us increase our ability to meet goals, resolve challenges or concerns, and discover and respond to newness. Ekvall (1987) indicated,

> Climate affects organizational and psychological processes such as communication, problem solving, decision-making, conflict handling, learning and motivation, and thus exerts an influence on the efficiency and productivity of the organization, on its ability to innovate, and on the job satisfaction and well-being that its members can enjoy. The individual organization member is affected by the climate as a whole, by the general psychological atmosphere, which is relatively stable over time. No single separate event produces this more lasting influence on behavior and feelings; it is the daily exposure to a particular psychological atmosphere. It is because of this overall and lasting effect that the climate concept is of interest and importance to our understanding of organizational life. (p. 183)

Dimensions of the Climate for Creativity

The basic question remains: "How do I know which guidelines are important for my specific situation?" Fortunately, a growing body of literature offers helpful insight into this question. There has been considerable progress in defining the essential aspects of climate in organizations.

Ekvall (1983) and his colleagues (Ekvall & Arvonen, 1984; Ekvall, Arvonen, & Waldenstrom-Lindblad, 1983; Ekvall & Tångeberg-Andersson, 1986) studied a number of organizations to determine if they could identify "organizational climate" and identified the main characteristics or dimensions of the organizational climate for creativity and innovation. Building on Ekvall's work, Isaksen and others (Isaksen & Akkermans, 2007; Isaksen & Ekvall, 2007; Isaksen, Lauer, & Ekvall, 1999) conducted research in a number of organizations that reformulated the climate factors into nine major dimensions. These are:

> *Challenge/Involvement:* This factor represents the degree to which people are involved in daily operations, long-term goals, and visions. When there is a high degree of Challenge and Involvement, people feel motivated and committed to making contributions. The climate is dynamic, electric, and inspiring. People find joy and meaningfulness in their work. In the opposite situation, people are not engaged and feelings of alienation and apathy are present. Individuals lack interest in their work, and interpersonal interactions are dull and listless.

> *Freedom:* Freedom refers to independence in behavior exerted by the people in the organization. In a climate with much Freedom, people are given the autonomy and resources to

define much of their work. They exercise discretion in their day-to-day activities. Individuals have the opportunity and take the initiative to acquire and share information about their work. In the opposite climate, people work within strict guidelines and roles. They carry out their work in prescribed ways with little room to redefine their tasks.

Trust/Openness: This dimension involves emotional safety in relationships. When there is a high degree of Trust, individuals can be genuinely open and frank with one another. People count on each other for professional and personal support. People have a sincere respect for one another and give credit where credit is due. Where Trust is missing, people are suspicious of each other, and therefore, they closely guard themselves, their plans, and their ideas. In these situations, people find it extremely difficult to openly communicate with each other.

Idea-Time: Idea-Time refers to the amount of time people can use (and do use) for elaborating new ideas. In the high Idea-Time situation, possibilities exist to discuss and test suggestions not included in the task assignment. There are opportunities to take the time to explore and develop new ideas. Flexible timelines permit people to explore new avenues and alternatives. In the reverse case, every minute is booked and specified. The time pressure makes thinking outside the instructions and planned routines impossible.

Playfulness/Humor: This factor involves spontaneity and ease displayed within the workplace. A professional, yet relaxed atmosphere where good-natured jokes and laughter occur often is indicative of this dimension. People can be seen having fun at work. The climate is seen as easygoing and lighthearted. The opposite climate is characterized by gravity and seriousness. The atmosphere is stiff, gloomy, and cumbersome. Jokes and laughter are regarded as improper and intolerable.

Conflict: This factor deals with the presence of personal and emotional tensions in the organization, and it is the only dimension that does not contribute positively to creativity; less Conflict is generally better than more. When the level of Conflict is high, groups and individuals dislike and may even hate each other. The climate can be characterized by "interpersonal warfare." Plots, traps, power, and territory struggles are usual elements of organizational life. Personal differences yield gossip and slander. In the opposite case, people behave in a more mature manner; they have psychological insight and control of impulses. People accept and deal effectively with diversity.

Idea-Support: Idea-Support refers to the ways new ideas are treated. In the supportive climate, ideas and suggestions are received in an attentive and professional way by bosses, peers, and subordinates. People listen to each other and encourage initiatives. Possibilities for trying out new ideas are created. The atmosphere is constructive and positive when considering new ideas. When Idea-Support is low, the automatic "no" is prevailing. Fault finding and obstacle raising are the usual styles of responding to ideas.

Debate: We define Debate as the occurrence of encounters and disagreements between viewpoints, ideas, and differing experiences and knowledge. In the debating organization, many voices are heard, and people are keen on putting forward their ideas for consideration and review. People can often be seen discussing opposing opinions and sharing a diversity of perspectives. Where Debate is missing, people follow authoritarian patterns without questioning them.

Risk-Taking: Risk-Taking has to do with tolerance of uncertainty and ambiguity in the workplace. In the high Risk-Taking case, bold initiatives can be taken even when the outcomes are unknown. People feel as though they can "take a gamble" on their ideas. People will often "go out on a limb" to put an idea forward. In a risk-avoiding climate, there is a cautious, hesitant mentality. People try to be on the "safe side" and often "sleep on the matter." They set up committees, and they cover themselves in many ways.

You may have noticed that a number of these nine factors appeared on your list of important aspects of the climate for creativity. When taken together, they will help you understand the climate for creativity in the context in which you are working. They will help you locate the factors that will support or inhibit creative productivity to make decisions about the readiness of the context for using CPS effectively and to plan how and when to proceed.

Implications of Understanding Climate

Understanding climate at an individual, team, or organizational level has a number of implications for Planning Your Approach, Appraising Tasks, or managing your CPS applications using any of the components or stages. At the individual level, increasing your awareness or perceptions of the work environment, or making the invisible a little more visible, will help you judge the costs and benefits of applying CPS and also to decide whether or not to initiate or participate in such efforts. Awareness of culture and climate may also lead to opportunities for you to contribute to shaping (or reshaping) the work climate by applying CPS strategically. In addition, examining the culture and climate carefully will help you understand how you, and others with whom you work, will perceive the importance and value of using CPS in relation to both positive and negative aspects of the work climate.

At the team level, awareness of climate perceptions can help you prepare for effective applications of CPS by promoting honest communication among team members. Examining the climate for creativity may also help all team members to uncover, make explicit, and resolve unappreciated or unproductive perceptions of team members that were previously unknown or implicit. Those efforts will help overcome obstacles to effective, productive group functioning and will help team members understand the importance of applying effective problem-solving methods and tools (Isaksen & Lauer, 2002). Of course, effective dialogue about climate among team members can also help uncover and build on strengths within the team that were previously unknown or untapped.

For the organization, deliberate investigation of climate dimensions enables leaders to identify areas of strength and opportunities for improvement that can be fertile to address using CPS. Recognizing the organization's climate can guide decision making that relates to the core purposes, vision, and mission of the organization. Understanding climate also helps organizational leadership emerge and direct its efforts to promoting success and well-being for the organization, its own people, and its clients or customers (Isaksen, 2007). Knowing about the organization's culture and climate will also help you plan your CPS approach by determining what organizational structures (procedures, offices, or people) will be most likely to encourage and support the use of CPS for specific tasks or as part of an overall strategy for managing change.

We have developed an assessment called The Situational Outlook Questionnaire® (SOQ), based on Ekvall's work, to help obtain insights regarding the climate (Isaksen & Ekvall, 2007). It can be used for teams, leadership development, and organizational improvement efforts. Understanding your climate can be helpful for managing all sorts of change and helping an organization meet the innovation challenge. You can find more information about the SOQ at SOQonline.net.

History

Appraising Tasks also involves understanding the historical experiences—the people, interactions, and events that have shaped an organization over time and on which it is important to build for the present and future. Considering the history for a task involves gathering data about a number of background themes and issues and sampling several different sources of information. Different people might have unique kinds of information to contribute or differing memories and views of the same history and events.

Understanding the historical background will help you be aware of the varying interpretations, perspectives, or points of view that surround or accompany many tasks. By being aware of the many and varied interpretations and attitudes people have about current and past events, you will be better able to assess their readiness to engage in new efforts. You will also be prepared to deal explicitly and constructively with varying interpretations and attitudes that might otherwise be implicit and inhibiting. Under some circumstances, you might find that the historical data reveals long-standing controversies and disagreements that might impair or limit the effectiveness of any new initiatives.

Some of the questions to help you explore the readiness of a context to support creativity and change include the following:

1. What has been attempted in the past in relation to this or similar tasks? Have those efforts been successful? Why or why not? How do people feel about or react to those historical efforts?

2. Have other people attempted previously to bring this task forward (or opposed efforts to address it)?

3. Have there been champions or opponents? Were they credible and respected? Are they still around? Involved? (Why or why not?)

4. What historical impressions, memories, or experiences might people have relating to this task, and will those support current efforts or inhibit them?

Are You Willing to Manage Change?

We refer to the next element of the Context as "willingness" or the extent to which you, and others in the case of a group setting, will actually be prepared to make the commitment to apply CPS to deal with a certain task. Willingness includes three major considerations:

1. Your strategic priorities (or those of a team or an entire organization)

2. The presence of leadership for change

3. Commitment and energy to carry out the needed work

To decide whether or not to apply CPS or how best to use CPS for a certain task, ask whether the task fits your priorities or your group's priorities in that setting. Also, ask yourself (or your group) how well the task fits your strategic priorities. You may also want to know whether there will be people to lead the work in the necessary directions and to provide the commitment and support for the efforts.

If the task is strongly related to high-priority needs and goals that are clearly evident, it is likely that efforts to apply CPS will meet with some support and encouragement. It is often helpful to be able to demonstrate the relevance or "fit" between the task and the vision, mission, or goals that already exist in the context. The linkages may be direct and explicit, or it may be necessary to do some initial preparation and development to identify them. Conversely, if you cannot see (or construct) such links in a plausible way, you can expect resistance to using CPS, if not open opposition to your efforts to obtain people, time, or resources.

Change leadership is also important to assessing the degree of willingness in the context. This underscores the interrelationships of "people" concerns from Chapter 7. Change leadership involves having people in the organization who are actively taking initiative to provide support and encouragement for people to change. They challenge what is going on now and excite people with visions about what things might be like. These may or may not be people in high-level management or administrative positions. However, willingness to change can certainly be helped by having senior people take on the change leadership role. They can often provide the authority necessary to legitimize change efforts, remove barriers to productivity, and enable people to use their talents to make a productive difference. Willingness also relates, of course, to considerations of ownership, the importance of clarity and support by a sponsor, and the need for well-established clientship (these issues have also been discussed in other chapters).

The third important aspect of willingness is energy. This involves the extent to which people are aware of the costs and demands of any deliberate change effort, and their willingness to accept them. Using CPS, or any other systematic, deliberate change method, to deal with complex, ambiguous, and important tasks makes heavy demands on people's personal energy and commitment. It requires a sense of conviction and commitment to the goal and to pursuing it, knowing full well that it might not be easy to accomplish. Energy and commitment also involve staying with the effort in the face of adversity, setbacks, or obstacles and pursuing the goal with courage and conviction. Before you decide to apply CPS, it is important to determine that people will be willing to make the necessary investments.

In assessing the willingness dimension of the Context, then, some of the questions you will certainly explore include the following:

1. Does the task relate clearly to a topic or area of high strategic priority as reflected in an established vision or mission statement?

2. Is it linked to specific goals or objectives that have been adopted?

3. Can you relate it directly to the needs, aspirations, or preferred future of the person, team, or organization?

4. Is there acceptance by those who will be working on the task that it is meaningful and worth doing?

5. Are people inspired and eager to work on the task?

6. Are there leaders to move the change forward?

7. Will the essential people be willing to invest the sustained energy, effort, and commitment to pursue the task?

Are You Able to Move Forward?

We have now looked at two important aspects of Context: readiness (the culture, climate, and history surrounding a task or new initiative) and willingness (the strategic priority of the task, change leadership, and energy for the task). The third Context factor to consider in Appraising Tasks is "ability" or the extent to which you can obtain or mobilize the people, space, time, equipment, and other resources that will be necessary to carry out any CPS application successfully. Too many people have learned through frustrating experiences that a positive climate, a high strategic priority, and some "cheerleaders" (people who say they're interested as long as someone else does the work) will not guarantee success for change and innovation.

We might also propose three areas of specific importance in assessing whether you are able to move forward with CPS for the task: (1) human resources, (2) physical resources, and (3) fiscal resources. Human resources include identifying the people with whom you will need to be able to work on the task effectively. However, identifying the people is not sufficient. You must also determine whether they will have (or be able to create) the time that will be necessary. (This can be especially important for complex tasks that will be high in the "energy" demands discussed under willingness.) It will also be important to know where the time will come from (in relation to other parts of their workload, for example) and the extent to which they will receive support and encouragement from others.

Physical resources include the space, supplies, technology, and other tangible resources that will be necessary to carry out the work. Sometimes, of course, everyone decides to take on a task or project that must be conducted "on a shoestring," or with the barest minimum of physical resources, at least in its initial stages. It is important to be aware of the availability or constraints in this area, however, in order to determine whether it is realistic to proceed. Similarly, fiscal resources involve budget support and determining whether or not you will have, or be able to attain, at least the minimum support that will be necessary to carry out the work that will need to be done.

Some of the questions you should be ready to explore in this aspect of Context include the following:

1. Is there time available for people to come together to work on the task? Is it genuine or time that people must "take out of their personal hide"?

2. Will there be space or facilities available? Are they conducive to working effectively on the task?

3. Will the equipment, supplies, technology, or other material needed for working on the task be readily available? If they are not already present, will it be possible to obtain them in a timely way?

4. Is there a budget for working on the task? Is it realistic? Will it support the work that must be undertaken?

5. Are there realistic goals and expectations about what will be accomplished, and by when?

Using Information About Context When Appraising Tasks

The Context element of our model for Appraising Tasks enables you to analyze several important aspects of the environment or setting in which people work in order to determine whether, or how best, to apply CPS for any task. These aspects—the readiness, willingness, and ability—are important to examine carefully to ensure that you are maximizing your chances for success (or, at least, minimizing the chances that you will be "set up" for failure before you even begin to work on the task). For this element of Appraising Tasks, as well as for the other elements discussed in Chapters 7, 9, and 10, there are several possible ways to use the information you gather as listed below.

Apply CPS

If, after considering your readiness, willingness, and ability to work on this task, you determine that the conditions are favorable or can be arranged or developed in a satisfactory way over time, you may decide to proceed with applying CPS.

Modify the Task

You may discover that one or more of the important aspects of Context suggest that it might be inappropriate to use CPS for the task as you have understood or defined it at the present time. Under these circumstances, one appropriate course of action might be to look closely at the task. You might be able to modify or restructure the task so that there will be a better match with the Context. If this is possible, you might decide to apply CPS for the modified task.

Modify the Context

If your appraisal of the Context factors leads you to conclude that the setting is not right, for any reason, to apply CPS for the task, another possibility to consider is to modify the Context. You might discover that certain gaps or obstacles, especially in relation to priorities or resource factors, could be modified through some focused efforts in that direction. One of the ways to prepare the Context for change and innovation is to apply the SOQ to assess the current status of the nine dimensions of climate. Since the SOQ also includes three open-ended questions, you can learn about what is working well, what needs to be changed, and specific suggestions for making that change happen.

Wait or Withdraw

If your appraisal of the important Context factors suggests that there will be major threats to applying CPS successfully, your best decision may be to withdraw from the task, to postpone action until a more appropriate Context exists, or to direct your efforts and energies to other tasks.

The Rest of the Story

Hearing that a major symphony orchestra wanted to transform itself was like music to our ears. We would be in a position to help an arts organization address fundamental challenges associated with a changing marketplace. We conducted an organizational climate audit with the staff of the symphony using the SOQ (Isaksen & Ekvall, 2007). We gathered the entire staff together to explain the case for change and to administer the instrument. We shared the results with the senior management team. It provided them insights about the working climate and its readiness to change and enabled them to plan how they could improve the climate and its readiness to support the vision.

The management team identified five climate dimensions that needed attention. They put a cross-functional project team together to get their involvement on what to do about the climate. The team provided a list of key activities they suggested would be helpful. They did not think that all the activities would be necessary but wanted to create a menu to increase the chances of better selections. The senior management team took the suggestions from the cross-functional team and evaluated them against the five climate dimensions that needed the most improvement. This resulted in the selection of the key projects for the cross-functional team to pursue. It also resulted in some short-term actions that were very visible. For example, the dress code was changed to make it more relaxed and comfortable. It resulted in longer-term projects that focus on challenges such as improving the flow of information throughout the organization and establishment of a human resource–type function. Informal feedback from the people in the organization indicates that they are already beginning to see changes in the climate. People are becoming more optimistic about changes being made.

This story illustrates that you can actually do something about building a context that supports change. In this case, we used an assessment to provide a targeted approach for senior management to improve the climate and its readiness to change. It also helped the team understand its role in planning and managing change. They now see the importance of establishing a climate that encourages people to use their skills and talents to make change happen.

Putting This Chapter to Work

This chapter has been focused on understanding the context surrounding the task to be addressed by CPS. The context or situation within which the task resides can provide you with insights about how ready, willing, and able the environment is to support and sustain your change and innovation efforts. We examined the distinction between culture and climate, and described nine dimensions that have been shown to be important for managing change and innovation. We also provided some questions you can use to explore how ready, willing, and able any particular situation might be for applying CPS.

Activities to Guide Reflection and Action

Work on one or more of the following activities to review your understanding of the material in this chapter and to practice applying the content in real situations. If you are using this book as part of a course or study group, you may wish to work individually, and then compare your responses, or to work collaboratively as a team.

1. Take the best- and worst-case situations you thought about from earlier in this chapter and see how you might score them on the nine climate dimensions. Develop your own scale and then compare the results. Think about what might be done to make your worst-case situation more amenable to change, innovation, and the application of CPS.

2. Take one of the tasks you have identified earlier, or an entirely new one, and practice asking the questions about readiness, willingness, and ability provided in this chapter to see what kinds of insights you can obtain about your situation.

3. Identify one of the most creative and innovative organizations you know about. It could be a specific business or school, or some other sort of agency. Think about what it has produced that convinces you that it is, in fact, successful at producing creative results, innovation, or change. Then, do a little research into its working atmosphere. How would you characterize the nature of the place? What implications might this have for where you work or apply CPS?

The Role
of Content

Nothing much happens without a dream. For something really great to happen, it takes a really great dream.

—Robert Greenleaf

The purpose of this chapter is to examine the Content element of Appraising Tasks. It will help you understand the role and importance of content and knowledge within the task domain in applying any Creative Problem Solving (CPS) component, stage, or tool. After reading this chapter, you will be able to do the following:

1. Define and explain the core issues examined by the Content element of Appraising Tasks.

2. Describe the relationship between the Content and Method elements of Appraising Tasks.

3. Describe five benefits of taking a balanced approach to considering the entire system of people, context, content, and method when making change.

4. Identify implications of overemphasizing either the method or the content.

5. Select the kind of novelty you will need in order to work effectively on a task.

6. Clarify the size of the impact you intend from CPS applications and the implications of that impact for applying the method.

7. Identify the influence of breadth and depth of impact on your decisions about using CPS.

(Continued)

(Continued)

8. Identify an appropriate leverage point on which to focus your CPS efforts.

9. Decide which elements of a task are important and meaningful to pursue and which are not.

10. Use your understanding of the content of a task to make a decision about the appropriateness of using CPS.

A state education agency needed to develop new policies and procedures for meeting the needs of high-ability students throughout the state. The key staff members recognized the complexity of their challenge. Current practices varied widely. Some school districts were actively involved in innovative programming, some offered limited, traditional services for a small group of students, and others offered no programming at all. The attitudes of teachers and administrators ranged from eagerness to embark on new directions to entrenchment in continuing to "do it the way we have done it for years." Different opinions also existed among parents, ranging from strong advocacy to opposition to any new programs or services. A number of competing demands for new programs added to the complications, and all this made many educators feel overwhelmed or "besieged by change," confronted with a parade of fads and the "latest buzz."

They wanted our help to move forward in meeting the needs of high-ability students, but in a systematic, soundly designed, and comprehensive way, rather than through a fragmented or disjointed series of "one time, one shot" events or activities. What information in this story would you consider to be most important in deciding how to assist this agency? What in the content might be essential in deciding whether CPS would be useful (and if so, in what ways)?

What Is Content?

Content is the driving force underlying any application of CPS. Put as simply as possible, "You have to use CPS about something!" The Content element of Appraising Tasks helps you understand what you want to change. It is the subject, the substance of a task, or the topic on which you are working. It is the area in which you want to make a change, the outcome or desired result you want to achieve. Knowing *what* you want to change will help you make a decision about whether or not CPS can help you create the change.

Understanding the content of the task goes beyond the specific facts or basic information about the task. Content also includes the general domain or field of knowledge, the perceptions and attitudes people hold implicitly or explicitly about the task, and the experience base on which the task rests (see Figure 9.1). Understanding the domain provides you with a more comprehensive view on the task and how it fits the

Figure 9.1   The Relationship Between the Task and the Task Domain

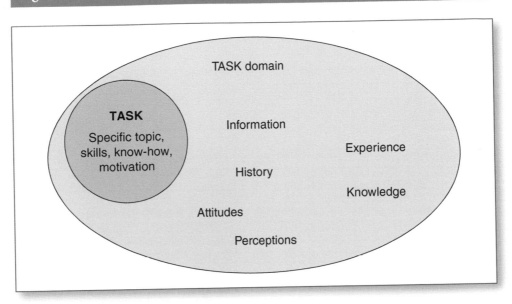

bigger picture. For example, if your task were to create a new chemical compound for a nylon fiber, the content of the task would include specifics such as the nylon product itself, the chemicals used to create it, the market opportunity being addressed, and the equipment involved in producing it. If your task were to develop a new history curriculum, the content might include specifics such as the time period to be examined and the major issues and themes to be addressed. It might also include the scope and sequence of the topics, the amount of instructional time available, and the ages of the students for which the curriculum will be used.

In both examples, the content includes the knowledge, information, and experience from the larger domains of chemistry and history, respectively. Understanding these domains can provide you with greater opportunities to create new and useful changes related to the specific task. It can also help you venture into domains outside the task area to get a fresh perspective on your needs related to the task.

The Role of Content in the System

Although it is important to focus on the content of a task, it is important to do so in relationship to the other elements of Appraising Tasks (People, Context, and Method). The four areas of Appraising Tasks make up the overall system that makes CPS work (as we discussed in Chapter 2). Since they constitute a system, the elements are related to each other, making it difficult to have one or two of the elements operating without the others. You need to consider the entire system to fully understand a task or to make a decision about the use of CPS.

Overemphasizing any one part of the system can result in an incomplete picture of the task or a misdiagnosis about the appropriateness of using CPS. It also threatens your ability to successfully address the needs of your task. We frequently notice people getting so excited about the method or content, for example, that they forget about the people involved or the context necessary to stimulate high-level creative performance. People in business often get so excited about their content (calling it innovation or the commercializing of new ideas) that they forget about the people who develop the innovations or the climate necessary to stimulate innovation. People frequently leave these organizations to work elsewhere (often for the competition), where they feel that they are treated better and provided an environment of trust and risk-taking. In education, people can get so excited about helping students get good results on tests that they forget about the learning process or the long-term welfare of the student. Assessing a child's learning is an important part of the overall approach to education. It provides an excellent opportunity for feedback and additional development of the student. However, when passing a test becomes the goal rather than a means, it threatens the long-term success of the child in society.

There are also examples of overemphasis at the method end of the method-content dimension in Appraising Tasks. We see people getting so excited about a particular method that the content of the task becomes irrelevant. We hear them refer to change efforts using the name of the method rather than the need being addressed. In these situations, the method seems to take on a life of its own. In educational settings, the curriculum or instructional plan can become such an important aspect of the approach to education that we overlook the welfare of the student learner.

Our point is fundamental. To get the best results for your task, maintain your focus on the entire system (your desired outcomes, the people with whom you interact, the context in which you work, and the methods you use to accomplish your desired results). Overemphasis on either the content or the method is likely to have the effect identified in the first two columns of Table 9.1. The benefits of focusing on the entire system are identified in the third column of Table 9.1.

Table 9.1   The Benefits of Focusing on the System

Implications of Overemphasizing Content	Implications of Overemphasizing Process	Benefits of Emphasizing the System
People become *disconnected from the process*, resulting in the need to spend more time later gaining their buy-in.	People have initial enthusiasm and excitement but lose interest when there are no worthwhile results to report.	People engage *early in the process*, resulting in buy-in and acceptance with less energy.
Process appears unplanned or ad hoc, resulting in less focus and a diffused approach to managing change.	Process becomes "play time" that people perceive as irrelevant to their "real work."	Deliberate and explicit *attention to the process*, resulting in opportunities to make it efficient and productive.

Implications of Overemphasizing Content	Implications of Overemphasizing Process	Benefits of Emphasizing the System
Quality issues *appear later in the process*, resulting in more fixing activities and lower overall quality.	People lose sight of the original purpose for the process and may fail to consider the quality of their work or the standards for productivity they are trying to reach. *As long as the process is enjoyable they think they're doing OK. Then, the crunch comes, and they discover they have nothing to show for all their process, and it's too late to do anything about it.*	People *catch issues earlier in the process*, resulting in overall higher quality results from the process.
People do not see their role in relationship to each other, resulting in diffused energy and unnecessary repetition and in greater costs.	People responsible for managing the process are viewed by others as irrelevant to the core purposes of the organization and not taken seriously. *They are just the "flip-charts, Post-its®, and dots people" who don't really contribute to the business.*	People understand how they fit the overall change process, resulting in synergy that lowers costs of all kinds.
The environment discourages risk-taking and trust, resulting in less creativity or in change that is close to what was.	People learn to distrust each other *and* the process; then they dismiss the process as "fun and games" or simply as a visible sign that something is being done to change things. *As a result, the real power of process goes untapped.*	There is an environment of trust and risk-taking, resulting in greater novelty that adds value to the change.

What are the most important issues to consider when exploring the Content element of Appraising Tasks? How can you use your understanding of the content to help you decide if CPS is an appropriate method to use on a task? There are three core issues to consider that will help you answer these questions: (1) the kind of novelty you need, (2) the size of the impact you want, and (3) the best place to focus your efforts.

Novelty: What Kind of Novelty Do You Need?

The Content element in Appraising Tasks helps you understand the novelty you need to introduce in order to make the change in the task you desire. *Novelty* refers to something new or unique that you're introducing into a context, system, or procedure. You can introduce novelty aimed at improving an existing context or system, or novelty that searches for or results in something completely different. Your challenge is to understand, clarify, and determine the kind of novelty you need to best produce the kind of change you want.

Some people find it surprising that the process of change involves a dynamic interaction among different kinds of change. Real-life situations do not involve just one kind of novelty or another. For example, consider this situation: Have you ever found yourself working to improve the speed or efficiency of a particular work process? As you work, some of the changes you introduce result in refinements or incremental improvements to the process. However, one day, the requirements for that process change to the point where they can no longer be met by making incremental changes in the process. You discover that you need to use an entirely different process for meeting the new requirements and build one. The change process doesn't stop there. As you introduce and use the new process over time, you learn new and better ways to make it work, too. This results in a new series of evolutionary improvements to the *new* process. This second round of improvements once again will take you only so far in increasing the efficiency of the process. Then, you find that it is time to create another, *different* process to lift your results to a new level, and the cycle continues, making the process both better and different.

Over the long term, the change process represents a natural, dynamic movement along a continuum from evolutionary to revolutionary change (see Figure 9.2). You have probably read about or studied the "ends" of this continuum using different language. For example, evolutionary change is sometimes described as continuous improvement, incremental change, or total quality. It focuses on making things better using novelty that typically fits within the given or current structure, systems, or procedures. It is typically quick to implement and often costs less than revolutionary change. Revolutionary change is often called step change, radical breakthrough, or "out of the box" thinking. This kind of change focuses on doing things differently with a total departure from the current approach or way of operating. Therefore, this form of novelty often creates the need for new or different structures, systems, or procedures. It is also likely to take longer to implement and typically costs more than evolutionary change.

Figure 9.2 A Spectrum of Change

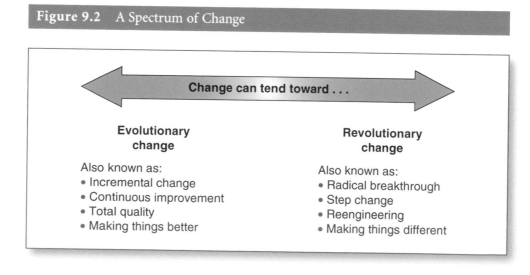

Evolutionary and revolutionary changes are both important and necessary to make the overall change process work. Over time, whether you are working on your own, in a group, or in an organization, the change process works best when these two complementary forms of change are allowed to happen in tandem, naturally, and organically. Imagine what your life would be like if there were only evolutionary change. There would be few or no *fresh* perspectives, no unusual new product lines, and no really new forms of technology. Or imagine life in the opposite situation, where every day things were entirely different from the day before; different clothes, a different way to get to work, a different job, a different home. Every day, everything was completely different than it had been the day before! These might be extreme and unlikely possibilities, but they illustrate the idea. You need both kinds of change, working in harmony with each other, to be productive and successful over the long term.

The challenge is to understand the kind of novelty you need at a particular time to meet the demands or constraints of a given task. This is not as easy as it sounds. Recall that in Chapter 7, we mentioned your preference for one kind of change or another and its influence on your perceptions about a task. If you have a more developmental preference, you are more likely to prefer evolutionary changes that result in continuous improvement. If you have a more exploratory preference, you are more likely to prefer revolutionary changes that result in step change or radical departures. If you have a moderate preference, you may look to the situation for help in making decisions about the kind of change that will be needed for a task. In any case, the danger is that people often identify the kind of novelty to pursue based on their own preferences rather than on the actual demands of the task, as illustrated in Figure 9.3.

Figure 9.3 The Change That Is Necessary Rather Than Personal Preference

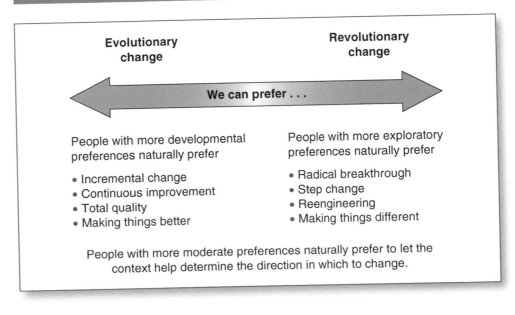

Evolutionary change — Revolutionary change

We can prefer . . .

People with more developmental preferences naturally prefer

- Incremental change
- Continuous improvement
- Total quality
- Making things better

People with more exploratory preferences naturally prefer

- Radical breakthrough
- Step change
- Reengineering
- Making things different

People with more moderate preferences naturally prefer to let the context help determine the direction in which to change.

When you consider the kind of novelty you need, look to the demands, opportunities, and constraints of the task rather than simply to the kind of change you prefer to introduce. Consider the following questions, and test them against your experience with real tasks. Would you have felt better prepared to introduce change if you had considered them? Of course, when you are actually working on a task, it can be difficult to be sure that you are not only asking these questions but also answering them candidly and accurately. You will probably find, however, that they are worth the effort.

1. Are you attempting to build on the current structures and systems or to create different ones?

2. Are you attempting to make incremental improvements or to come up with something totally different?

3. Do you have room to "play" outside the current systems or do you need to work within clear constraints?

4. Are you looking for something that fits within an existing system and is quick to implement, or do you have the necessary resources (time, money, etc.) to introduce entirely new approaches?

5. Are you looking to revolutionize how work gets done?

Size: How Great an Impact Do You Want?

The size of the impact you want to have will have an influence on many decisions about people, content, and method. For example, your approach to making small cosmetic changes in a limited area of your personal life is likely to be different from your approach to transforming the purpose or structure of an entire department, function, or organization. The size of impact will help you understand the level of energy and commitment you will need as well as the time it will take to complete the task. It will also help you understand the impact you will have on the context and the number and kinds of methods you will need to learn and use to meet the demands of the task.

The Content element of Appraising Tasks will help you analyze how great an impact you want to create and thus help you determine whether CPS is appropriate to help you create it. You can understand the size of impact by examining it from two perspectives: its breadth and its depth.

Breadth of Impact

Breadth concerns how wide or broad an area you want to change. For example, in narrow breadth, your attention will probably be on an individual rather than a group, a team rather than an entire department, or a division rather than the entire organization. When the breadth or range of impact is wide, you are likely to focus on changing many facets of your life or influencing multiple groups or systems. Changing a unit of study for one class would be narrow; changing the curriculum in a certain area for an entire school system or for all the schools in a state, province, or country would be broad. As demonstrated in Figure 9.4, changing an entire product or service line would be broad, while changing a particular product or service might be narrow.

Figure 9.4 The Breadth and Depth of the Desired Change

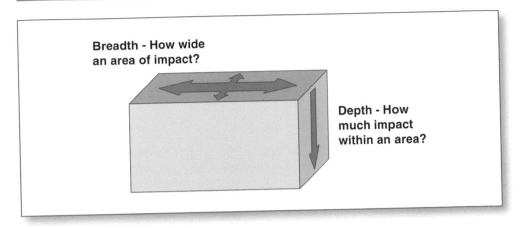

Depth of Impact

Depth concerns how deep or thorough a change you want to make within a particular area. For example, if you are interested in a low level of depth or surface change, then you might focus your attention on making cosmetic, partial, or restricted changes within the task. If you want great depth, then you are likely to focus your efforts on making structural, extensive, or complete changes within the particular area (see Figure 9.4). Repositioning a soap product in the marketplace would be a surface change; changing its positioning along with its chemical ingredients, function, and delivery systems would be getting below the surface into deep or more fundamental change. Updating the book used to deliver a course would be surface change, while updating the book, instructional activities, and support materials might be getting under the surface into deep change.

People often underestimate the impact of a change on themselves or others. Consider transformational and transactional change (Taffinder, 1998). Transformational change in an organizational setting is typically large-scale change because it involves both a wide range of change (breadth) and an extensive amount of change (depth). Whether you are part of a school district, a local church, or a global manufacturing company, change at this level can have profound implications. It involves changing an organization's vision of the future, its purpose for existence, its mission, and its values. Transformational change can even affect the kinds of products and services that are developed, the kinds of people hired and retained, and the processes used to make work happen throughout the organization.

Transactional change, on the other hand, involves changing things such as organizational processes, procedures, skills, or people in an organization. These changes are more likely to be concentrated in particular areas and may have limited or no impact on other parts of the organization. Therefore, they are likely to be smaller in breadth and depth than transformational changes. For example, changes in a purchasing system will be likely to affect mostly those people directly involved in purchasing, with little or no impact on other people. Changes in the curriculum for physical education in a school may or may not affect the math or science curricula in that school or any of the curricula in other schools or school districts.

Small and large change can happen by taking either an evolutionary or a revolutionary approach. However, transformational change is likely to require more time, energy, and resources because of the size of its impact in contrast to transactional changes. Therefore, in the Content element of Appraising Tasks, your opportunity is to be clear about the size of the change you want to create and to consider its implications for the work that will be necessary to get the change implemented. The implication of size will become more relevant as we continue through this chapter and when describing the Designing Process stage in Chapter 11.

When you consider the size of the impact you want or need to create, consider the following questions. Test them against a task you worked on previously to see if they might have helped you clarify the task or to understand better what you were getting yourself into.

1. How great an area do you want to affect?

2. Will the impact be restricted to a particular group of people, system, or area, or will it affect many groups or systems?

3. Are you looking to make a change centralized in a particular area or one that has widespread implications?

4. Do you want to make transactional changes or transformational changes?

5. Are you looking to make minor cosmetic changes or complete structural changes?

Leverage: Where Is the Best Place to Focus Your Energy?

Of all the places you *could* focus your energy, where *should* you focus your energy? The Content element of Appraising Tasks helps you identify the *leverage point,* the place in the task where you believe that you will have the greatest chance of making valuable progress toward your goal. It helps you cut through all the excitement, opportunities, confusion, or threats you might be sensing and enables you to identify where you have the power to act effectively and productively. You can identify where you should act before you begin working on a task or when you are in the middle of the task looking for the next steps to take along your journey. In either case, knowing where you should focus your efforts is key to being successful with a task.

Your understanding of the domain in which your task rests can help you know where to focus your efforts. However, knowing where to focus can be difficult because of the pace at which change happens in many domains. For example, if you want to make a change that involves the use of computer technology, you will need to move fast because the computer industry changes at an extremely fast pace. An expert in a group with which we worked recently presented this rather startling piece of information. He said that, on average, a new piece of computer software or hardware enters the world market every 8 to 12 seconds. We then heard the same piece of information from two other organizations within the computer technology field. If this is true, it means that all your computer hardware and software might move from being "state of the art" to being obsolete in a very short period of time. In technology today and in many other areas as well, what we understood to be impossible one day becomes common practice the next.

Other domains might move more slowly, enabling you to understand the relevant information for your task more accurately. For example, some equipment in the medical field has a life span of 12 years. Exploring the Content element of Appraising Tasks in this domain will be different than for tasks in the computer industry. It is important to know the pace and rate of changing content for any task on which you might consider working.

Identifying Key Leverage Points

How do you know the best place to focus your efforts? The content of a task is often made up of many different parts or elements. Some of these elements will be more *important* to address than others. You will also likely be more *capable* of addressing some of the elements than others. These two issues make up the Leverage Grid contained in Figure 9.5. This grid builds on the work of Treffinger (1992) and provides an approach to help you identify where in the task you should focus your efforts to be successful on important issues.

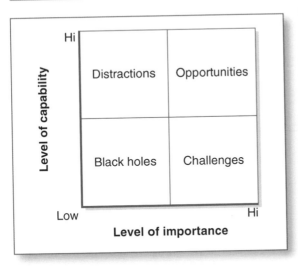

Figure 9.5 A Model to Help You Identify the Best Leverage Point(s)

Level of Importance. The importance dimension is about identifying the most meaningful parts, elements, or areas of the task content to address. Task elements high in importance are significant, worthwhile, or critical to approach with new thinking. They are areas that, if successfully addressed, would provide you with substantial benefits or represent excellent progress in accomplishing your desired outcome. Task elements low in importance are insignificant, inconsequential, or even trivial. However, be careful to identify and recognize the elements of the task that are important versus urgent. For example, you may consider a telephone call urgent because the person is on the phone at that moment in time. However, the subject of the phone call may not be important or of high priority.

Level of Capability. The capability dimension is about having the capacity, skill, or know-how to get something done successfully. You have a high level of capability for tasks when you are confident that you can complete them or that you can acquire the skills, technology, or information you need to make them happen. Tasks with low capability are those you believe that you do not have the capacity to do, those for which you don't know where to go to get the know-how, or those for which the capacity to complete the task does not yet exist. Exploring the level of importance and the level of capability together will help you identify the greatest leverage point for the task (see Figure 9.5). Your perceptions of the task in relation to these two dimensions will help you identify black holes, distractions, potential challenges, and opportunities to pursue.

Task elements low in importance and low in capability are known as *black holes*. Black holes pull or draw energy in from the surrounding area. They are so strong that not even light can escape. Black holes in a task, although probably not as strong as those in outer space, pull energy and effort into areas of the task that result in little or no productivity. You do not have the capacity to address such tasks, and even if you did, the outcome would not be important enough to add value to your efforts. They are areas of the task for which you will be wasting your time and effort; avoid them! Do not get trapped into thinking about these as opportunities or challenges for which you can create a breakthrough.

Elements of the task that are high in capability, but low in importance, are known as *distractions*. They may capture your interest because they are easy to do. Unfortunately, doing them would be a waste of time, energy, and resources because the work will have little or no significance or worth. As a result, they will misdirect your energy and attention away from the more important and meaningful areas of the task on which you could be working. As Covey (1989) suggests, be sure to put "first things first."

Opportunities are elements of your task that are high in both importance and capability. They provide you with an opportune place to invest your energy because they are important enough to provide meaningful results and areas you can accomplish successfully. They build on your existing skills, strengths, or knowledge or those of others in your group, team, or organization. They can be quicker to address than the task elements that require a great deal of capacity building.

Challenges are elements of the task that are high in importance, but low in capability. These are interesting elements in that they can provide you with unique possibilities to make progress, *if you only had the necessary capability*. They may require you to move into new domains, new skill sets, or new content areas for which you do not currently have an existing capacity. You can get breakthroughs in this area by finding ways to make something possible that now seems impossible. This requires a high level of commitment to increasing your fundamental capability.

Although you may address opportunities more quickly, there may be other reasons why you might choose to pursue the challenges; don't dismiss them without careful consideration. For example, imagine that you are part of an organization that needs to make itself profitable within 2 years. You may choose to develop products for which you have the existing capability and that are likely to bring in additional revenue (opportunities on our matrix). Then, consider another business with a strong financial base, but for which increasing competition is becoming a problem. Rather than pursuing new products using their existing capacities, they might decide to build the internal capacity (i.e., a black box operation, a parallel new product development system, or even a new research and development function) to pursue entirely new products or services. The context in which your task rests (in this case, an organization with financial or competition issues) will have an impact on determining the best leverage point for a task.

Use the following questions to help you determine the best leverage point(s) for a task. Test them to see if they work for you by considering a task you addressed in the past. Would they have helped you understand where to focus your efforts?

1. What are the most important parts of the task? Least important?

2. What area of the task is most likely to give you the greatest benefit? Least benefit?

3. What parts of the task currently seem impossible, but would enable you to accomplish your desired results if you could address them?

4. Where is the greatest potential for new insights that would be productive?

5. What is the highest priority element of the content?

Using Your Understanding About Content

The Content area of Appraising Tasks is only one of four areas to consider when determining the appropriateness of applying CPS. However, it provides you with important input for your decision. As a result of your examination of Content, you might decide to do the following:

Apply CPS

You might decide that CPS is appropriate for the task because you understand the kind of novelty desired, the size of impact needed, and the best leverage point in which to begin working on the task. However, the major factor that influences the appropriateness of CPS is the need for novelty. If you found that novelty was unnecessary, but that the task required some energy to deal with a problem using a solution that already existed, you might use an alternative method. CPS is unique in that it will help you create a new response to a complex and ambiguous situation. We will talk more about the unique qualities of CPS in Chapter 10.

Modify the Task

You may find that the part of the task you chose to address has no room for novel thinking (e.g., the definition of the task is either too constraining or overly general). Tasks that are too tightly constrained will make it difficult to use your creativity because there is "no room to play." Tasks that are too general or abstract may make it difficult for you to apply CPS powerfully because the "target" for your thinking is unclear. Therefore, you may need to adjust your definition of the task, open the task more to novel thinking, or focus the task to create a clear target.

Adjust the Expectations You Hold for CPS

You may find that you are not the ultimate owner of the content and that someone else has final decision-making responsibility for it. In these situations, you might apply

CPS. However, you might need to adjust your expectations because the best you can do in this situation is provide the ultimate task owner with recommendations for what he or she might do. You will not really be able to use CPS to make decisions about the task or to implement the results of your CPS efforts.

Use a Different Method

If you decide that there is no need or desire for novelty to accomplish the outcome, the task is probably not appropriate for CPS. In this situation, you would look for alternative methods that are better suited to help you accomplish your desired outcome.

The Rest of the Story

The state education agency clearly needed novelty. The client wanted to use recent advances in understanding human abilities and talents to guide schools toward contemporary models and approaches to educating high-ability students. However, we had to proceed cautiously, recognizing, affirming, and building on the initial and varying levels of expertise of people in the field. We had to make new knowledge and information available to many people *before* they were expected to support and implement new policies and program requirements.

The initial stages of our work were more incremental (building on current expertise and acknowledging concerns). As our work continued, we added new content challenges but we also provided additional process training and support. We gave people in the field exposure to and experience with new content and new process tools and skills. We brought people into the project gradually, over a period of several months, rather than "springing" new requirements and expectations on them suddenly and with little preparation or follow-up support. We also worked with the state agency's staff to acknowledge and involve key leaders from within their department and from schools and communities throughout the state early in the overall project.

Finally, these efforts helped the leaders in the state create an effective plan for managing change creatively. As a result of considering many issues about both content and process, the overall project expanded beyond writing and developing a prototype set of guidelines, policies, and procedures. Leadership teams from various regional areas within the state participated in combined review and advanced training sessions. They received newly developed and established materials and resources, as well as structured training programs. These programs were followed by additional advanced training sessions that combined sessions on new approaches to programming for high-ability students (content) with training in learning styles and CPS. The groups were better prepared for their new roles because they worked during the training on real problems and challenges that they expected to encounter in working with schools (in relation to working with students or with other adults). Recognizing the importance of both depth and breadth of impact, the state also provided continuing support for some districts to build model programs that could be used to serve as sites for other districts to visit and as a springboard for continuing development.

Putting This Chapter to Work

The goal of this chapter was to help you understand the role content plays in deciding whether or not to apply CPS on a particular task. We explored in particular the issues of novelty, size of impact, and best leverage point and their implications for your approach to making that decision.

Activities to Guide Reflection and Action

Use the following activities to deepen your understanding of the information and to practice using the material examined in this chapter. If you are using this book as part of a course or study group, you may wish to work individually, and then compare your responses, or to work collaboratively as a team.

1. Think back to a meeting you participated in where the group leader put so much attention on the content of the meeting that the process went unmanaged. Make some observations about what took place during the meeting. Consider how you know attention was more heavily focused on content and not balanced with attention to process. What impact did the emphasis on content have on the process of the meeting, the people, and the outcomes of the meeting overall? What might have been done differently to create a more balanced emphasis during the meeting?

2. Think back to when you were part of a group that implemented a successful change. Consider what actions the group took to make the change happen and what impact they had on the people, the context, and the methods involved in the situation. What kind of change was implemented—more evolutionary, or more revolutionary? What observations or insights can you make about what it takes to make that kind of change happen successfully?

3. Think back to a situation in which you were part of a group that successfully implemented a change that was at the opposite end of the evolutionary–revolutionary change spectrum from the change you identified in #2. Consider what actions the group took to make *this* kind of change happen and the impact those changes had on the people, the context, and the methods involved in the situation. What observations or insights can you make about what it takes to make this kind of change happen? Compare and contrast your insights with those from #2.

4. Identify a situation you are currently responsible for that is requiring you to make some new changes. Considering the qualities of the change you believe will best serve the needs of the task:

   a. Describe the nature of the novelty you need to create. Is it more evolutionary or revolutionary? Explain your rationale for that conclusion.

   b. What do the qualities of the change tell you about the depth and breadth of impact you need to create? Identify the implications of pursuing that level of depth and breadth.

   c. Identify the best leverage point for beginning your application of CPS in addressing the needs of the situation. What is your rationale for starting there?

CPS as a
Change Method

Nothing is permanent but change.

—Heraclitus

This chapter examines the Method element in the Appraising Tasks stage of the Planning Your Approach component. It will identify the key issues you need to consider as you decide about the appropriate use of Creative Problem Solving (CPS) and plan for its effective application. As a result of reading this chapter, you will be able to do the following:

1. Define what change methods are and show how they can help you address tasks.

2. Identify four reasons why it is important to be explicit and deliberate about using change methods.

3. Distinguish between method and content when Planning Your Approach to CPS.

4. Identify four task characteristics for assessing the appropriateness of using CPS.

5. Identify how the CPS framework, language, and tools can be used to help you address tasks with different characteristics.

6. Identify why you can be confident in your use of CPS as a method for managing change.

7. Identify the costs and benefits of applying CPS and their implications for your use of the method.

8. Make a decision about the appropriateness of CPS based on your exploration of the Method area of Appraising Tasks.

I magine that you're a manager in a large consumer goods company making products such as laundry soap and paper towels. What would you do if your competitor started producing new products that threatened to take your customers away from you? The laundry sector of a global consumer goods company was in this situation and asked us to help. They wanted us to use CPS to help them develop and implement an approach to leapfrog ahead of their competitors by developing new products that no other company in the world was thinking about. The way in which they wanted to do this was by identifying unknown and unmet consumer needs.

We knew that the company was facing a difficult situation. The task called for a high level of novelty because they wanted to identify new consumer needs that their competition would not even know about. As a result, they wanted to find new ways to discover new needs and concepts for meeting those needs. The task was highly complex because the company wanted to identify basic human needs and desires of consumers in different cultures around the world, requiring the involvement of people from different functions, disciplines, and cultures, within and outside the company. The task was also ambiguous because the company wanted to conduct exploratory consumer research, an approach to new product development that no one in that organization had tried before because of the heavy investment and use of a more confirmatory approach. The classic marketing research function was dominant in the organization.

How would you decide whether CPS is appropriate for this kind of task? Can CPS help you develop new products or new ways to serve customers? The focus of this chapter is to help you be deliberate and explicit about your selection and use of CPS as a method for accomplishing the desired results examined in Chapter 9.

What Is a Change Method?

Change, or sometimes just the thought of it, can stimulate feelings of excitement about opportunities or new beginnings. It can create energy or enthusiasm over the possibilities of doing something novel, different, or better. The uncertainty that often accompanies change can also make you feel anxious or apprehensive about what your future might hold. It can result in a state that makes you hesitant about what to do in a given situation. Change (when it is productive) involves moving from your current state to some desired future state. That future state may be somewhat ambiguous or contain some level of complexity and ambiguity. Whether you are developing a new product for your customers, creating a new curriculum or instructional approach, or changing your personal behavior or perceptions, change is often accompanied by novelty, ambiguity, and complexity.

You may see change as an opportunity to be seized or a threat to be avoided or, sometimes, as both. Whatever your situation or reason for change, explicit tools and methods can help you harness your energy (and the energy of others) and channel your efforts in positive directions that result in productive change. *Change methods* are specific ways or approaches you can use to make something better or different. They are frameworks or structures that help you think or act on a task in ways that help you create productive transformation. A change method is creative when it implies that you are attempting to develop something new, in an unstructured situation, on an open-ended kind of problem or opportunity. It requires you to engage your imagination because there are no ready-made answers available. Change methods can be implicit or explicit and deliberate or unintentional. You can use them proactively to address a task early, or you can use them to react to a situation that is already on you. You can use change methods individually or in a group setting.

Of course, CPS is not the only change method. Isaksen and Tidd (2006) identified more than 30 such methods. Some of them work best by themselves, and others can be integrated or woven together. Some are powerful approaches that can be used in many different kinds of situations, while others are best used for a particular kind of task. Some are best for personal or individual application, while others are better for group/team or organizational application. Whereas CPS is a method that emphasizes developing novel solutions to situations and challenges, Isaksen and Tidd described the emphasis of the following methods in this way:

- *Kepner/Tregoe*® (Kepner & Tregoe, 1981). Uses "rational" approaches to situations where fault diagnosis and repair is the goal.
- *Lateral thinking and Six Hats* (DeBono, 1970, 1986). Develops solutions for intractable problems using methods that would typically be ignored by logical thinking.
- *Six Sigma* (Brue, 2002). Provides measurement-based strategies for process improvement and variation reduction to improve business capability.
- *Total quality management* (Deming, 1986). Enables long-term success by engaging all the members of an organization in improving the processes, products, and services in ways that improve customer satisfaction.
- *Lean manufacturing* (Womack & Jones, 1996). Eliminates all waste in the manufacturing processes.
- *Strategic planning* (Mintzberg, 1994). Employs disciplined efforts to produce fundamental decisions and actions that shape and guide what an organization is, what it does, and why it does it, with a focus toward the future.
- *TRIZ* (Altshuller, 1996). Uses an algorithmic approach for solving technical and technological problems.

Whereas each of these methods has its own unique history of development, there are also a number of different versions of CPS that share a common history with our CPS Version 6.1™. Each of these derivations of CPS has been developed to meet the specific needs of specific contexts. For example,

- *Simplex*® (Basadur, 1994). Focuses on specific organizational applications of tools that emphasize balance of ideation and evaluation.
- *Creative Problem Solving: The thinking skills model* (Puccio, Murdock, & Mance, 2007). Provides systems and processes that help leaders be more deliberate in how they think and act.

With so many change methods available, how do you identify the best change method for a task? What would you need to know about that method to be confident in its application? Why would you consider using CPS instead of, or in addition to, the other 30 or more methods? The Method element of Appraising Tasks helps you answer these questions. It helps you determine whether or not CPS (or any method) is appropriate for a given task. Most important, the Method element helps you be deliberate and explicit about the method(s) you use to accomplish the objectives of a task.

Being Deliberate About Method

Being deliberate about the methods you use to address tasks can pay big dividends. For example, one person we trained used CPS to help his organization create a new business. He used deliberate and explicit methods to help the group develop an approach to solving customers' problems. His focus on method shifted the group's attention away from developing a specific solution to a client's need to building a business method that enabled them to solve problems for many different clients. Being deliberate about method in this situation led to the development of a $15 million a year business.

Although it can have powerful results, investing time and energy in being deliberate and explicit about the method or the way you accomplish a desired result of a task can be difficult. Sometimes, you pay so much attention to the content of a task that you invest little or no effort in differentiating, understanding, or managing the method used to address it. Most of your attention focuses on *what* you need to get accomplished (content), rather than on *how* you will get it accomplished (method). For example, focusing your attention on the content of a task enables you to think and act on things such as:

1. Who else needs to be involved to get the work done?

2. What is the most important task to be accomplished and how should you channel your energy in that direction?

3. What strategies and priorities are most important?

4. Where should you focus your efforts to get the highest quality results?

5. When is the best time to address the task?

6. Why are you working on the content in the first place?

It is not surprising that people tend to focus so heavily on the content of the task. We are typically rewarded for getting something done that accomplishes a desired result. Whether you are helping children learn, getting a new product to the market, or building a house, most organizational pay structures, as well as their reward and recognition programs, are focused on encouraging people to accomplish results, not on the change methods used to get the job done. Given a choice, therefore, most people will choose to focus on the results or content of a task, with little or no deliberate attention paid to the method.

In Appraising Tasks, you have the opportunity to be deliberate about distinguishing method from content and then managing the unique contribution that each makes to your productivity. Take, for example, a tennis coach. An effective tennis coach (or any coach for that matter) focuses attention on both the *output* of performance (Did the student win or lose? What games or sets were won or lost? How many times were certain shots made or missed?) and the *form* of the performance (How well did the technique aspects of the game work? What strategies did the student use? How well did the student handle distractions on the tennis court?). Coaches integrate their attention on both these issues to understand their unique contribution to the overall performance and in finding ways to improve it the next time.

Distinguishing method from content means understanding them as unique, but interdependent, and identifying the contributions that each provides in making change happen effectively. Being explicit and deliberate about Method enables you to do the following:

- Make conscious, purposeful decisions about the best method(s) for dealing with a task.
- Identify and plan to use the best approaches to understanding the challenges and opportunities that exist within your work, generating unusual and valuable ideas for solving your problems, and putting effective plans in place for getting your ideas accepted and implemented.
- Identify and use powerful tools that enhance your capacity to think creatively, make decisions effectively, and solve problems productively.
- Plan and implement how you will involve others, stimulate their commitment to accomplishing your desired results, and focus their energy in productive directions.

The nature of the task itself will help you determine when to spend the energy and time necessary to distinguish method from content. Although CPS can be helpful for tasks both large and small, you may benefit most from distinguishing and managing method explicitly when you are working on larger, more complicated tasks that require some form of new response or approach. Let us consider the characteristics of the task that are most appropriate for CPS.

CPS as a Change Method

Chapters 7, 8, and 9 identified the key issues about people, context, and content to be considered in diagnosing your use of CPS. What issues should you consider about CPS itself to determine if it should be used on a task? The following three sections of this chapter will examine the core issues you need to consider about CPS as a change method when determining the appropriateness of its use. These issues include the purpose and unique qualities of CPS, how you know it will work, and the potential costs and benefits of its use.

Do You Need the Purpose and Unique Qualities of CPS?

The *purpose* of any method identifies the core reason for its existence. It clarifies the original intent or aim of the method and helps you understand the characteristics of a task for which it is best suited. Its *unique qualities* help you understand how the method differs from other methods and how it might be helpful in ways that other methods are not and under what conditions. Knowing a method's purpose and unique qualities will help you set appropriate expectations for its effectiveness. You will be in a better position to know when you are using the method in a way where you can be confident in its use, and when you might be stretching the method beyond its potential effectiveness.

You can use CPS on a wide range of tasks from many different areas of your life. It can be used on personal and professional tasks, tasks that involve only you or tasks that involve many people. It can be applied on technical issues, people issues, organizational process issues, and environmental issues. It is a dynamic and powerful process. However, the purpose and unique qualities of CPS make it more naturally suited for tasks that have particular characteristics.

Figure 10.1 identifies four task characteristics to help you assess when CPS will be an appropriate choice as a method. Other factors might influence your choice of a method for a specific task. These four characteristics will be important to consider across many different situations. Keep in mind that CPS is not an elixir or all-purpose method, suitable for any and all tasks. Examining these four task characteristics will help you be effective in choosing tasks for which CPS will be most helpful and appropriate. For these characteristics, we intend the "bars" in Figure 10.1 to depict broad ranges of applicability, not specific, quantitative rating scales. The four factors may interact with each other, and under some conditions, one or two of the factors might outweigh the others in importance. Consider these factors to be general guidelines, not specific "standards" or precise indicators to be measured. We will describe each of the four task characteristics and discuss its relevance in choosing CPS as a method.

Some tasks require answers that already exist and that simply need to be located or researched. Other tasks may require you to create your own answers because no suitable responses currently exist. The *need for novelty* focuses on whether or not you need to invent, design, or construct a desired outcome and pathways to reach it. They are tasks that require more imagination than memory or awareness during problem

Figure 10.1   The Best Application Range for CPS

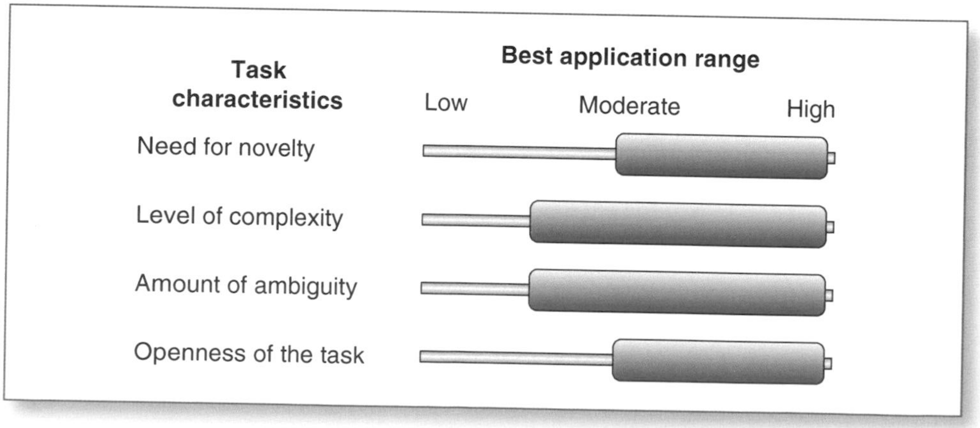

solving. The novelty you need may be evolutionary or revolutionary, incremental or step change. In any case, the need for novelty concerns the necessity to pursue or create something new, better, or different.

The *level of complexity* deals with the extent to which elements of the task are interrelated, the number of layers, or the number and variety of issues or themes that might exist in a task. You will face tasks that are low in complexity. These have few or no interrelated elements, few layers, or little or no diversity of elements with which to contend. The elements or layers are clearly prioritized and are likely to stand on their own. They have solution pathways that are known, predetermined, or relatively simple. Tasks that are high in complexity have a large number of interrelated elements or layers, many of which conflict or are "tangled" in some way. The elements also depend on one another so that you can't change one element without influencing the others. The solution pathways are unknown, undetermined, or highly complex.

The *amount of ambiguity* concerns the degree to which the task is defined. Tasks low in ambiguity are well-defined and clearly structured. You have a clear understanding of the need you must address. Tasks that have a high level of ambiguity are fuzzy, or ill defined. You find them perplexing or puzzling because the need is unclear. You find it difficult to get to the *heart* of the matter and, therefore, need to dig in and muddle around to create a clear image or definition of the task.

The *openness of a task* focuses on the amount of room you have to generate possibilities. Tasks that are low in openness are those for which there are preconceived notions of what the correct or appropriate responses for them will be like. They leave little or no room for generating alternatives since the *answers* are self-evident, leaving few choices possible. For tasks with a high level of openness, nothing is pointing you to a particular viewpoint, option, or course of action. The space within the task is open enough for you to make decisions or move in any direction you think appropriate.

CPS is designed for tasks that have moderate to high levels of novelty, complexity, ambiguity, and openness (see Figure 10.1). Since we are concerned about solving problems in creative ways (new ways that add value), we developed the CPS framework, language, and tools specifically to help you access your creativity (or the creativity of others) and apply it in productive and meaningful ways to meet your needs.

The CPS Framework

The CPS framework is unique in that it builds on more than 60 years of continuous improvement and development. The business world gave birth to it, the academic world developed it and teaches people how to use it, and now people in many kinds of settings and organizations are actively using it for managing change, increasing innovative productivity, and building creative capacity within their organizations.

The unique flexibility of a contemporary CPS framework enables you to tailor its use to respond better to the multiple and often conflicting priorities that come with complex tasks. It enables you to change quickly in response to unexpected events that can arise when you are working on new tasks. The process components help you take a highly ambiguous task and turn it into focused action. One component

(Understanding the Challenge) helps you gain clarity from ambiguity, another component (Generating Ideas) helps you create ideas for addressing the task, and yet another component (Preparing for Action) helps you prepare to take focused and powerful action on the task.

The CPS framework is also unique in that it represents a complete system. It enables you to think continuously about and plan for issues that may influence your success, positively or negatively. Its management component (Planning Your Approach) is "on" all the time to help you consider the people, the context, the content, and the method(s) involved. This continuous monitoring enables you to move about in the open areas of a task space while maintaining your focus and understanding of where you are at all times. It also enables you to know where you are and determine where you need to go to continue making progress.

Part of the power of CPS arises from its integration of two fundamental forms of thinking necessary for creative productivity: generating and focusing. The framework includes two sets of guidelines that establish best practice norms for both kinds of thinking. The heartbeat of CPS (the generating and focusing phases of each stage in the process components) helps you stretch beyond obvious or standard thinking. It also helps you manage your natural desire to reject novelty in order to select, develop, strengthen, and implement the newness you seek.

The design, clarity, and flexibility of the CPS framework make it possible for you to integrate other methods within CPS. We designed the CPS framework recognizing that no single change method can do everything. Larger, more complex tasks will often require you to use multiple methods to reach your final desired outcome. Each component and stage of CPS has a clear and distinct purpose. Any tool from any change method can also be used within CPS (or separately) to help you accomplish the major purpose of any CPS component or stage. In short, the contemporary approach to CPS works well with others. It can be easily integrated into project planning, analytic problem solving, and many other methods.

The CPS Tools. CPS contains a balanced suite of tools that have been carefully developed or selected for inclusion in the framework. The toolbox is uniquely balanced, in that it contains tools for both generating and focusing options. Each set of tools helps you engage in a wide range of different kinds of thinking. For example, some of the generating tools help you think of large quantities or many different categories of alternatives, while others help you generate highly original options or help you expand or elaborate on your thinking. The focusing tools help you analyze, evaluate, and prioritize your options, as well as develop and strengthen your alternatives.

The CPS tools can be used to help you or a group target your thinking for the kind of novelty you want to produce—whether you need new thinking inside the box or new thinking outside the box. Some of the tools will help you produce evolutionary or incremental change, while others will help you create revolutionary or step change. The toolbox also contains two unique selection models that will help you know when to use the different tools for generating options (see Chapter 4) and focusing options (see Chapter 5).

Each tool is written with a clearly defined purpose, description, and outcome that is distinct from the CPS framework. This means that you can plug each tool in to different components and stages of the framework, as well as use them independent of the CPS framework. It also means that you can easily supplement them with other tools, adjust them to fit unique needs, or modify them to fit a specific context or group of people.

The CPS Language. Language and thinking are strongly linked. The specialized, yet natural, CPS language helps shape your thinking to be focused more on possibilities (emphasizing what might be) rather than impossibilities (emphasizing what "can't be"). This is particularly helpful because you do not always know where the pursuit of novelty will take you. The specific CPS language helps remind you to focus on the possible, the plausible, and the probable, rather than on the impossible, the implausible, or the improbable—even in uncertain or unclear situations.

Because the language of CPS is simple, natural, and easy to use, you are not likely to get bogged down learning many new or obscure technical terms. You can focus most of your attention on addressing the subtleties and complexities of your task or gaining clarity about what you want to create within a task. The language invites you to play in the open space rather than focus on inappropriate and self-imposed constraints.

The CPS language is also clear, concise, and consistent. The language is simply defined, to the point, and descriptive. Therefore, CPS is easily used to create a common language for addressing complex tasks that require involvement of different people, from across functions and cultures. The language can help you consider and integrate different perspectives, pieces of information, elements, and directions and decrease the chances of missed opportunities for solving complex problems creatively.

These four task characteristics will help you decide if CPS is appropriate for your task. To help make this determination, ask yourself the following questions. Try them on a task you faced in the past and see how they might have influenced your selection of CPS as a method.

1. What was my need for novelty? Was it more evolutionary or revolutionary?

2. What level of complexity or ambiguity was I dealing with?

3. How would the purpose of CPS have fit with the unique characteristics of the task?

4. How open was the task space, and did I have room to use my creativity in coming up with responses?

5. Would it have been necessary to "stretch" CPS beyond its known capacity to make it work on the task?

How Confident Am I in Using CPS?

You can be confident in the use of a method when there is information, people, and experiences supporting its effective application. There is plenty of support for CPS within all three of these areas. For example, Isaksen and DeSchryver's (2000) list of more than 700 citations supporting the effectiveness of CPS gives us justification to say that CPS provides a sound approach for making innovation and change happen. The power behind the evidence is that it provides both research-based support and evidence of the powerful results people have created using CPS. We also have a large amount of data from research we conducted on the impact of CPS on the organizations with which we work. We also continue to hear stories and discover reports about its powerful impact. We maintain an up-to-date compendium of the evidence that you can download from our Web site (cpsb.com).

Some of our confidence in the use of CPS comes from the fact that people have been using it successfully to deal with a wide range of topics with individuals, groups, and organizations in educational, government, not-for-profit, and business settings for decades. A growing number of networks around the world use CPS as their core method for managing innovation and change. There are many stories about its effectiveness at helping people manage change, several of which we will share in Chapter 12.

We focus on increasing our confidence in CPS by continually modifying and updating our understanding of it. Throughout this book, we have been illustrating the power of CPS by sharing stories of our experience with its use and impact. However, one of the best ways to understand whether CPS can work for you is to try it yourself. Although there are many books, articles, and courses you might attend, your personal experience will be one of the most convincing ways to understand what works, what doesn't, and when you should try something else.

We encourage you to practice using CPS on tasks that are appropriate for using language and tools that are new to you. These might be low-priority tasks that do not require the involvement of others or have a profound impact on them. Then, move up to larger or more important tasks once you have some personal experience and additional confidence in your use of the tools, language, and framework.

When you consider using CPS, ask yourself some of the questions below to see if you are ready to try it:

1. How confident am I that CPS will work on this task?
2. What evidence is there about the potential impact from using CPS on this kind of task?
3. Can I access the necessary CPS support materials to learn more about its use?
4. Can I get the help if I need to effectively apply CPS on this task?

CPS can be effective for a great many kinds of tasks, as we have tried to demonstrate with our stories throughout the book. More often, the important question seems to be "Are you willing to invest the costs to get the benefits from applying CPS?" rather than "Does CPS actually work?"

What Are the Benefits and Costs of Using CPS?

Using any method places demands on you, your group, and your organization. However, your gain or reward from its use should outweigh the costs of its application.

Considering the benefits and costs of using CPS before you decide to use it will help you decide whether or not it is worth the energy to attain the benefits. It will also help you understand and set appropriate expectations for its use.

What are the benefits of using CPS? Table 10.1 illustrates some of the benefits your use of CPS can yield. You will notice that the benefits build on the characteristics of the framework, language, and set of tools described above. However, additional benefits that come from using the specific stages are worth keeping in mind, too. For example, CPS helps you focus your attention and energy in positive directions. It helps you focus on what you want, not on what you don't want. Unfortunately, people too often pay more attention to what they want to avoid, rather than to what they want to create. CPS helps you understand the situation surrounding your task in a way that prevents you from being distracted from your goals. It enables you to frame problems in ways that build motivation and commitment. It also helps you stimulate effective teamwork and collaboration when used in a group setting.

CPS can help you stretch your imagination in many, varied, and unusual ways to stimulate ideas for solving problems in new and productive ways. However, having a good idea is not always enough to enable you to solve a problem or make a change. Therefore, CPS also enables you to turn interesting ideas into powerful solutions and then helps you put plans in place for their successful implementation. Using CPS can provide you with these benefits while also enabling you to have higher quality results, at less cost and in shorter amounts of time, than when it is not used.

Table 10.1 Some Benefits of Using CPS

Increases likelihood of yielding productive results on new and complex opportunities and challenges
Provides common problem-solving language—promoting teamwork and cooperation across functions, cultures, and disciplines; decreasing time and costs associated with change
Provides a natural, flexible framework for organizing tools and strategies—easy to learn and use because it fits people's natural approaches to creativity, decision making, and problem solving
Encourages a dynamic balance between creative and critical thinking when generating and focusing on options—resulting in useful novelty that fits your needs
Stimulates group ownership—building commitment for implementation and encouraging the consideration of more factors, information, and experiences
Enables resource group involvement—encouraging your use of diverse perspectives, expertise, and information and decreasing the likelihood of gaps or missed opportunities

What are the costs of using CPS? Getting to the benefits of CPS does have its costs, too. For example, as Table 10.2 suggests, using CPS requires honesty and openness on the part of all involved. CPS gets to the core of the issues. Therefore, you will need to be ready to put the necessary information on the table to ensure success. It also requires you to be clear in your communication and coordination when involving others because it is possible for others to try to "take the ownership" of the topic from you. Unclear or unknown expectations about who actually owns the task can result in confusion or conflict of expectations among the people involved in the task. They may think that they have more decision-making influence than they really do.

Tailoring CPS for the best possible application requires thoughtful and deliberate planning. You will get the best from CPS (or any method) when you invest your energy in planning and preparation, before using the method. This takes commitment and energy, and you or your group must be willing to invest that energy. Although the language is natural and easy to use, it does require some learning on your part to ensure effective and efficient use of the method. You will also need to invest energy, time, and commitment when working to make high levels of novelty happen. This is particularly the case when you involve others of equal decision-making responsibility.

CPS requires self-control and courage on your part to work beyond traditional, patterned, or habit-bound ways of thinking. CPS is about creating *new* approaches that result in productive change. You must be ready, willing, and able to face the changes you pursue. You may also need to be ready to deal with organizational resistance to the use of CPS as an approach for creativity, decision making, and problem solving that may or may not be different from what is currently done in the organization.

Table 10.2   Some Costs of Using CPS

Requires honesty and openness on the part of the client
Takes commitment and energy for individuals and teams to learn and use the CPS framework, language, and tools
Requires thoughtful and deliberate planning to structure opportunities and environments for its effective application
Takes self-control and courage to work beyond traditional, patterned, or habit-bound ways of thinking
Takes more time and energy for focusing, decision making, and reaching agreement when using with a group of clients than when using with a single client
Requires effective and efficient communication and coordination with resource group members to prepare for, carry out, and follow up its use

When considering the costs and benefits of using CPS, some questions to ask yourself include the following:

1. Do I understand the costs and benefits of using CPS on this task?

2. Do the benefits of using CPS outweigh the costs?

3. Is the task important enough for me to invest in effectively applying CPS?

4. Am I willing to accept the costs of using CPS?

5. Do others involved understand the costs and benefits of using CPS?

Your Options From Exploring Method

You might make any number of decisions as a result of exploring the Method element of Appraising Tasks.

Apply CPS

You might find that the purposes for which CPS was designed fit naturally with your task, making it an appropriate method to apply. You may have the evidence you need to show that CPS can work for your kind of task. You may find that you have the support you need to get the best from a CPS application. Under these conditions, you would decide to apply CPS and begin to plan how to optimize its use for the task.

Combine CPS With Other Method(s)

Your examination of Method might result in the decision that CPS fits some of the needs of the task but that some other methods also offer additional, important, or necessary contributions. In this situation, you might decide that it is best to combine your use of CPS with another method or other tools. Your next step would be to identify what other methods to use (applying the Appraising Tasks model to confirm their appropriateness) and begin planning how they can be integrated for optimal productivity.

Wait or Withdraw

You might decide that CPS is not the best or most appropriate method to use on the task or under your specific set of circumstances. You might have found that you do not have sufficient ownership of the topic to deal with the novelty needed, its complexity, or its level of ambiguity. You might find that the task is simple or clear enough and that it is not fruitful to invest in the costs necessary to get the benefits. For these tasks, it might be more appropriate to use some method other than CPS. For example, if you believe an answer exists, but you need to find it, then research methods might be an appropriate use of your energy rather than constructing or inventing the answer using CPS. Your next step would be to determine what other methods are better suited for the task and then explore their potential application.

The Rest of the Story

CPS was perfect for the laundry division of the consumer manufacturing company that needed to understand consumer needs before the consumers themselves could even express them. CPS is designed for situations that are highly novel, complex, and ambiguous, as this one was. We designed and implemented a 1-year project that involved gaining insights about customers and their needs. The project included the use of CPS as the umbrella or overall framework for the project. This enabled us to integrate other more common approaches to gaining customer insights (such as focus groups) and identifying unarticulated consumer needs as well as to invent some new ones.

In the 1-year project, we used CPS to take the laundry sector's list of concepts to develop into products from 25 (collected over the past 7 years) to 76. These concepts are now being turned into new products that are changing the way in which people do laundry. We also used CPS to develop new exploratory research methods that are now in use for identifying unknown, unarticulated, and unmet consumer needs. Using CPS also helped them substantially reduce the errors and the rework previously made necessary by misdiagnoses of results from focus group research activities.

One of the unique outcomes of the project was that the organization identified consumer needs that did not fit into the organization's existing product categories. It resulted in the need to engage in greater cross-divisional cooperation—taking advantage of the core competencies of different divisions. For example, one concept required the capacities of the laundry division in combination with capacities of the paper division. This one concept alone resulted in an entirely new product and $8 million net revenue in the first year of sales.

Another lesson from this example is that CPS can be blended with other innovation and change methods. This project included the use of ethnography, archetype research, futuring, and some new forms of market research. The ease with which these methods were incorporated within the CPS framework allowed the company to transform the way they did market research. It also led to the development of a unique application of CPS to help organizations discover unmet, unknown, and unarticulated consumer needs. (This method is called GEMagination™, and you can contact CPSB for more information about it.)

This project also helped us reaffirm the power of CPS for addressing tasks that are new to you, that are complex, and for which there is uncertainty or ambiguity about what might result. We had information about the people involved, the situation they were facing, the need they wanted to address, and CPS as the core method for use. One of our key challenges was to design the best possible application of CPS. We needed to construct the most appropriate combination of components, stages, and tools to get the job done. In Chapter 11, we will turn our attention to that aspect of the Planning Your Approach component (the Designing Process stage).

Putting This Chapter to Work

Our goal for this chapter was to explore the Method element of Appraising Tasks and its implications for helping you make a deliberate decision about whether or not to use

CPS to address the needs of a specific task. In particular, we examined how understanding the unique qualities of CPS as a method, the level of confidence you have with its application, and costs and benefits associated with its use can influence your decision about whether or not to apply CPS.

Activities to Guide Reflection and Action

Work on one or more of the following activities to review your understanding of the material in this chapter and to practice applying its content in real situations. If you are using this book as part of a course or study group, you may wish to work individually, and then compare your responses, or to work collaboratively as a team.

1. Consider a situation you faced in the past that required you to develop a new approach to addressing a challenging problem. Identify what factors in that situation might have caused you to benefit from the use of CPS and what factors might have hampered its effective application.

2. Identify a problem-solving or change method (other than the approach to CPS described in this book) with which you are familiar. Consider the potential strengths and limitations of that method and its application. Describe the qualities a task would need to have in order to make this method uniquely suited to address it.

3. Compare and contrast CPS with the method you identified in #2. Identify the key factors you would use to decide the use of one method over the other for any given task.

4. For the two methods identified in #3, consider potentially blending the two methods and applying some combination of them on a task. Identify the qualities of a task that would benefit from a blended application of CPS and the other method. Explain what the implications might be in taking this kind of approach.

Designing
Your Way
Through CPS

Chance favors only the prepared mind.

—Louis Pasteur

The purposes of this chapter are to help you understand the Designing Process stage of Planning Your Approach and use it to customize or tailor your applications of Creative Problem Solving (CPS). As a result of reading this chapter, you will be able to do the following:

1. Identify and describe the purpose and outcomes of Designing Process.

2. Use the data you have about people, outcomes, context, and methods to tailor your CPS application in ways that will enhance its effectiveness and power.

3. Match your choice of the CPS components, stages, or tools with your particular needs and purposes.

4. Use the natural language for describing the purpose of CPS to help you identify the component or stage in which to focus your efforts.

5. Monitor the effectiveness of your choices of components, stages, or tools in relation to their helpfulness as you proceed with any CPS application, and modify those choices when necessary.

6. Analyze the results of any CPS application and determine what actions should occur, and what CPS components, stages, or tools to apply next (if any).

7. Identify designs for using CPS in a single session, during a project, or in a large-scale initiative.

The story about the laundry division of the consumer goods company in the previous chapter had a happy ending. The company figured out what consumers were looking for and developed new products to meet the demand. They tripled the number of concepts they were planning to develop into products for customers. They even sold some of their insights to other companies for substantial sums. What process design did we use to help make the project so successful? What information did we use to make decisions about the design?

To understand how to respond to these questions, review the "raw material" at your disposal. Chapters 2 to 5 gave you the information you will need about the use of the components, stages, and tools of CPS. Chapters 6 to 10 gave you some insights into what to look for when appraising the task. This chapter will help you integrate what you learned in those two sections of the book so that you can design the best application of CPS for the task at hand. We will examine Designing Process as the link between what you learned when Appraising Tasks and your specific application of the CPS process, language, and tools.

Some of the power of CPS comes from the fact that you can integrate it easily into your daily thinking and behavior. For example, the next time someone approaches you with an idea for which they want your feedback, challenge yourself to use the ALUo tool in preparing your response. Start by identifying at least three things you like about the idea. Then, identify three concerns or limitations you see in the idea. Remember to phrase these as questions beginning with a How to . . .? Next, identify one or two things that seem unique about the idea as you understand it. Then, give the person a few suggestions for overcoming at least one of the limitations you identified. We think that you will be pleasantly surprised at the impact your feedback will have. This is an example of an informal or spontaneous application of CPS. Many parts of the CPS tools and language can be applied in this way. However, in this chapter, we will concentrate on opportunities for you to be more deliberate and systematic in your use of CPS.

Linking Needs to Process

If you only use the parts of CPS that are necessary for a given task, how do you know what parts to use? Customizing your use of CPS involves linking the needs of the task to the component and stage that are best designed to address them. Specifically, this involves linking your knowledge about your Content with the parts of CPS (as the Method) that will work best.

Appraising Tasks and Designing Process are stages within the Planning Your Approach component of CPS. We refer to Planning Your Approach as a management component because its purpose is to help you navigate your way through CPS. It functions in a similar way as the operating system on your computer. The operating system is always on when you are working on your computer. Should you need to write a report, you would likely choose an application such as Microsoft Word. If you were trying to analyze some numbers, you would likely choose Microsoft Excel. If you had to prepare a presentation, you would choose to use PowerPoint. In a similar way, Planning Your Approach helps you choose and use only the component(s) of CPS that will best meet your needs. Otherwise, we go back to the mind-set of believing that we need to use *all* the elements of CPS *all* the time for *all* tasks. And that is not the best way to get the full power of CPS.

Three important steps help you link the process effectively to your need. First, know what your need is and the best place to begin to address it (see Chapter 9). The need may come from your work on Appraising Tasks (particularly the Content element) or it may be evident from your general understanding of the task. Second, know the specific purposes fulfilled by each CPS component and stage. And third, link the task need to the most appropriate component or stage based on the purpose it fulfills.

It is easiest to begin developing a link between CPS and your needs by considering the three process components. Each component and stage has a specific and unique purpose. At the component level, CPS can help you gain *clarity* about the challenge you have, generate *ideas*, or put ideas into *action* (using Understanding the Challenge, Generating Ideas, and Preparing for Action, respectively) as identified in Figure 11.1. These represent the three core purposes of the CPS process components.

When you know what component to use, you will also be in a better position to identify what stage or stages to use. Each stage also has its own purpose that is linked to the component purpose. For example, the Constructing Opportunities stage helps you gain clarity about the *future*. The Framing Problems stage helps you gain clarity about the specific *problems to address*. The Developing Solutions stage helps you *transform ideas into promising solutions*. Finally, the Building Acceptance stage helps you *transform ideas into promising action*. Let's try an example to practice selecting components and stages (see Figure 11.2).

Figure 11.1   The Core Purposes of CPS Process Components

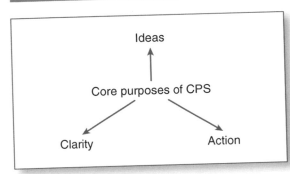

Figure 11.2   The Core Purposes of CPS Process Components and Stages

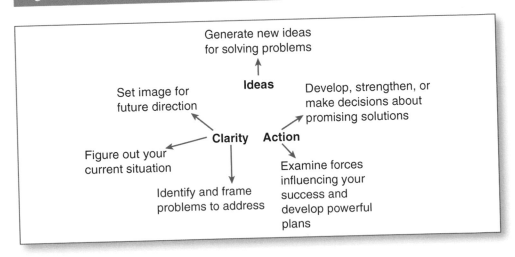

An Example of Matching Process to Need

This small example will help demonstrate what we mean by linking CPS to the needs of a task. Read the paragraph below and imagine that it is your task situation. What CPS component and stage will best help you address the task? Consider the information in the following three sections to help you make your decision. Remember that you are making your best assessment or estimation of the component or stage in CPS to direct your efforts.

> You have a great idea to share with members of your work environment improvement planning committee. You know that it will work because you have tested the idea with a few members of the committee and they liked it. However, you know that the idea needs to be improved before it is ready for implementation. You know the committee will be able to help you strengthen and develop the idea at your next meeting.

What is the task need? What component deals with the purpose suggested by that need? What specific stage or stages might best help you meet that need? What component or stages would you decide to use? (We'll discuss the answer later in this chapter.)

You will make your diagnosis at two levels. First, identify which component is best likely to meet the person's needs. Use Figure 11.1 to refresh your memory of the three possible component needs CPS might address, once you know what component you are in. Second, examine the stages within that component to decide which is the most appropriate stage to use. Use the three component descriptions below to help you determine which stage you would use.

Using Understanding the Challenge. Figure 11.3 identifies specific needs (on the left side of the figure) you can address using each stage in the component (on the right side of the figure). The needs on the left are linked to the stages on the right. Start with the top need and ask yourself if that need best describes what the person wants in the task description above. Read all three need statements in the figure before making your assessment. If the CPS need (on the right) fits with your description, look to the right side of the figure and that will be the recommended stage in which to begin.

Using Generating Ideas. Figure 11.4 provides you with the specific need addressed by the Generating Ideas component and stage. Generating Ideas will help you when you need to produce many alternatives, a wide variety of options, or a number of unusual possibilities. If you need to find ideas for solving a problem, you would use the Generating Ideas component and stage.

Using Preparing for Action. Figure 11.5 provides you with the needs and stage descriptions for the Preparing for Action component. If you need to develop and strengthen a solution, you would use the Developing Solutions stage. If you want to examine the forces influencing your success or to develop a specific plan for managing change, you would use the Building Acceptance stage.

Figure 11.3 Specific Needs Addressed by Understanding the Challenge

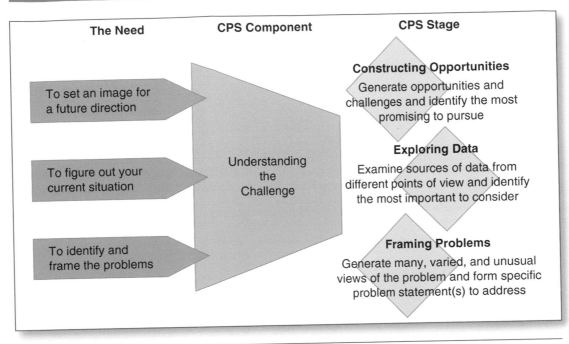

SOURCE: Copyright © 2009. The Creative Problem Solving Group, Inc. and The Center for Creative Learning, Inc. Reprinted with permission.

Figure 11.4 Specific Needs Addressed by Generating Ideas

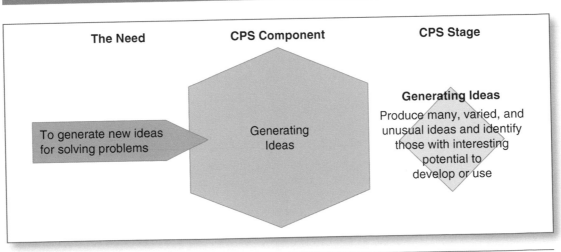

SOURCE: Copyright © 2009. The Creative Problem Solving Group, Inc. and The Center for Creative Learning, Inc. Reprinted with permission.

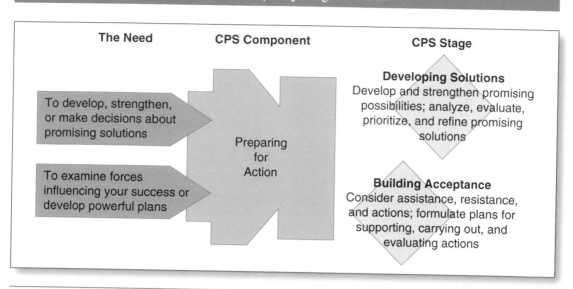

Figure 11.5 Specific Needs Addressed by Preparing for Action

While working, keep two things in mind. First, use this approach to link your need to the process *whenever* you are trying to determine what parts of CPS to use. This may take place when you are planning the initial use of CPS or at any time during your work on a task. Second, be prepared to reassess the situation and to change if you find that your original assessment was not "on target."

Returning to Our Example

Now that you have reviewed the core purposes of each component and stage, go back to the example. Can you identify the best component and stage to use? Briefly, the task statement was "We need to improve our office environment." According to the example, you have an idea that needs to be developed and strengthened before it can be implemented. Your need is to get ready for action. Therefore, the component to use would be Preparing for Action. However, the idea needs to be developed and strengthened before it is ready to be implemented. Therefore, the stage you would use is Developing Solutions.

Making an appropriate assessment about the component or stage to use is a skill that comes with experience. The more you practice, the better you will become. And the more you do it, the better your results will be. It is an essential activity within CPS that makes the method uniquely powerful for stimulating innovation and change.

What Is Designing Process?

Have you ever had the experience of working on a task that was like a dream—a best-case scenario where everything just worked? The task fit with your personal priorities and those of your group. You had clear images of how you were going to work your way through the task. You were clear about your responsibilities and the results you needed to create. People around you agreed about the importance of the task and provided you with the support you needed. You were able to work around people who resisted your efforts. When you encountered obstacles, you handled them in creative ways. Ideas seemed to flow naturally and without much effort. You implemented changes, learned from your mistakes, and made improvements that worked like a charm. The resources you needed were available when you needed them, or when they were not available, you found different ways to get the job done.

Unfortunately, things don't always happen that way. In the worst-case scenario, have you ever worked on a task where you were sidetracked, distracted by low or frequently changing priorities, or constantly bombarded by unforeseen issues? You were unclear about priorities associated with the task, or how others were to be involved. You did not understand your decision-making responsibilities or the need to keep others informed of your work. You felt like you were taking two steps forward and one step back every time you tried to make progress.

Designing Process is the stage in CPS in which you outline a flexible and dynamic plan to help bring your journey on a task to a successful destination (by creating the best-case scenario and avoiding the conditions of the worst case). In a nutshell, you map out your plans and procedures for using CPS to realize your aspirations for a task in three ways as shown in Figure 11.6: (1) linking your need to the process, (2) determining the level of application you need, and (3) designing the scope of application.

Figure 11.6 Designing Process in a Nutshell

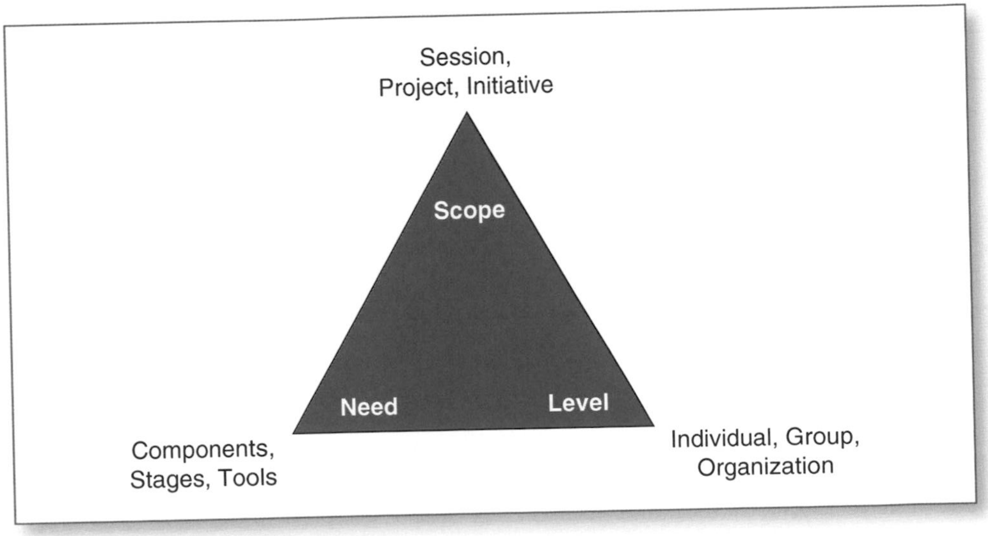

SOURCE: Copyright © 2009. The Creative Problem Solving Group, Inc. and The Center for Creative Learning, Inc. Reprinted with permission.

Although the Designing Process stage is not always explicitly linked to the Appraising Tasks stage, it often functions as a bridge between what you learn when Appraising Tasks and how you will implement CPS. *Input* into Designing Process includes the decision that CPS is an appropriate method to use on the task. With that in mind, you will want to be certain that you have a need for novelty, that you have ownership for the task, and that the task is a priority for you, your group, or your organization. You should also be certain that you are willing to invest the costs to get the benefits CPS can provide.

Your work within the Designing Process stage involves four key areas of processing. These may take place informally or formally and include:

1. determining the scope of CPS application (a session, project, or initiative) necessary to accomplish your desired results;

2. linking your need to the CPS process to determine the most appropriate CPS components, stages, and tools to use;

3. determining your level of application (individual, group, or organizational) so that you can identify and prepare the necessary people for their involvement in CPS application; and

4. using your understanding of the context to choose, locate, and access the appropriate resources to accomplish the task.

The output of your work in Designing Process is a plan for how you will use the CPS framework, language, and tools to help you accomplish your goal. This plan includes how you will involve people and deal with the impact of the context as you pursue the desired results. Although you will have a deliberate plan for using CPS, it is important to keep it flexible so that you can respond to unexpected issues as they arise during your CPS application.

Like the Appraising Tasks stage, the Designing Process stage is part of the "operating system." Therefore, your work in Designing Process is ongoing during your planning and use of CPS. Whether you are at the beginning of a task or halfway through, Designing Process enables you to develop new plans or modify existing plans for how you will use CPS. For example, a special education center within a university participated in an initiative to help redefine state and local government (Reid & Dorval, 1996). The part of the project in which they were involved focused on helping families and children in need receive special assistance from government agencies. We prepared a team from the center to provide training in CPS to caseworkers in their state. These caseworkers were the people who would actually work with the different government agencies to provide services to the families and children in need. The project was originally funded for 1 year. However, because of the positive feedback it received and its impact, it was extended for a second year, then a third year, then a fourth, and ultimately a fifth. Each time the project was extended, its focus shifted to accommodate new issues. The project underwent continuous change during that 5-year period. More people from new organizations received training, the project served new clients, and the participants dealt with a variety of different tasks.

Our ongoing work with the Planning Your Approach component helped us be successful throughout the 5 years (Freeman, Wolfe, Littlejohn, & Mayfield, 2001). It enabled us to monitor and redesign our plan for supporting the special education center's initiative as our work continued. Each time we engaged in Planning Your Approach, we refined and enhanced our plans. The success of the project also laid the foundation for numerous other initiatives (Littlejohn & Mayfield, 2005). The next four sections of this chapter will help you engage in the Designing Process stage. They will help you link the CPS process to your content needs, design your scope of application, design ways to involve people, and consider the impact of the context on your design.

Setting the Scope of CPS Application

Linking your need to the CPS process tells you what parts of CPS to use; designing your scope of application helps you estimate how long and how often you will use CPS on the task. The size or extent of the impact you envision will have a strong influence on how you design your application of CPS. Figure 11.7 identifies three possible levels of application. A small change is one in which there is impact on a limited part of your life or on the people and systems around you. Often, it may be accomplished with a single session using a CPS stage or tool. A larger outcome may have impact on a greater number of people, structures, systems, rules, and policies and, therefore, might require multiple applications of CPS or other approaches over time as part of a project or as an initiative. You need to think about which of the three levels of application you are considering and then design a process for making it happen. Let's examine these three levels in more detail.

Figure 11.7   Three Levels of CPS Application

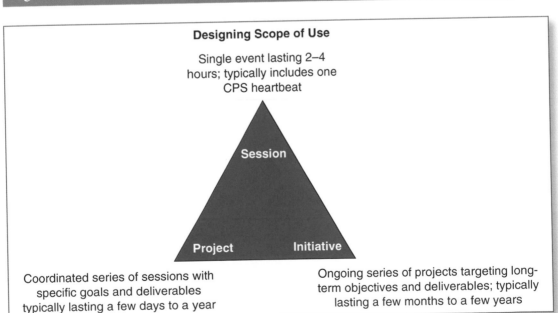

Designing a Single Session

You can design CPS for use in a single session. A session is a single event or meeting designed to use CPS to help accomplish a specific goal or objective related to a task. It typically lasts 60 to 90 minutes and involves one stage of CPS. It is usually best for a task that needs a quick burst of energy or a kick start to get momentum going. It may also be a task on which you are "stuck," have reached a key decision point, or have come across a barrier that needs special attention.

A session has a specific focus or application with a well-defined start and end point. It might take place at your desk, during a group meeting, or during a retreat away from work or home. A session might also take place during a workshop or conference in which problem solving and creativity are needed. In fact, oftentimes, workshops and conferences have multiple sessions taking place over one or more days.

The single session is a very common and productive way in which many people apply CPS. A single session can be useful since it is easily planned, arranged, and implemented; sometimes, it provides ample time to deal with a task successfully. To make any CPS session productive, consider the following factors in your planning.

The Session Purpose and Outcome. It's always important to know what you need to accomplish; therefore, begin by confirming the purpose and outcome of the session. Almost everything else comes from having this clarity of purpose. It tells you why you are holding the session and helps you make decisions about what needs to take place for it to be productive. It will also help you select the appropriate components, stages, and tools. The outcome tells you what you can expect to have as a result of applying CPS. It should be specific and measurable so that you can determine whether you were successful in your application. Having a specific target also helps you know whether you need to apply additional CPS to better hit your targeted outcome.

The CPS Component and Stage to Use. There is no prescribed order or sequence in which to use the CPS components and stages. In fact, you do not usually need to apply all the elements of CPS. Designing a session means identifying which CPS component(s) or stage(s) will help you best meet the needs of the task. We discussed this in greater detail in the Linking Needs to Process section earlier in this chapter.

The Tools to Apply. Different tools accomplish different purposes. Select the generating and/or focusing tool(s) that will enable you to accomplish the specific objectives for the session. Be sure to allow enough time to get maximum productivity from the use of the tools. Resist the temptation to build more tools into your plan than you will have time to use. It's usually better to use a smaller number of tools well than many tools too quickly. Use only the tools you need rather than including tools simply because you prefer them or get excited about their use. Use the models for choosing tools in Chapters 4 and 5 to help make your choices.

Group Involvement. Using CPS in a session includes determining whether you need to involve others in your work. Are you working on an individual task, a task involving a group/team, or a task requiring organizational involvement? If you know that others need to be involved (at a team or organizational level), determine who they are and the roles and responsibilities they will take on. We will discuss this in greater detail in the "Designing Ways to Involve People" section of this chapter.

The Plan for the Session. Be certain to take this step whether you are working on your own or with a group. Developing an actual plan for your personal application of CPS may seem a bit strange. However, being deliberate and explicit about your approach to applying CPS can be very helpful in being efficient and productive, particularly if time is short. Once you know the components, stages, and tools you will be using, create an explicit plan for applying those elements of CPS. Your plan should include what you will do, how you will do it, and by when. Give yourself a deadline with specific results to create by a certain deadline or completion date.

Explicit plans (such as the one in Figure 11.8) become even more important if you involve others. A session plan or agenda helps create a shared understanding of what will happen by when and helps keep people on the same page during a CPS application. Use an agenda or plan to also respond to people's desire to know what they will be doing in a meeting. Be sure to design enough time into the session plan to allow for productive generating and focusing activities for the component(s) or stage(s) you plan to apply.

Figure 11.8   A Design for a Session

> ### Agenda
>
> - Welcome, purpose, and overview
> - Roles and responsibilities
> - Task summary
> - Generating options
> - Focusing options
> - Next steps, closing comments

Tips for Designing a Single Session

Consider the following two tips as you plan and implement your CPS session.

Plan an appropriate balance of generating and focusing. It can be easy to emphasize the generating side of CPS because generating is often fun and energizing for an individual or group. However, people tend to get more value when generation is followed by some form of deliberate focusing, even if the focusing is "light" and will be followed by additional generating activities. This allows time and opportunity for productive incubation of possibilities.

Have other stages and tools ready for use. Surprises or insights often emerge during any CPS session that can stimulate interests that take you in different directions than planned. Although it can be difficult to "know" in advance what other stages might be used, have a general level of readiness (i.e., support materials) to move into other parts of CPS.

Designing a Project Application

Projects are unique tasks involving organized sets of activities directed toward specific goals and objectives. They often include a coordinated series of sessions designed to obtain a specific result or deliverables within a limited time frame. Projects, particularly those that require ongoing creative thinking and problem solving, are fertile soil for your application of CPS. Projects can last anywhere from a few days to about a year. Frequently, they involve interactions with other people, who in their own right may have different priorities, goals, and objectives. Projects also require resources to get them accomplished. Therefore, they often have specific mandates or "charges" attached to them and may also have milestone plans (specifically stated outcomes that will be accomplished at certain times over the life of the project).

Projects often involve bringing novelty into existence. They are typically complex and often have a moderate to high level of ambiguity. Although CPS is not necessary in all aspects of a project, you can use it to support or enhance the efficiency and productivity of various aspects of a project. To make any project productive using CPS, consider the following four factors in your planning.

The High-Level Project Plan. Develop a general plan for how the project will take place. The plan should include the key outcomes you need to accomplish during the project. It should also identify the specific time frames in which they would be produced. These outcomes provide the specific targets that are necessary to be accomplished along your journey through the task. They should be organized and sequenced in a plan that enables the overall outcomes to be accomplished in the time frames required.

The Parts of the Project Involving CPS. Some parts of a project can benefit from CPS, while others may not. As Figure 11.9 demonstrates, some parts of the project (the boxes in the figure) have a CPS element within them and others do not. Identify those parts of the project where you need help developing new thinking that require untangling of complex issues or clarifying ambiguous situations. Identify what the particular part of the project needs and then plan to use the component or stage of CPS that meets that need. Then, design your use of CPS for those as you would for designing a session. Remember that you can also use CPS to address unexpected issues or surprises that arise during the project.

Figure 11.9 A Design for a Project

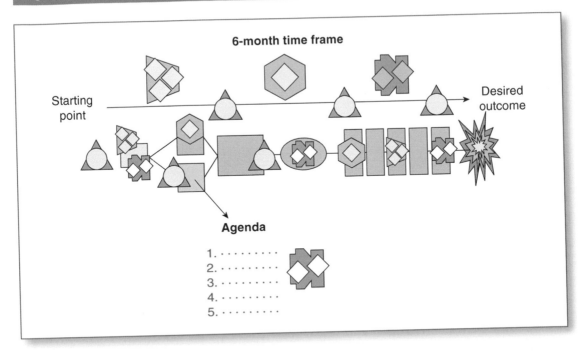

The Involvement of Different People Along the Way. Projects often involve other people. However, they may be involved in different ways. Some steps may require certain people to be involved (e.g., with particular task expertise). Others may benefit from having a diversity of people involved. Identify how you want to involve people in each step of the project. Be prepared to inform people about the roles and responsibilities they will take on when involved.

Scheduling (People, Time, Locations, etc.). Managing the use of CPS at a project level involves the typical logistics associated with managing meetings. Develop plans and schedules for who needs to be involved, when the meetings will take place, where they will be located, and so on. Be sure to inform all involved about these plans and details.

Tips for Designing Project Applications

Consider the following three tips as you plan and implement your use of CPS.

Design flexibility into your project plans. We've mentioned it before, and we're mentioning it again: It is important to be flexible in your planning and use of CPS. You may know this from personal experience participating in or managing projects. The longer a project takes to complete, the greater the likelihood that things will change; new people get involved, people leave, project objectives change, new project opportunities present themselves, new constraints emerge, and so on. Since unpredicted events happen, build your plan to predict, understand, and capitalize on changes and ensuring successful outcomes. This can be done by designing your use of Appraising Tasks and Designing Process throughout the project.

Plan links between multiple sessions. Project applications of CPS involve the added challenge of linking various sessions and activities together. Although it is not always necessary to use CPS on every aspect, a project is likely to involve multiple and repeated applications of CPS. It involves using whatever components, stages, or tools are necessary to address issues as they arise. You may face similar issues more than once and, therefore, require multiple use of the same CPS elements.

The outputs from one session should help you define the inputs into the next. Therefore, your design for any one session should serve as a springboard to guide you in planning additional work or another session. Rather than thinking about a self-contained application that results in total resolution of the issue or completion of the project, each session should contribute to the momentum and keep you engaged in the project.

Design for extended effort. Projects provide you with a unique opportunity to build extended effort into your design. Extended effort is the concept of investing the sustained time and energy necessary to increase the likelihood of obtaining the novelty you want. You can extend your effort during generation by working deliberately to get beyond everyday thinking and stretching to create unusual options. Extending effort during focusing involves spending the time needed to screen, select, develop, and strengthen the novel options you generated. Therefore, if the project on which you apply CPS involves high levels of novelty, remember to provide sufficient time to think up novel responses and then to analyze and develop the options fully to make them useful. Extended effort can involve time during specific sessions or additional time between sessions.

Designing an Initiative

Some tasks are so large that they require a large-scale change effort to get them accomplished. For example, an organization may need to develop and strengthen its existing product and services portfolio, or a school system might seek to modify its management and administrative organization and structure at all levels. We use the term *initiative* to refer to a long-term approach or effort taken to accomplish a high-level strategic goal, purpose, or imperative. Initiatives can last from a few months to a few years and often involve introducing change that has far-reaching or transformational impact on an individual, a group, or an entire organization (or even a nation). President Kennedy set a very large-scale initiative in motion when he said that "We would put a man on the moon by the end of the decade" (1960s).

Initiatives differ from projects in that they are typically much longer in duration. They involve outcomes that are larger and also more complex and ambiguous than projects. They are ongoing in that they do not have predetermined, clear endpoints or completion dates. They involve multiple and different kinds of projects—each with its own start and end time. They involve many different kinds of activities, events, procedures, or actions taking place during simultaneous projects or projects that happen one after the other. As a result, they often involve more people, a variety of functions, several departments, or an entire organization. There are some unique issues to consider when designing the application of CPS at an initiative level.

The Goals and Strategies for the Initiative. It is important to have a clear understanding of your goals and objectives whenever you invest your time, energy, and resources to make a change happen. This is particularly the case when planning and implementing an initiative, since initiatives often require large amounts of investment to complete. Identify goals and objectives explicitly and use them to make decisions about what is done during the initiative.

The General Plan for Guiding the Initiative. Use your understanding of what needs to take place during the initiative to create a plan for guiding the overall initiative. The plan should include the general stages that will be completed throughout the initiative. Then, use your understanding of the purposes for each part of the initiative to select the CPS component to guide that particular part.

Time Frames and Outcomes of Projects. Initiatives usually include multiple projects. These projects may take place in sequence or in parallel. In either case, be sure to schedule the different projects so that the outcomes of one project lead into or support work conducted in subsequent projects. Also, be sure that the outcomes of each project link with the overall objectives for that part of the initiative.

Plan for How People Will Be Involved. It is not always possible or necessary to have the same people involved in every aspect of the initiative. You will need to consider as part of your plan who is to be involved at what parts of the initiative. You should be clear about the roles they will play and the responsibilities they will take on during the project.

Tips for Designing an Initiative-Level Application of CPS

Consider the following four tips as you plan and implement an initiative using CPS.

Keep your general plan at a CPS component level. If things change during projects, imagine how much they can change during an initiative. Having a design helps you guide the overall direction of activities associated with accomplishing the initiative's strategic goal. However, it is likely that the elements you design into the overall process will need to be changed in some way during the life of the initiative. Keep the initiative design at a high level of abstraction, focusing on the CPS components (see Figure 11.10 for an example of a high-level initiative design). The general-level design is more likely to be stable over time

Figure 11.10   A Design for an Initiative

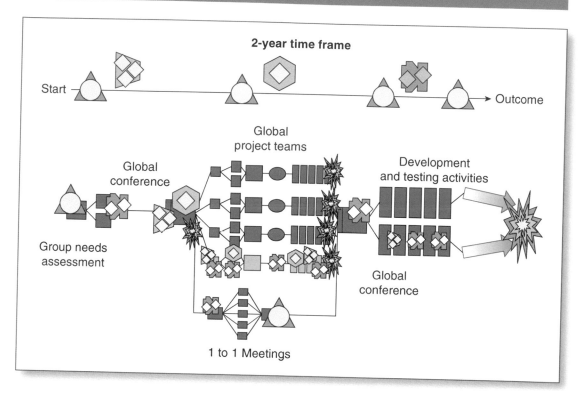

than the specific elements contained within. Be ready to plan the stage applications as the initiative progresses.

Design for consistent project outputs. Initiatives consist of different projects. Therefore, one of the additional challenges of designing at an initiative level over a project level is to ensure that the outcomes from different projects are consistent with the overall goals and objectives of the initiative. When outputs of different projects are woven together, they need to fit.

Plan for changing involvement of people. As initiatives live on, the people involved in them often change. It is also important to design into your plan guidelines for how you will integrate new people into the initiative, as well as how you will deal with the gaps created from people leaving the initiative. Remember that when new people become involved, you will need to bring them up to speed both with the initiative itself and with how you are using CPS. You may also want to build steps into your design where you can educate people who join the initiative.

Plan check-in points throughout the initiative. The longer an initiative lives, the greater the likelihood that it will go astray from its original purpose or intent. Check-in points enable you to take stock of the current status of the initiative, check to ensure that changes desired are actually taking place, reexamine its goals and objectives, and consider potential changes in people or priorities to ensure its continued productivity. A natural place to schedule these check-in points is at key milestones throughout the general plan for the initiative.

Designing Ways to Involve People

There are also a number of issues to consider when you plan to involve people in your use of CPS, many of which were presented in Chapter 7. Designing how to involve people will depend on whether you plan on using CPS alone, in a group, or at an organizational level. If you decide to involve others, you will need to determine the best way they can support your efforts. This section will take the information from Chapter 7 and help you consider its implications for using CPS at the three levels. We will also help you clarify the roles and responsibilities people will need to assume if you decide to involve others.

Determine Your Level of Use

Part of the power of CPS is that you can use it personally, within or across groups, or at an organizational level (see Figure 11.11). Designing process is about knowing the level at which you will be using CPS and then designing your journey through the process in a way that best fits the level of application you intend. To determine whether

Figure 11.11 From an Individual to an Organization: Designing Level of Use

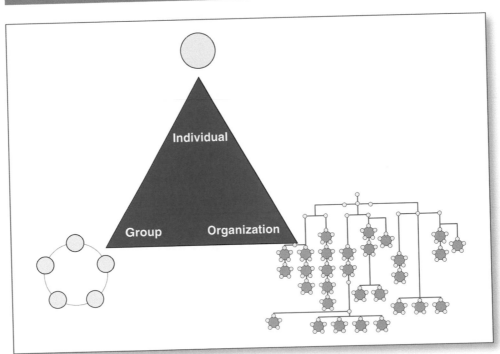

you have a task that is best handled alone, might benefit from using a group, or needs to take place at an organizational level, consider the following issues.

Using CPS at an Individual Level. Some tasks are best handled alone. For example, the task may be meaningful only to you, too personal to share with others, or involve a level of confidentiality that does not allow you to share it with others. In these situations, CPS can help you get the best from your own thinking by being explicit and deliberate in your own creativity and decision making. At a personal level, you can design your use of CPS to

- help you improve your understanding and use of your own creative abilities,
- understand your own skills and style preferences,
- address life management challenges,
- engage in career and financial planning, and
- develop and maintain personal relationships or even to engage in self-renewal.

In these situations, design your use of CPS depending on what you want to accomplish personally. Use CPS flexibly wherever and whenever you want. It will usually be helpful if you invest the energy to be deliberate and explicit about your use of the CPS framework, language, and tools. You already know how to solve problems using your natural process (as you discovered in Chapter 2). Therefore, challenge yourself to enhance or expand your natural skills by using CPS explicitly and deliberately.

Using CPS at the Group or Team Level. In other situations, you can benefit from involving others in your application of CPS. Groups and teams alike can benefit greatly from your use of CPS. In fact, Osborn created the early versions of CPS to help people get the best from groups.

We have been using the words *group* and *team* almost interchangeably throughout this book. It may be helpful to mention here that there are some fundamental differences between groups and teams and that CPS can be used with either. As Katzenbach and Smith (2003) described, a group is a collection or assembly of individuals. Groups can be small or large with group members getting together because of common needs and interests. In some cases, nothing more may hold them together than a common zip code. A team, on the other hand, is a small number of people with complementary skills who are committed to a common purpose, set of performance goals, and approach for which they hold themselves mutually accountable. High-functioning teams have members who can think and act interdependently when problem solving. As teams develop, their members build emotional connections to each other that help raise the individual performance level of each individual team member. As a result, effective teams think creatively, make decisions, solve problems, and implement action more efficiently and productively per unit of time than low-functioning teams.

You can use CPS to help both groups and teams engage in creative thinking and problem solving. In fact, one benefit of applying CPS with groups is that it can help turn them into high-functioning teams. At a group or team level, you can design your use of CPS to

- help improve interactions among team members,
- get better productivity from people's individual strengths and styles,
- manage team projects more efficiently, and
- increase collaboration in team decision-making and problem-solving activities.

In these situations, design your use of CPS to get the best from all the people involved. By using CPS, you can increase the quality of a group's decision making and problem solving by considering diverse viewpoints and avoiding gaps in information. However, using CPS with groups may also require you to do more planning. You may need to clarify people's roles and responsibilities, schedule their time to use the process, or weave CPS into existing meetings. You may also need to find common space in which people can come together to use the tools. You may even need to plan time for the group to learn some of the CPS language and tools so that they can be productive with its application.

If you have an interest in learning more about using CPS to enhance the power of groups, read Isaksen and Dorval (2000) or Isaksen and Shephard (2008). Additional references about CPS facilitation are included at the end of this book. You may also want to attend one of our Igniting Creative Potential: A Focus on Facilitation courses (check out CPSB's Web site at www.cpsb.com for the current schedule).

Using CPS at the Organizational Level. Still other tasks may best be addressed at an organizational level. CPS can be used when the tasks become so large that you need the involvement and interaction of people from across different departments, functions, or cultures. At this level, CPS can help you to

- drive organizational change efforts,
- develop new products and services,
- bring new life into existing products and services,
- invigorate your organizational research and development work,
- develop human resources, and
- appreciate and manage diversity.

For these tasks, design the CPS application to take into account the full range of the organization's diversity, both in people (as we described in Chapter 7) and in context (as we described in Chapter 8). CPS can help you build collaboration and productivity across the boundaries of function or culture that often occur among people. Your design should support learning about the language and tools on a broad scale. Your plan should also show how you will gain support from the groups involved in using CPS—particularly when you will be developing and using CPS as a common approach to solving problems across functions and departments.

Clarify People's Roles and Responsibilities

You may choose to involve other people for any number of different reasons: for general energy and support, for their task expertise, because they own part of the task, because you need their help with implementation, for novel perspectives to shift your mind-set, or for help in managing process. Whatever the reason, be certain to clarify who takes on what roles and responsibilities and prepare them for doing so. Have you ever been involved in a project where you thought you had more decision-making responsibilities than you actually had? This can be terribly frustrating, and it can seriously hamper the motivation and productivity of the people involved. Clarifying roles and responsibilities may not be an issue if you are using CPS on your own. However, it becomes essential when others are involved. We examine these roles in more detail in Isaksen and Dorval (2000) and Isaksen and Shephard (2008).

You can involve people in the role of client, facilitator, or resource group member (see Figure 11.12). These are specific social roles, not "permanent" titles or positions; they are only meaningful in particular social settings in which CPS is involved. You take on one of these roles when you are involved in planning or applying CPS. You might be a client for one application of CPS and a resource group member for another. Design your application of CPS knowing that people's roles can change as they work on different parts of a task and be ready to let people know the specific roles and responsibilities they will have at any time.

Figure 11.12 The Roles of Client, Facilitator, and Resource Group Member

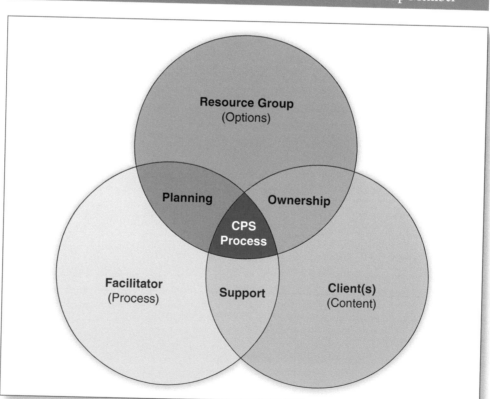

Involving Clients. Some tasks may require you to take on the role of client or the person who is responsible for the task itself. You will need the authority to make decisions about the content, and you must be capable of driving the content in different directions. Clients are also responsible for taking the results of the CPS application forward. Therefore, you must have ownership (interest, influence, and imagination) to be an effective client (as we described in Chapter 7).

For some tasks, you might be the only client involved, but for other tasks, you might share your clientship with others who have equal responsibility. Your CPS design must consider whether or not you have sole clientship or shared clientship with others because decisions about the content will determine the design for applying CPS. Everyone involved in the client's role needs to understand the plan for using CPS to address the task. This usually means an explicit use of the Designing Process stage involving all the clients. Often, the most valuable outcome is aligning the group of clients so that there are clearly shared outcomes.

Involving Resource Group Members. Some situations require you (or whoever is the client) to have the help of others in providing you with alternatives and energy for getting your task accomplished. In these cases, it is appropriate to involve a resource group. Resource group members should be selected based on their ability and desire to provide the client with input, suggestions, or feedback on the task at hand. They provide energy, interest, and imagination to help the client work successfully on the task. You will need to design your process so that you (or the client) get the best from resource group members' contributions. Some people may be resource group members for certain parts of a CPS application and not for other parts. However, when you do involve people, they need to know their roles and responsibilities in order to contribute productively.

Although using a resource group can be productive, it is not necessary to have one when you use CPS. Table 11.1 identifies the benefits and liabilities of using resource

Table 11.1 Some Assets and Liabilities of Using CPS With Groups

Potential Assets	Potential Liabilities
Provides extensive availability of knowledge and information	Limits contributions and increases conformity due to social pressures
Increases the likelihood of building and improving on the thinking of others	Encourages focusing on options with greatest agreement, regardless of quality
Provides a wide range of experiences to stimulate novel perspectives	Provides dominant individuals undue influence and impact on outcome
Increased understanding improves acceptance and commitment	Reduces accountability, allowing for riskier decisions
Provides opportunities for communication, teaming, and group development	Causes unproductive levels of competition from conflicting opinions

groups. For example, they can help provide varied perspectives that the client may not have. However, they also require additional energy to manage in order to use everyone's time wisely.

In considering the makeup of a resource group, it can be difficult to know who should participate. You might select people who can provide highly novel perspectives on the task. You might want to involve people who will be key to implementing the results of the CPS application or people who are available for multiple meetings in which the task will be addressed. Use a resource group only when their involvement will contribute to your primary purposes and goals and when the benefits make the costs worthwhile. Figure 11.13 identifies some of the guidelines to consider when selecting resource group members.

Figure 11.13   Guidelines for Selecting Resource Group Members

Will the person:

- Provide novel perspectives on the task?
- Be involved in the implementation of the task?
- Have domain-relevant knowledge of the task?
- Be at the same level in the organization as other resource group members?
- Commit to taking on the role and responsibilities of a resource group member?
- Be able to work effectively with other resource group members?
- Be able to take the needed time for the meeting, session, or other form of CPS application?
- Have the willingness, ability, and opportunity to bring something to the application of CPS that the client may find both novel and useful?

Involving Facilitators. If you take on the role of the facilitator, you will be responsible for leading the process. Facilitators are responsible for designing, planning, and managing the use of the CPS framework, language, and tools. They identify the needs of the task, develop a process plan for accomplishing the desired outcomes, select tools, and implement the tools to get the work done. They identify the components and stages of CPS to be used on the task. They also identify and plan for the use of specific tools to enable the kind of thinking necessary to get the work done.

Whether you use CPS on your own or in a group setting, encourage all the people involved to give their best efforts to using their creativity and decision-making and problem-solving skills. An effective resource group requires a supportive climate. The facilitator plays an important role in establishing and maintaining that climate. Thus, the facilitator should have a general understanding of the issues discussed in Chapter 8 and their implications for using CPS.

You can take on the facilitator's role when you apply CPS on your own or when you are helping others with their task. If it is your task (i.e., you are the client) and you want to involve a resource group, we recommend having someone else assume the facilitator role. It is usually best for you to be able to concentrate on one thing at a time, and do it well. Leading the direction of the content, making decisions about the process, managing the people in your group, and building a context for creativity is too much for one person to handle.

As you develop your design for using CPS, be sure to identify who should participate and in what role in each activity. Remember, taking on any one role is often enough for one person to handle at a time. Therefore, identify one role per person at any point in your design.

Designing for the Impact of Context

Whether you use CPS personally, in a group, or at an organizational level, for a session, a project, or an initiative, your CPS efforts will be affected by all the context issues we discussed in Chapter 8. Designing for the impact of context means that you use your understanding of the specific context (its readiness, willingness, and ability to change) to guide and manage your CPS efforts. You can have a very exciting image of what you want to create, but if the context is not supportive, you will have a difficult time getting it implemented.

The context for your task involves many different forces that will have an influence on your work, some of which you know and understand, and others which are unknown, unexpected, or untested. You may know about these forces from conducting a task appraisal, or they might simply be apparent from your general knowledge of the context surrounding your task. To help you plan for the impact of context, consider the following three issues when you design your process.

Designing for Readiness

Have you identified the impact the climate, culture, and history surrounding the task will have on your efforts? Consider the readiness of people in the context to accept your use of CPS. You may find that some people or groups are more open and accepting of your use of CPS than others. Designing Process involves using your understanding of the context surrounding your task to design the optimal use of CPS. This includes taking into account the pockets of support or resistance within the context. These sources of support or resistance may come from people's historical experiences with the task, a culture that does not support what you are trying to accomplish, or a climate that resists new thinking or problem solving in creative ways. Your plan should identify proactive and affirmative ways to address these issues. You may even consider the application of the Situational Outlook Questionnaire® to obtain a more detailed understanding of the climate.

How can you involve people who are supportive of your efforts? How can you address any resistance in ways that turn the resistance into assistance? For example, you might plan to use CPS in informal ways where there is resistance and more formally where there is support. Your plan might include specific steps to link or pair the people who are resistant with others who are supportive.

Designing for Willingness

Consider the priority of your task or its connection to the support of key leadership groups. If the task is high in priority and supported by key leadership in the group or organization, you may have the opportunity (and the need) to concentrate your time and energy on getting it done in a timely and efficient manner. However, this is not always the case, and you may need to find the time and energy to get the job done—over and above your real work (the official tasks for which you are responsible). How are you planning to access the leadership support for your efforts to promote change? What can you do to involve key players who share your goals? On the other hand, if the task is lower in priority, you may need to design into your process smaller, less time-consuming applications, over a longer time frame, to conserve energy and concentrate your efforts on the highest leverage points.

Designing for Ability

Your CPS design must also consider the resources available to support your application of CPS. You may have the desire, need, and time to design a CPS plan but not have the time, attention, or resources necessary to implement it. Lack of time, attention, and resources may result from too many demands on you or others, which makes it difficult for them (or you) to commit the necessary support to accomplish your task in the desired time.

You may need to build into your design how you will acquire the necessary sponsorship from key change leaders to support the implementation of your design. You may need to craft your design to allow for actually applying CPS when the resources become available. You may also need to plan for using CPS in less supportive parts of the organization to build long-term commitment to your efforts.

Your challenge is to understand enough about the context in which your task resides so that you can "optimize" your efforts (or give yourself the best possible chances for success) when you implement your plans. Designing for the impact of context will help you avoid being surprised or sidetracked by unexpected issues that detract from your ability to accomplish your desired outcomes when you implement your plan.

Designing Your Work Space

At a more specific level, it will be important to design the work space in which you will be applying CPS. There may be tasks for which a very informal design is best and others when you find a more formal design to be more suitable. Your decisions about items such as space, setting, and furniture can be very important in setting an appropriate tone for the work you will be doing. For example, some environments are better suited for applying creative thinking and problem solving. If the topic is serious, you may want to select an environment in which you are comfortable thinking about serious topics. If you are looking to create a playful environment, find a site that encourages playful thinking and acting.

When you involve a group in CPS, you will need to consider a greater number of issues. These include things such as the participants' ability to get to the site, sufficient space for everyone to be comfortable, and an environment in which everyone can feel ready, willing, and able to use their creativity. The space should be large enough for people to work in various groupings (individually, in pairs and small groups, or as a whole group) and should usually have ample wall space to display information the group might need or generate during their work together. An informal design often involves soft chairs, sofas, or similar informal furniture, with small tables or work areas, and it resembles a "living room" or "den." A more formal design often uses a conference room, with straight chairs and round or rectangular conference room tables.

You may face the challenge of working with others who do not share a common space (distributed teams, numerous locations, etc.). When this is the case, it is even more important to be well organized and deliberate for when you are at the same place and time. There are also numerous collaborative software programs you can use to hold virtual CPS sessions. Many organizations have intranet resources that can be applied or modified to allow for this as well.

Some Suggestions for Designing Process

Designing effective CPS applications requires careful planning and the consideration of many different factors, particularly as tasks become larger and more complex. We showed you how to link your need to the CPS process so that you know what parts of CPS to apply. We examined three different levels of scope of application (session, project, and initiative) to help you plan your effort and energy efficiently. We also looked at how you might involve people in using CPS, as clients, resource members, or facilitators. Finally, we identified several ways to consider context factors as you plan your use of CPS.

The following three suggestions will help you increase your power and productivity when you design and implement your plans.

Design With Purpose in Mind

Clarity of purpose requires being mindful in your planning and implementation of CPS. Have a clear purpose in mind whenever you decide to include anything in your plan. Be clear about why you intend to use any of the CPS components, stages, or tools at any point in your work. In addition, be clear about why you might involve any particular individual or group, or why you might choose to focus your efforts on a particular leverage point in the task. If you are unclear about why something or someone is part of your design, question yourself and get the clarity you need. Lack of clarity can result in wasted time, energy, and effort by working in ways that do not add value to your results. If, when you are part way through your plan, you realize that some steps are not needed, or no longer add value, then remove them, change your design, and restructure your approach before you continue along your journey.

Design a Straightforward Pathway Through CPS

Oftentimes, the most productive way through a situation is the most obvious and straightforward. As you plan, look for the shortest and simplest path. We use the word simple here not to mean trivial but to mean clear, transparent, and easy to understand and follow. For example, if you can accomplish an objective in two steps rather than three, then plan for two steps. If you can accomplish it with one other person rather than three other people, plan for involving one other person. Avoid the temptation to apply components, stages, or tools just because you want to see how they work or because you really enjoy using them. Use only what you need to accomplish your desired results.

Be Ready to Change Your Plans

Remember that your plan represents your best understanding of the task at that moment in time. As your understanding of the task changes, or as you make progress on the task, your plans may need to change as well. Therefore, be ready to change your plans as you move forward. Simply because your design is written on a piece of paper or in your computer doesn't mean that it is (or should be) permanent or unchangeable. In fact, we suggest that you look for opportunities to change, update, modify, or improve your design. Method serves content, so as your understanding of the content changes, so too might your use of the method. We often explain this to our participants in our courses as "preplanned flexibility."

The Rest of the Story

Remember the consumer goods company we spoke about at the start and end of Chapter 10? We learned some important lessons about Designing Process during our work with that organization. As you recall, we had our hands full with a very complex situation. We had 35 highly competent people, working on a global challenge to leapfrog ahead of the competition with the development of fundamentally new products. We had people from a variety of different disciplines who brought their unique knowledge, expertise, and methods to bear on the task. Our challenge was to design a process that would integrate all these factors in a way that accomplished the goals and objectives of the project effectively and efficiently.

We used CPS as the overall framework to integrate all the activities, people, and methods. We broke the project down into phases and confirmed the outcomes associated with each phase. We used our understanding of the desired outcomes to weave CPS into each session. Unexpected issues emerged throughout the life of the project, providing us with many chances to apply CPS on new challenges. The process we designed for the original project was clear, deliberate, and repeatable, so much so that we were able to return 5 years later to plan and implement a session to help the project managers develop another round of testably different new product concepts. The process plan for that follow-up session fit nicely into the original project design.

Today, the project has turned into a self-sustaining initiative to develop radically new product concepts for the organization. People in the organization gained so many powerful insights from the work that they continue to train new researchers in the exploratory approaches to consumer research developed during the project. People involved in the project are also training people from other organizations in the use of the proprietary approaches to new product development.

This chapter has been about helping you design your journey through CPS. Since CPS is aimed at enhancing your natural creative process, you can apply it in many different ways. The Designing Process stage of the Planning Your Approach management component can help you consider many of the key factors that will help you consider successful applications of CPS.

The following chapter outlines some examples of CPS application and illustrates how the Planning Your Approach component guides the use of the framework, guidelines, and tools. It also includes a few resources to continue your learning about our current version of CPS.

Putting This Chapter to Work

The goals of this chapter were to explore the Designing Process stage of CPS and to tailor your application of CPS to the needs of a task. We highlighted three key issues associated with tailoring CPS application—setting the scope of your application, designing how you involve people with its use, and determining your level of application.

Activities to Guide Reflection and Action

Work on one or more of the following activities to review your understanding of the material in this chapter and to practice applying the content in real situations. If you are using this book as part of a course or study group, you may wish to work individually, and then compare your responses, or to work collaboratively as a team.

1. Reflect on two situations in which you were a member of a group working on a task. The first situation was a best-case scenario in which everyone on the team was on the same page about the process to address the work being done. The group's focus was clear and productivity was high. The second was a worst-case scenario. The group was filled with members who had their own unique perspectives for how the work should be done. Their multiple and conflicting processes caused productivity to suffer. Consider what the core qualities of the situation were that caused it to be a best- or worst-case scenario. Compare and contrast the two situations. How did the concepts we discussed in this chapter play out in each situation?

2. Identify a situation in which you experienced the leader of a group take on the roles of both content and process leader. Consider what took place during the group's work when the leader held both the facilitator and client roles. Identify what worked for the leader and what challenges the leader faced when holding both roles. Identify what actions the leader might have taken to better manage the multiple roles. What are the implications for taking on both roles?

3. Identify a situation you are currently facing for which you have ownership (interest, influence, and imagination) and on which CPS could be appropriately applied. Considering the needs of the task, identify which component you believe would be the most appropriate place to begin CPS application. Explain your rationale for the decision. Considering the component, identify the stage best suited as your starting place and present a rationale for that decision.

4. For the situation in #3, consider whether you would be designing the use of CPS for a session, a project, or an initiative. Identify the factors that would influence your decision and why those factors are relevant. Describe how you would need to alter your design if your focus were a session versus a project versus an initiative?

Applying CPS

Destiny is not a matter of chance, it is a matter of choice; it is not a thing to be waited for, it is a thing to be achieved.

—William Jennings Bryan

The purpose of this chapter is to provide you with examples of Creative Problem Solving (CPS) application and recommendations for helping you apply CPS successfully. As a result of reading this chapter, you will be able to do the following:

1. Describe the importance of focusing on the people, context, method, and outcome to improve your application of CPS.

2. Use real-life accounts of CPS applications to illustrate the impact of people, context, and content on your application of CPS.

3. Explain and give examples of CPS applications at the session, project, or program level, and describe their implications for effective practice.

4. List 10 suggestions for applying CPS effectively into your own plans to increase your productivity and success in using CPS.

Some earlier versions of CPS were applied only in a lockstep, sequential manner. You started "at the beginning" of the process (typically called "fact finding") and worked your way through each of its stages. You "ran through" the entire process each time you used it. As a result, the process often seemed to take on a life and special importance of its own. Through research, development, and practical experiences, however, we have continued to learn new ways to apply CPS effectively. Today, following the "one size fits all," lockstep approach would be like using an abacus or a slide rule instead of a calculator or computer to do mathematical operations (see Figure 12.1).

Figure 12.1   From the Abacus to the Computer

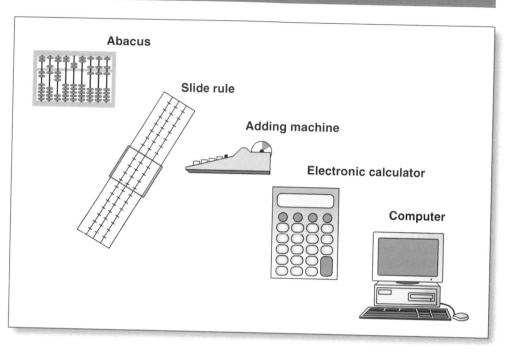

To be sure, you could use the abacus or the slide rule, but in most cases, today's engineers or scientists are much more likely to use the most effective and efficient tools available to them. The same holds true with our contemporary version of CPS; the power of CPS today is far greater than that of its earlier versions.

Contemporary versions of CPS approach the process differently from their predecessors. The emergence of the Planning Your Approach component is probably one of the most significant ways that CPS today differs from earlier versions. It is the component of CPS that enables you to determine whether it is appropriate to use CPS at all, and if so, to decide what components and stages you need initially and throughout your work. This addition to CPS is important because it helps you make an informed, deliberate decision about how to tailor your use of CPS, which may be particularly helpful when not all the components and stages are necessary. Using the Planning Your Approach component enables you to examine, understand, and consider four important elements (people, content, context, and the CPS method itself) in order to make decisions about CPS and its application.

Effective people and organizations focus their attention on all four elements when they make change happen. For example, Davis (2000) pointed out that top-performing organizations created products (and services) by paying attention to the people involved, the climate for creativity and change, and the methods associated with innovation (the commercialization of new ideas). One key message from this study is that these organizations concentrated on all those elements, not just one or a few of them. When they didn't pay attention to the entire system, things did not go as well as planned. We believe that the same principles apply to educational, nonprofit, and government organizations as well as to businesses.

From our experience, people pay a great deal of attention to the desired outcomes they pursue. And why not? Content performance is usually the main indicator of our success or failure. Whether it involves students' test scores and academic achievement or the revenue generation from a product or service, we pay intense attention to the results we want to create—sometimes to the extent that we pay far too little attention to the people, the context, or the methods involved in creating the results.

A study conducted by Arthur D. Little (Loos, 1994) demonstrates this point. Researchers interviewed 350 top executives from a variety of North American industries in which there were major change efforts. The top six barriers or hurdles to the success of their change efforts all focused on the buy-in and acceptance of the change by the people involved. When asked what he would have done differently, one executive said he would have helped managers and employees see what was in it (the change) for them. Lack of attention to the change methods they used was another common barrier. For example, some of the senior executives suggested that they thought they knew the best methods to use for a project but discovered that they had really failed to think through the likely stumbling blocks along the way.

Similar challenges arise when an organization loses its focus on the context. Have you ever been in a situation where organizational changes were taking place that made it somewhat "dangerous" to try something new or different (e.g., during downsizing, rightsizing, or cost-reduction exercises)? We observed this within a global petroleum company. They engaged in a 2-year initiative to implement a new vision in one of their departments of 3,200 people. We measured the climate for creativity 18 months into the initiative and noticed significant decreases in people's perceptions of risk-taking behavior. Many people had lost their jobs or were outsourced. As a result, those who remained in the department were afraid to take risks because they learned during the downsizing activities that if they failed, it was not a big step for the company to lay them off (since they were letting people go anyway). As a result, the senior management team initiated efforts to positively affect the working climate after the change initiative in order to rekindle people's desire to try new things, take risks, and use their creativity in the business.

There are many examples of what happens when people do not attend to all four elements when creating change. More important, however, there are also examples of the value of focusing on all the elements. We will share three such examples to illustrate how you can focus on all four and to highlight the impact you can have with CPS when you do. They demonstrate how you can use CPS in a single session, within a project, and to support an initiative. They also provide examples of how you can use CPS at an individual level, within a group or team, and at an organizational level. After presenting the stories, we will offer four recommendations to help you prepare to use CPS and 12 suggestions for increasing the power and impact of your work with CPS. Additional case studies and examples are available on our Web site (www.cpsb.com).

Lost Prizes

This is a story about the application of CPS by a group of educators who were concerned about the problem of at-risk adolescents dropping out of school. It involves an application of CPS in a single group session.

In a regional consortium of several school districts, several administrators were concerned about the number of at-risk students who had either dropped out of school or were about to do so. These students were capable of being successful learners, but they often found the school setting socially, emotionally, or intellectually unpleasant and not motivating. The greater their dissatisfaction grew, the more frequently they became involved in behavioral problems and conflicts with teachers and with other students, which, in turn, heightened their dissatisfaction and often led to poor academic performance. The concerned adults realized that the future life and career prospects were very poor for young people who became school dropouts. Students who failed to complete their education would seriously harm their future career prospects, and many dropouts were at risk of becoming involved in gangs or criminal activities. The adults also knew that many of these young people had talents and potentials that might go unrecognized and undeveloped to the youths' disadvantage as well as to the ultimate disadvantage of society.

What Did the Participants in the Session Do?

The participants, who were all professionals from the consortium districts, applied CPS to explore ways to deal with this unproductive situation and, if possible, to identify steps to prevent the problem in the future. In a 2-day session, they used the Understanding the Challenge component to clarify the situation and to frame a problem statement to guide their future efforts. They compared their current reality and desired future state and considered many possible Opportunity Statements. As they used the 5WH tool in Exploring Data, the term *gift* was used frequently, and the group members observed that, far from "gifts," these students were often viewed by others in the schools as nuisances, troublemakers, or misfits, or in other undesirable terms. The group members also observed that many of the students had become so negative and lacking in self-esteem that they did not view themselves as having any worthwhile strengths or talents. As the group applied focusing tools, such as Highlighting, the concept of "reclaiming lost prizes" (as it was expressed by one of the group members) began to emerge as a key issue. The students had lost the sense of their own personal "prizes" (their own strengths and talents), and if they could not be reclaimed, valuable prizes would be lost to society, too.

The session led to the development of the idea for the Lost Prizes project. The initial session led to a constructive and forward-looking understanding of the challenge. As part of their preparation for the session, the administrators had studied the content by reading about at-risk students and by talking with a number of students, teachers, parents, and community leaders. They also decided that, given the need for new solutions and a broad level of impact, CPS offered a promising method. They determined that they had ownership for the task and that they had the expertise within their consortium to plan an innovative program and to prepare a funding proposal.

What Challenges Did the Participants Face?

This task, like so many complex social problems and issues, was initially surrounded by frustration, negative experiences and attitudes, and anxieties for many different stakeholders. The students were unhappy, as were the school personnel, the parents, and other community members and agencies. By using the Understanding the Challenge components and stages, the group was able to create a constructive approach to framing the task and to approach their future efforts in a positive way. The administrators also knew that they would face several challenges—overcoming resistance from some teachers and students, arranging activities outside the typical school setting, and establishing a positive climate for learning, for example.

What Impact Did CPS Have?

Subsequently, the group worked on a number of other tasks that led to extensive government funding for a multischool, multiyear initiative, the results of which have been reported elsewhere (McCluskey, Baker, O'Hagan, & Treffinger, 1995; McCluskey & Treffinger, 1998, 2002; Place, McCluskey, McCluskey, & Treffinger, 2000). The project has been successful in helping many young people from the participating communities complete their secondary education (using a variety of alternative pathways), to develop effective life management skills, to find employment or move into postsecondary study opportunities, and to discover and apply their personal talents. Through the project or one of its subsequent "spin-off" programs, recidivism among youthful offenders was reduced substantially, and many young people have been able to turn their lives in positive directions.

The flexible structure of CPS helped the educators select and use the components, stages, and tools they needed to work effectively on this task, and on other challenges that arose over a period of more than three years. The CPS language promoted more effective and productive communication among the group members, and the emphasis on constructive, or positive and forward-looking efforts made it possible to identify an approach to the project that helped everyone involved participate. People felt that they knew where they did want to go, whereas too many previous efforts focused only on what was wrong, missing, or deficient.

The group used generating tools to explore many aspects of the data in the task and to find novel opportunities (where so often groups looked only at a long list of "things that were wrong"). Specific tools for Exploring Data (such as the 5WH tool) helped people "stretch" their thinking. Focusing tools, and especially Highlighting, enabled the group to establish a clear, positive direction for the project.

Members of the group found great benefit in their use of CPS. So much so that the use of CPS was woven into the Lost Prizes program itself. The instructors of the program use CPS when they work with the students. The students also learn CPS to help them develop and use their strengths and talents and continue to do so well after the program.

Creating Computer Software

This is a story about the application of CPS by a manager involved in leading a project to develop new computer software. It involves his personal application of CPS as well as the manager's use of CPS tools when interacting with other members of the project team.

A consulting company saw trends emerging in the marketplace focusing on globalization, e-commerce, and the fast-paced integration of new technology. Many of the consulting company's clients were already moving toward more "virtual" work patterns. The clients wanted the benefits of face-to-face interaction without the costs of bringing people together in person. They wanted to work in global or cross-functional project teams, conduct consumer research, engage in organizational improvement initiatives, and train employees at a national and international level, while limiting the amount of time, energy, and resources necessary for meeting travel.

To meet these changing market demands, the consulting company initiated a project to develop a Web-based software application focusing on their best practices. Using such applications, people would not need to be in the same room, or even in the same time zone, to work together on important tasks. The virtual interaction could reduce costs associated with travel, lodging, and meeting space and reduce the amount of time away from the office or home.

The company collaborated with a software development organization that had the technical experience necessary for the development and implementation of the product. Project team members were designated from both organizations, although they were located approximately 400 miles apart.

What Did the Project Manager Do?

The project manager used CPS in working with the members of the project team to state the project's goals and objectives and then to develop and commercialize the software. The group used the Brainstorming tool to generate milestones (goals along the action plan) and specific actions that needed to be accomplished to reach each milestone. Eventually, they selected key milestones and actions, sorted them, and sequenced them using focusing tools such as Selecting Hits and SML. Both organizations shared a commitment to the final project plan, using the Preparing for Action component. This contributed to using human resources efficiently on the project.

During the project, the project manager used CPS in a variety of ways, both formal and informal. For example, CPS was built formally into each stage of the project, when significant new developments were added to the product. At the beginning of the project, the Exploring Data stage was helpful in understanding the landscape of products that were similar to their proposed new software product. The Generating Ideas stage was helpful in identifying the name for the product.

The team also used CPS informally throughout the project. For example, a number of problems arose during the initial software development activities. The project manager used the CPS language of problem statements (e.g., "How to . . . ?" and "How might . . . ?") to identify the root problems clearly and to prepare the team for generating ideas to solve them.

What Challenges Did the Project Manager Face?

In developing the software, more than 90% of the collaboration took place virtually—through teleconferences, e-mail, and instant messaging. The project manager faced the challenge of giving feedback about software developments to the software programmers. This was particularly important because the programmers had the expertise to make the software work well. However, they were far removed from the potential customer or end user of the software. Therefore, the project manager had to give feedback to the programmers about their insights and suggestions for development in a way that kept them motivated and engaged in the project. However, the project manager also had to channel the development of the software in the direction of the customer needs (which he, as project manager, knew best).

Figure 12.2 provides an example of how the project manager used the ALUo tool to provide structured feedback on the developments. He applied the tool informally throughout the project as well as during scheduled times within each stage of the project. It was particularly useful since it acknowledged the strong points of the

---

Figure 12.2   Feedback Using ALUo

Concept: Using a new technology to develop a specific function of the software

Advantages:

- The function would accurately emulate what happens in real-time applications of CPS.
- The interface of the function would be intuitive and easy to use.

Limitations:

- How might we incorporate this technology in time for the first release?
- How to assist online facilitators in managing group dynamics when using this function?

Unique qualities:

- This function would help to differentiate our software from the competition.

programmers' ideas in a way that was affirmative and consistent with their organizational culture. It also empowered them to improve their ideas because he phrased the limitations or drawbacks in their ideas as questions beginning with "How to . . . ?" This provided them with the stimulus to strengthen the product and gave the project manager additional insight about what actions needed to be added to the project plan. As a result, the speed and efficiency of the project team increased.

What Impact Did CPS Have?

Overall, using CPS to develop the software helped the project manager engage in decision making and problem solving that kept everyone excited about and engaged in the project. The flexible structure of CPS helped in developing the initial plan of action as well as in modifying plans when unexpected challenges emerged during the project. It also helped them address problems as they emerged. Using the CPS language promoted more effective and productive communication among project team members. As a result, the amount of time necessary to communicate accurately and concisely about the project decreased. This was particularly helpful since much of the communication took place via e-mail.

The ALUo tool was helpful in establishing a climate for creativity during interactions with team members throughout the project. By seeing their input accepted, the programmers felt that they were contributing beyond their primary role of producing code. This made it easier for programmers to implement needed features that they were reluctant to code due to difficulty or time needed to complete. The software met its scheduled launch date and has been a commercial success.

Developing New Products

This is a story about using CPS to support a global organizational initiative to develop new products. It involves the use of CPS in small groups and at an organizational level.

A global publishing company faced major changes in its marketplace. They recognized that the world is becoming increasingly digital. Their competitors were developing products that threatened their financial stability. The company needed to get new products to the market quickly and efficiently. They had 2 years to return to profitability, and time was running out.

We were called in to support the company in the development and implementation of a new product development initiative. The company's short-term strategy was to strengthen the portfolio of products in their core business. Once successful in this area, they would have the finances to develop new business and long-term growth with products that stretched the core business or were outside it.

They faced a number of challenges in this initiative. Like most organizations, they needed to find a way to speed up the product development process, while decreasing the costs associated with it. At the same time they wanted to take advantage of global synergies and increase their work together on a global level. Therefore, we had to design an approach for using CPS that would meet these objectives as well as help the organization develop high quality new products.

What Did We Do?

We designed the application of CPS at two levels. At one level, we used CPS to design a high-level overview of the 2-year initiative for new product development. We did this using the components of the CPS framework to map the general purposes for each stage of the initiative. We started the initiative by developing an understanding of the market opportunities and the customers' needs, using the Understanding the Challenge component. Next, we used this understanding of the marketplace to create preliminary product ideas (using the Generating Ideas component) that might meet the customer needs they identified.

The group then worked intensively for about 4 months to confirm the customer needs, transform the ideas into concepts that met the needs, and build business cases for investing the resources needed for full development and testing. Finally, they needed to transform their initial concepts into real products that they could test with customers. Once the group tested and received feedback about the products, they were able to develop, strengthen, and introduce the new products to all their customers. This part of the process took approximately 10 months. We structured these activities using the Preparing for Action component.

At a second, more specific level, we designed the initiative to enable small-group project teams to use CPS in response to their unique situations. Each team worked on two to four new product concepts. Each concept was large enough in scope to be considered a project in itself. The project teams included members from different functions and cultures. Each team worked in a different country (context), on different products (content), and ran its project meetings (method) in unique ways.

Therefore, we did not want to preset or prescribe any uniform approach to CPS for all the teams. We designed this level of application to enable different teams to use stages and tools that addressed their unique issues. At the same time, we needed to design for consistency in the type and format of the outcomes required for that phase of the overall initiative, such as the completion of a standardized business case for every project. The high-level design we used enabled the teams to be flexible at the project level, while maintaining their overall purpose and objectives at an organizational level.

What Challenges Did We Face?

We faced several challenges throughout the initiative. One of them involved designing a series of meetings, conferences, and interventions to keep the initiative on track. Historically, these meetings had been considered competitive and relatively unproductive. People felt that the meetings took too much energy away from more beneficial work. At any one of these meetings, we would be working with a diverse group of up to 25 people from different organizational functions and levels, as well as at least six different countries.

The overall time frame for the initiative was tight, and each global meeting was costly—not only in terms of money but in terms of time and other resources. Therefore, we needed to run these global meetings with careful precision to make them as productive as possible. Prior to a meeting, for example, we sent participants a brief containing the overall purpose, background information, and expected outcomes of the meeting. It included a general outline or plan for the meeting, a description of their roles and responsibilities, and descriptions of what they needed to do before and after the meetings. Typically, the project teams were asked to complete prework and send it to their colleagues for review before the meeting. This enabled us to be productive right from the start of the meeting.

In one global meeting, the goal was to make decisions about the concepts on which to move forward (and invest a large amount of organizational resources). The prework included all the teams preparing business cases of approximately 70 pages each for the concepts they were developing—a total of nine cases among the four teams. Each person reviewed all nine cases prior to the meeting and came prepared to address questions from the other people present. During the meeting, the cases were reviewed and additional feedback was given (using an ALUo format). Each concept was placed in an Evaluation Matrix like the one in Figure 12.3, and all 20 people evaluated each product concept one at a time.

Figure 12.3   The Evaluation Matrix Used in New Product Development

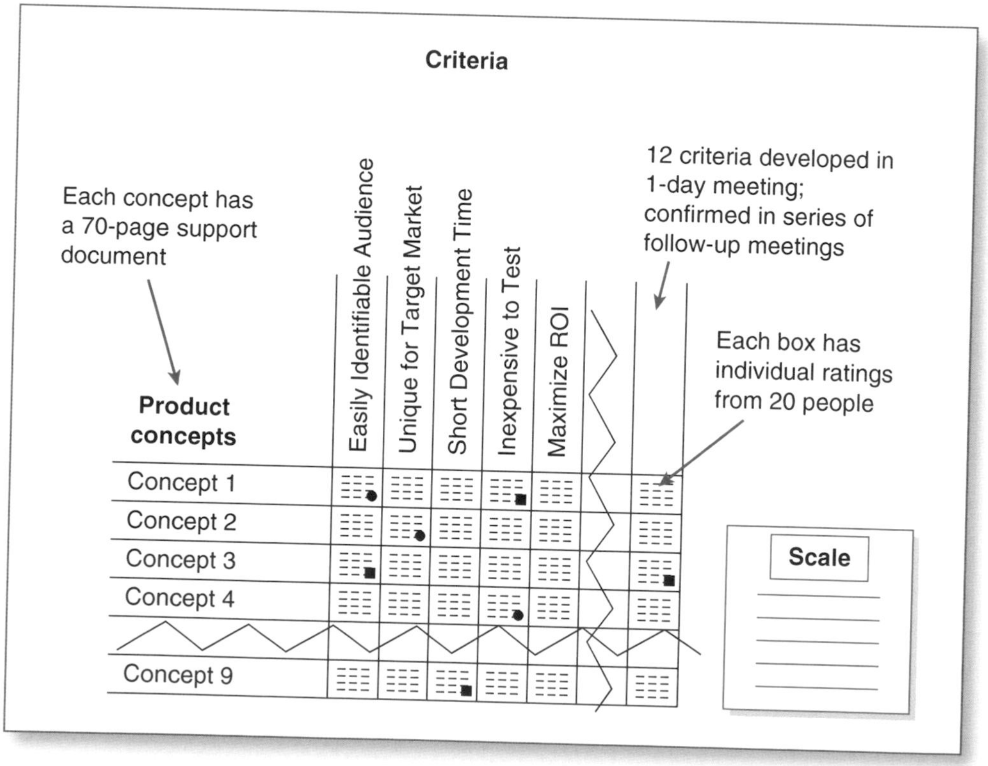

This meeting provides an example of how even one tool can be very powerful. This entire 3-day meeting revolved round the use of one Evaluation Matrix to help the group understand their concepts, develop and strengthen those that needed help, and make decisions about which to carry forward (Stead & Dorval, 2001). Just preparing for the Evaluation Matrix alone took 2 days of the senior management team's time (to develop and clarify the criteria for evaluation) and 4 months of the four project teams' time to develop the concepts evaluated in the matrix. Does an Evaluation Matrix always take this long? No. In this case, the group was making decisions about the future of their new product development efforts for which they were about to invest $5 million, so the stakes were high enough to justify the time and effort.

Given that we were working with people from different cultures, we also faced the challenge of different levels of English proficiency. As a result, it was very important to ensure that everyone had a common understanding of the language used throughout the meeting. Using natural CPS language helped a great deal, in that it gave people a common working language and helped everyone understand where we were in the process at any given time.

What Impact Did We Have?

We were able to affect the speed and productivity of the company's work in new product development. In the past, their process had involved developing a product concept first, then taking it to customers to see if they liked it, and then testing it. Products were developed for one of the four markets only, without knowledge of the real customer or their needs. It typically cost about $40,000 per product to get the ideas to the first round of decision making. Much of the money would be spent on creating product presentations to sell the concepts internally. On average, 24 ideas would be presented, 10 would be developed, and 2 would be launched successfully 18 months to 2 years later.

After the integration of CPS, products were developed on a global level and were focused on specific customer needs. Now, the cost was approximately $13,000 to move an idea to the second round of decision making, with the investment being made in exploring customers' needs. This time, nine products were presented, five accepted for testing with a view to launching within 8 months, one to be explored and tested within 9 months, and the other two to be revisited when the market had greater readiness for them. Just in the first idea phase, the new process saved the company a quarter of a million dollars (over the nine products) and reduced the development time from concept to market by approximately 1 year (see Figure 12.4).

Figure 12.4   The Impact of CPS

Results of new process	• Focused product development based on customer needs
	• Cross-functional, cultural development of product concepts
	• Development <u>time</u> reduction: over 50%
	• Idea development <u>cost </u>savings: 88%
	• Increase in <u>success rate</u>: estimate 401%

As one participant in the process put it, "Finally!!! We started quickly, came together, worked hard, and came up with a consensus of ideas and focused vision without wasting a lot of time, money, and emotional investment, as was done in the past." At the time of printing this book, seven of the nine concepts developed in the initiative were going to test in the marketplace. That is a very high percentage for the organization. The success from this initiative reminded us that it is possible for an organization to have things better, faster, and cheaper (Dorval & Stead, 2000).

Preparing to Apply CPS

Your preparation for CPS will depend greatly on the type of application and the number of people involved. We suggest that you follow four general guidelines to help improve the impact you obtain by using CPS deliberately and explicitly.

Prepare the People

As we discussed in Chapter 7, personal characteristics and preferences can have a strong impact on the results you obtain using CPS. If you are going to use CPS on your own, be clear at the outset about why you are planning to use CPS and about the outcome(s) you want to create. Consider how your preferred problem-solving style may point out some particular strengths and weaknesses. Think about your experience with the task and whether or not you need the support or help of others. If you plan to involve others, it is wise to let them know in advance about your purpose and desired outcome(s). Inform them about their roles and responsibilities, as well as what you expect them to do before and after your application of CPS.

Prepare the CPS Process

Whether you are alone or working with a group, know what components, stages, and tools you want to apply. At the component and stage level, remember that CPS is flexible and that it is wise to be prepared to use different components and stages as necessary and to have several different tools ready to use when you need them.

At the CPS tool level, begin by identifying the tools you think you may need to use. Remember to select the tools you *need* to use, not just the tools you *want* to use or *enjoy* using the most. For example, when you determine the kind of novelty you need, select the generating tool(s) that will be most likely to help you get that result. (Review the model for choosing tools in Chapter 4.) When you are considering different quantities of options to focus on, consider the model for choosing focusing tools in Chapter 5. Second, gather the appropriate support materials you will need to use the tools effectively. Be prepared to improvise when necessary! For example, if you do not have pictures to use with the Visually Identifying Relationships tool, then just ask people to look out the window or to go for a walk.

Preparing the process should result in an agenda or working plan. The agenda should contain the general flow of activities, the elements of CPS that will be applied, and the amount of time designated for each. If other people are involved, send the agenda to them before your meeting.

Prepare the Topic to Be Addressed

Sometimes we get so busy doing things that we lose track of where we are, what we have accomplished, or where we are going. Preparing the topic means pulling together the relevant information about why you are applying CPS and to what end. This *Task Summary* includes a statement of the need being addressed, the key background information associated with the task, and a statement of the desired outcomes. It should also have a definition of the working statement on which you will be focusing your attention. You will have acquired all this information during your Appraising Task activities.

If you are working alone, it may not be necessary to create a formal Task Summary. It is particularly helpful when you are working with a group in your application of CPS. For a group, provide some samples of the kinds of options that you hope they will generate for you. Also, send the Task Summary to them in advance.

Prepare the Working Environment

As we discussed in Chapter 8, the environment in which you apply CPS may have a powerful impact on your results. You might have the best tools in the world, but if the environment is not conducive to using your creativity, the likelihood of a creative result will be very low. Consider the physical space you will need to carry out your work. Select a space that you or others involved find stimulating but functional.

Once you have the space, prepare it for using CPS efficiently. For example, consider hanging some pictures or prints on the wall; using posters presenting the CPS guidelines, definitions, and framework; creating some open space for people to walk around; or using different kinds of seating areas for different work styles. Preparing the environment also includes ensuring that you have the appropriate equipment, supplies, and resources you will need.

General Suggestions for Getting Started

The following dozen suggestions come from a number of experienced professionals whom we asked to generate recommendations for those of you just getting started with CPS (see Figure 12.5), whether you are planning to use CPS personally or with colleagues.

Figure 12.5 Suggestions for Getting Started With CPS

- Use personally to demonstrate its effectiveness.
- Demonstrate the benefits of CPS.
- Use CPS soon after reading this book.
- Continue your learning.
- Debrief your use of CPS.
- Use the CPS framework flexibly.
- Start by using CPS on low-risk tasks.
- Integrate CPS into your current activities.
- Find a sponsor for your CPS application.
- Find a safe group with which to practice.
- Team up with someone who knows CPS.
- Use outside experts to get help.

Use CPS Personally to Demonstrate Its Effectiveness

We have observed participants in our own courses and workshops become much more proficient and comfortable with the CPS tools after applying them on a real task. Demonstrate the effectiveness of CPS to yourself first, before you try using it with others. Try practicing the language and tools first, so that you will feel more confident when you apply them with others.

Demonstrate the Benefits of CPS

One of our colleagues was part of a team involved in a change initiative. Different team members used different methods to manage their part of the overall initiative. Our colleague used CPS on three projects for which he was responsible. Each of his projects was accepted as delivered. Other colleagues needed to rework their projects. The differences in productivity demonstrated clear benefits for using CPS to the CEO of the company and resulted in a large initiative to integrate CPS skills within the organization. Demonstrating and documenting the added value and benefits can help create confidence in your knowledge of CPS and provide the stimulus to learn and apply it more.

Use CPS Soon After Reading This Book

One of the keys to supporting your use of what you read in this book is to have a supportive manager who encourages you to use what you have learned. Make deliberate plans with your supervisor, manager, or colleagues for opportunities to use the language and tools. You might also want to apply the method and tools in the book to help you develop explicit plans for applying the information. Our impact research suggests that the best time frame in which to try what you have read is about 2 weeks. After that point, the likelihood of you using this information begins to fall off dramatically.

Continue Your Learning

A book, an article, or a training course can provide you with exposure to CPS. This may be enough to start you on your way. However, none of these alone is likely to provide you with the depth of learning and insight that spans more than 55 years of research and practice on CPS. Many of our clients and colleagues pursue their interest in developing advanced skills in the use of the CPS framework, language, and tools. In fact, interest is so strong that we had to develop a CPS-skill-based development program that moves people from awareness of tools through learning how to facilitate CPS with groups. Consider this book to be a starting place on your journey or an initial step in enhancing your proficiency and productivity with creative approaches to problem solving.

Debrief Your Use of CPS

Many of our colleagues tell us of the powerful benefit they receive from the approach to debriefing what and how they learn on our courses. They learn faster and improve the impact of their CPS application. We were involved in a global workshop focused on new product development. At the end of each day, we identified insights from the day and their implications for modifying our plans for the remaining days. The debriefing sessions allowed us to make changes that added significant value to the meeting that responded to emergent needs throughout the workshop.

Set aside some deliberate time to examine the pluses or strong points, the needs for improvement, and the novel aspects or qualities of your work. Then identify what you might do differently the next time you use a tool, a stage, or a component. Reflecting on your use of CPS is one of the most powerful ways to continue your learning. (By the way, you may recognize these debriefing questions as an application of the ALUo tool!)

Use the CPS Framework Flexibly

Although you may currently see CPS as a general system containing four components and eight stages, the most appropriate use of CPS is flexible and dynamic. For example, a colleague told us of his use of simply the language of the Framing Problems stage. He was in a meeting in which two people were arguing with each other—to the point where it stopped any productivity in the meeting. Our colleague noticed that the two people seemed to be arguing about two different things. He stopped them, turned to one person and asked, "What problem are you trying to solve?" and the person answered. He turned to the other person and asked, "What problem are you trying to solve?" It turned out that the two problems were different. The people in the meeting then focused their attention on both problems, one at a time. This subtle intervention unblocked the meeting and resulted in excellent productivity. If you search for the opportunity to use all the components and stages at once, you may never get your chance to use CPS. Use pieces or parts of the process where you think they may be useful. Use a specific tool for a personal task or introduce a tool or a stage to a team or small group.

Start by Using CPS on Low-Risk Tasks

We know of one consultant who soon after attending one of our Igniting Creative Potential™ courses was asked to work on a globally significant project where the stakes were high. Fortunately, he was successful in his efforts but readily indicated that he would have preferred a few opportunities for practice before taking on that kind of challenge. Try using CPS on something that is not a "life or death" issue or that will not be job threatening for you or others. A "safe" task may help you be playful with CPS and to be less concerned about what might happen if you do not use the framework, language, or tools in the "correct" way.

Integrate CPS Into Your Current Activities

One of the strongest messages people have shared with us is the importance of weaving CPS directly into the work they are already doing. Rather than establishing a special situation for using CPS, it can be very helpful to begin using CPS on everyday challenges and tasks (at home as well as at work). You might try it for things such as deciding on a babysitter, buying a car, selecting a vacation spot, or simply figuring out the best way to spend a Saturday. You might use it to prioritize work tasks, give feedback to an employee, or set the direction for a new project. This will also help you see the value of CPS when applied to real personal or organizational needs. The integration can happen easily, particularly if you use CPS in a transparent and natural way.

Find a Sponsor for Your CPS Application

Some of the participants in our courses are sent for very good reasons. They often have the support from those who have approved and supported their attendance. These sponsors often invite them to use their new skills on a specific project or for a task appropriate for CPS. Some of these sponsors are alumni of the course or have received appropriate coaching. Others are just intuitively "smart" about getting a return on their investment. Identify an influential person around you who is interested in making things work better or differently. Offer to apply CPS on something that this sponsor wants to change or improve to help you gain support or "permission" to use the CPS framework, language, or tools.

Find a Safe Group With Which to Practice

A person from the United Kingdom attended a course and was able to use what she learned with a group of work associates with whom she had positive and productive relationships. They were curious about what she learned and offered an excellent "safe group" on which she could practice her new skills. If you are thinking about using CPS for the first time with others, do so with a small group of five to seven people with whom you are comfortable, and who you know will be supportive. Sometimes, offering to share a tool with this group and then experiencing a small degree of success can pave the way for more extensive future use and success.

Team Up With Someone Who Knows CPS

One of the participants from a course was lucky enough to be asked to work on a project in which one of our certified facilitators was involved. They found out about their common skills and knowledge and worked together to find many opportunities for successfully applying CPS. They were so good that the client for the project was certain to include them on the next big project and eventually sent many more of his direct reports to the training. Many people have been trained in CPS. You may find support in using CPS (especially when using it with a group) by teaming up with others in your network who know and use CPS. Having someone else with you who knows the framework, language, and tools can provide additional support to ensure productivity as well as help capture insights and learning from its application.

Use Outside Experts to Get Help

Although we are often available to help others successfully apply their CPS tools (see about CPSB [Creative Problem Solving Group] and CCL [Center for Creative

Learning] below), you can often benefit from using someone from within your own organization who may be from a different unit, department, or function. They qualify as *outside experts* but may be more available to you, especially if your organization supports cross-functional or interdisciplinary ways of working. If you own a task and you or your team needs help, bring in outsiders who know CPS to get things rolling. It will probably be difficult for you to be the owner of the task and the person who manages the use of CPS when working on the task. Outside experts might be experienced, trained facilitators, or simply people who have some training and experience in the use of the tools to help you get started.

Additional Resources

Some additional resources that you might find helpful are mentioned below. They may provide you with additional understanding of CPS as well as support your specific application of the framework, language, and tools.

- Treffinger, D. J., Isaksen, S. G., & Stead-Dorval, K. B. (2006). *Creative problem solving: An introduction* (4th ed.). Waco, TX: Prufrock Press.

This book provides a concise introduction to and overview of the most contemporary approach to CPS. It's based on extensive research, development, and field experience using CPS in education, business, and other organizations. *Creative Problem Solving: An Introduction* is also an excellent choice for use as a participant's textbook in introductory workshops, courses, training programs, or seminars. The book is available through www.creativelearning.com, www.cpsb.com, and www.prufrock.com.

- Isaksen, S. G., Dorval, K. B., & Treffinger, D. J. (2005). *Toolbox for creative problem solving: Basic tools and resources* (3rd ed.). Orchard Park, NY: Creative Problem Solving Group, Inc.

Toolbox came about when one of the facilitators we trained (a retired U.S. Air Force jet pilot) looked at our training materials and said, "You should make a preflight checklist like I used to have when I flew in the Air Force. The checklist would summarize what I need to do when I use the tools." So we created this resource.

Toolbox for Creative Problem Solving (provided in a three-ring binder) is designed for people facilitating CPS groups. It provides 16 removable tool booklets. These four-page booklets identify when to use the tools and the key steps to take in using them effectively. Each booklet provides a list of suggestions for modifying that particular tool and a reproducible worksheet for supporting your use of the tool. The tool booklets contain guidelines for generating and focusing your thinking and models for helping you select and use the tools. You will find this a valuable resource in supporting your work in the field.

- Isaksen, S. G. (Ed.). (2000). *Facilitative leadership: Making a difference with Creative Problem Solving* (1st ed.). Dubuque, IA: Kendall/Hunt Publishing.

Facilitative leadership is leadership that focuses on service—helping, developing, and strengthening others in ways that inspire motivation and shared commitment.

This book, filled with practical recommendations and resources, pulls together everything we know about facilitative leadership and what it takes to unleash the creative talent of others. It examines the challenges you will face when encouraging teamwork, managing group dynamics, and setting the climate for creativity and change. It describes a CPS facilitator skill base in detail and provides extensive support for the effectiveness of CPS as a method for change. You will find this resource valuable when you need to lead and enable others to make a real difference in organizations.

- Isaksen, S. G., & Tidd, J. (2006). *Meeting the innovation challenge: Leadership for transformation and growth* (1st ed.). Chichester, UK: Wiley.

This book is all about the core system that drives successful application of CPS to help those who lead and manage organizations meet their innovation challenges. It provides a comprehensive summary on leadership and management for innovation and outlines how CPS can be applied for a variety of organizational outcomes.

- CPS 101: A Distance-Learning Module

The Creative Problem Solving 101 (CPS 101) distance-learning course is designed to enhance the creative, innovative, and facilitation skills of practitioners from all lines of business. CPSB developed CPS 101 through collaboration with IBM's Executive Learning Center. It offers a variety of different opportunities to build core CPS Version 6.1™ skills and provides you with an overview of which tools, methods, and techniques are available to enhance your facilitation capabilities. You can contact CPSB to acquire pricing and log-in details (www.cpsb.com).

About Our Organizations

We have also provided a brief description of our two organizations. If we can be of service to you in your efforts to use creative approaches to problem solving, please let us know.

Creative Problem Solving Group, Inc.

CPSB is committed to bringing dramatic results to organizations by enhancing the creative talent of the people within them. We do this by conducting integrated research and development activities aimed at providing people who lead change efforts, consultants, and project or line managers with a full spectrum of products and services they can use to address their customers' needs and meet the innovation challenge.

The group includes top researchers from disciplines such as industrial and organizational psychology, cognitive psychology, organizational leadership, sociology, and learning and education. These scholars conduct scientific research to help us find answers to our clients' questions by extending the frontiers of our knowledge about creativity, leadership, and change. The group also contains highly trained facilitators and trainers. These certified practitioners use their knowledge and skills to help you or your organization address important challenges and opportunities.

Contact us if you need to develop products and services, design and drive changes in organizations, develop leadership potential, or enhance people's creativity and problem-solving skills. We offer a variety of services and resources to help you unleash the creativity within your organization.

> The Creative Problem Solving Group, Inc.
> Post Office Box 648-6, Grand View Trail
> Orchard Park, NY 14127
> Phone: (716) 667-1324 • Fax: (716) 667-6070
> e-mail: info@cpsb.com • Web site: www.cpsb.com

Center for Creative Learning, Inc.

The mission of CCL is to be a primary source of *ideas and information* that will inspire, inform, and enable people to foster creative learning and to recognize and nurture the unique and varied strengths and talents of every person. Our approach to creative learning and CPS builds on more than four decades of theory, research, and practical experience with schools and other organizations worldwide. We offer a variety of products on creative learning, Creative Problem Solving, talent development, and learning style, including books, brief reports, and trainer's resources. We offer training programs and consulting services on CPS with a specific focus on education, churches, and other nonprofit organizations.

> Center for Creative Learning, Inc.
> 4921 Ringwood Meadow
> Sarasota, FL 34235
> Phone: (941) 342-9928 • Fax (941) 342-0064
> e-mail: info@creativelearning.com • Web site: www.creativelearning.com

An Invitation

We hope that we have provided you with the information, understanding, and confidence you need to be productive in using CPS to reach your goals and aspirations. We are always interested in new stories about how CPS can be used, so if you have stories that you want to share, please contact us. We wish you all the success you can create in using CPS to make your home and work life richer, more satisfying, and more productive.

Visit Our Web Sites

You can obtain more information about our organizations, the professionals who are associated with us, and the services we provide by browsing our Web sites at www.cpsb .com and www.creativelearning.com. Both organizations' Web sites provide numerous downloadable resources as well as periodic newsletters.

Attend a Course

CPS Version 6.1™ is the most contemporary approach to creative problem solving we know of. Our team, as well as an international network of licensees, provides work-shops and training courses that can deepen your knowledge and skill in applying and facilitating CPS. More information about our Igniting Creative Potential™ line of service is available on our Web site (www.cpsb.com).

Putting This Chapter to Work

The goals of this chapter were twofold. First we wanted to provide you with examples of CPS applications in order to demonstrate how the different parts of CPS can be put together to create a successful outcome. Second, we identified specific recommendations and resources that can help prepare you to get the most from the information contained in this book.

Activities to Guide Reflection and Action

Work on one or more of the following activities to review your understanding of the material in this chapter and to practice applying the content in real situations. If you are using this book as part of a course or study group, you may wish to work individually, and then compare your responses, or you may wish to work collaboratively as a team.

1. Search your personal, academic, and professional life, and identify a few pressing issues or opportunities you might want to address. Identify two potential issues or opportunities that might be appropriate for CPS application and two issues that might not be appropriate for CPS. Compare and contrast the two lists and determine the main reasons why each task is or is not appropriate for CPS application.

2. Take an idea you are considering for solving a problem you are currently facing. Conduct an ALUo on the idea. Identify at least five to seven advantages, five to seven limitations, and three to five unique qualities. Identify the top two limitations to the idea, and generate a list of many, varied, and unusual ways in which you might overcome each limitation. Once completed, interpret the results of the ALUo tool by making observations and insights about the original idea, given what you learned from applying ALUo. Identify key actions you would take as you consider moving forward with the idea.

3. Select one of the tasks identified in #1 for which you have ownership (interest, influence, imagination). Conduct a Task Appraisal on the task and determine whether or not it is appropriate for CPS. If it is not appropriate, go back to your list of tasks in #1 and conduct another Task Appraisal. Repeat this process until you have a task that is appropriate for CPS application.

With the task in hand, design the most appropriate way through the CPS framework. Identify the component and stage in which you would begin to apply CPS. Apply the components, stages, language, and tools on your task. Debrief your application of CPS using the ALUo tool. Describe the impact of your CPS application in the form of a short story that you can share with others. Include in the story the need you addressed, the process you used to address it, and the outcomes of that application. Also include the impact those outcomes resulted in.

4. Find an individual who has a need, an issue, or a challenge he or she could use some help with. With this person as your potential client, and his or her issue as the task, engage in the same series of activities as those described in #3.

References

Altshuller, G. (1996). *And suddenly the inventor appeared—TRIZ: The theory of inventive problem solving.* Worcester, MA: Technical Innovation Center.

Amabile, T. M., & Gryskiewicz, S. S. (1988). Creative resources in the R & D laboratory: How environment and personality affect innovation. In R. L. Kuhn (Ed.), *Handbook for creative and innovative managers* (pp. 501–524). New York: McGraw-Hill.

Babij, B. (1999). A study in change: From bedsores to quality care. *Communiqué, 7,* 8–9.

Barker, J. A. (1990). *The power of vision.* Burnsville, MN: Charthouse Learning Corporation.

Basadur, M. (1994). *Simplex®: A flight to creativity.* Buffalo, NY: Creative Education Foundation.

Besemer, S. P. (1997). *Creative product analysis: The search for a valid model for understanding creativity and products.* Unpublished doctoral dissertation, University of Bergen, Norway.

Besemer, S. P. (2006). *Creating products in the age of design: How to improve your new product ideas.* Stillwater, OK: New Forums Press.

Besemer, S. P., & O'Quin, K. (1987). Creative product analysis: Testing a model by developing a judging instrument. In S. G. Isaksen (Ed.), *Frontiers of creativity research: Beyond the basics* (pp. 341–379). Buffalo, NY: Bearly.

Besemer, S. P., & O'Quin, K. (1993). Assessing creative products: Progress and potentials. In S. G. Isaksen, M. C. Murdock, R. L. Firestien, & D. J. Treffinger (Eds.), *Nurturing and developing creativity: The emergence of a discipline* (pp. 331–349). Norwood, NJ: Ablex.

Besemer, S. P., & O'Quin, K. (1999). Confirming the three-factor creative product analysis matrix model in an American sample. *Creativity Research Journal, 12,* 287–296.

Besemer, S. P., & Treffinger, D. J. (1981). Analysis of creative products: Review and synthesis. *Journal of Creative Behavior, 15,* 158–178.

Blanchard, K. (1985). *The situational leadership SLII model.* San Diego, CA: Blanchard Training and Development.

Boden, M. A. (1991). *The creative mind: Myths and mechanisms.* New York: Basic Books.

Bognar, R., Guy, M., Purifico, S. B., Redmond, L., Schoonmaker, J., Schoonover, P., et al. (2003). *Practical tools for creative and critical thinking: Applications for Destination ImagiNation®.* Glassboro, NJ: Destination ImagiNation.

Brue, G. (2002). *Six Sigma for managers.* New York: McGraw-Hill.

Burnside, R. M., Amabile, T. M., & Gryskiewicz, S. S. (1988). Assessing organizational climates for creativity and innovation: Methodological review of large company audits. In Y. Ijiri & R. L. Kuhn (Eds.), *New directions in creative and innovative management: Bridging theory and practice* (pp. 169–185). Cambridge, MA: Ballinger.

Carroll, J. B. (1993). *Human cognitive abilities: A survey of factor-analytic studies.* New York: Cambridge University Press.

Couger, J. D. (1995). *Creative problem solving and opportunity finding.* Danvers, MA: Boyd & Fraser.

Covey, S. R. (1989). *The seven habits of highly effective people.* New York: Simon & Schuster.

Davis, G. A., & Roweton, W. E. (1968). Using idea checklists with college students: Overcoming resistance. *Journal of Psychology, 70,* 221–226.

Davis, T. (2000). *Innovation and growth: A global perspective.* London: PricewaterhouseCoopers.

DeBono, E. (1970). *Lateral thinking: A textbook of creativity.* Harmondsworth, UK: Penguin.

DeBono, E. (1986). *Six thinking hats.* New York: Little, Brown.

Deming, W. E. (1986). *Out of the crisis.* Cambridge: MIT Press.

Dewey, J. (1933). *How we think: A restatement of the relation of reflective thinking to the educative process.* Lexington, MA: D. C. Heath.

Dietrich, A. (2007). Who's afraid of a cognitive neuroscience of creativity? *Methods, 42,* 22–27.

Dorval, K. B., & Stead, S. (2000). New product development: Changing the rules of the game. *Communiqué, 10,* 1–3.

Eberle, B. (1971). *Scamper.* Buffalo, NY: DOK. (Reprinted in 1997 by Prufrock Press, Waco, TX)

Ekvall, G. (1983). *Climate, structure and innovativeness of organizations: A theoretical framework and an experiment.* Stockholm: The Swedish Council for Management and Organizational Behaviour.

Ekvall, G. (1987). The climate metaphor in organizational theory. In B. M. Bass & P. J. D. Drenth (Eds.), *Advances in organizational psychology: An international review* (pp. 177–190). Newbury Park, CA: Sage.

Ekvall, G., & Arvonen, J. (1984). *Leadership styles and organizational climate for creativity: Some findings in one company.* Stockholm: Swedish Council for Management and Organizational Behaviour.

Ekvall, G., Arvonen, J., & Waldenstrom-Lindblad, I. (1983). *Creative organizational climate: Construction and validation of a measuring instrument.* Stockholm: Swedish Council for Management and Organizational Behaviour.

Ekvall, G., & Tångeberg-Andersson, Y. (1986). Working climate and creativity: A study of an innovative newspaper office. *Journal of Creative Behavior, 20,* 215–225.

Elliott, P. (1987). Knight's move: A new technique for stimulating creativity and innovation. *Creativity and Innovation Network, 12,* 2–12.

Fobes, R. (1993). *The creative problem solver's toolbox.* Corvalis, OR: Solutions Through Innovation.

Foster, J. (1996). *How to get ideas.* San Francisco: Berrett-Koehler.

Freeman, T., Wolfe, P., Littlejohn, B., & Mayfield, N. (2001). Measuring success: Survey shows how CPS impacts Indiana. *Communiqué, 12,* 1–6.

Fritz, R. (1999). *The path of least resistance for managers: Designing organizations to succeed.* San Francisco: Berrett-Koehler.

Gardner, H. (1993). *Creating minds.* New York: Basic Books.

Geschka, H., Schaude, G., & Schlicksupp, H. (1973, August). Modern techniques for solving problems. *Chemical Engineering,* 91–97.

Ghiselin, B. (1952). (Ed.). *The creative process.* New York: New American Library.

Gryskiewicz, S. S. (1980). *A study of creative problem solving techniques in group settings.* Unpublished doctoral dissertation, University of London, UK.

Gryskiewicz, S. S. (1987). Predictable creativity. In S. G. Isaksen (Ed.), *Frontiers of creativity research: Beyond the basics* (pp. 305–313). Buffalo, NY: Bearly.

Gryskiewicz, S. S. (1988). Trial by fire in an industrial setting: A practical evaluation of three creative problem-solving techniques. In K. Grønhaug & G. Kaufmann (Eds.), *Innovation: A cross-disciplinary perspective* (pp. 205–232). Oslo, Norway: Norwegian University Press.

Gryskiewicz, S. S. (1999, December). *Positive turbulence: How to use creativity to manage change and sustain healthy organizations.* Paper presented at Fit for the Future: The Sixth European Conference on Creativity and Innovation, Lattrop, The Netherlands.

Guilford, J. P. (1977). *Way beyond the IQ.* Buffalo, NY: Bearly.

Hall, D. (1995). *Jump start your brain.* New York: Time-Warner.

Higgins, J. M. (1994). *101 creative problem-solving techniques.* Orlando, FL: New Management.

Isaksen, S. G. (1984). *Organizational and industrial innovation: Using critical and creative thinking.* Paper presented at the Conference on Critical Thinking: An Interdisciplinary Appraisal sponsored by Kingsborough Community College, New York.

Isaksen, S. G. (1987). *Frontiers of creativity research: Beyond the basics.* Buffalo, NY: Bearly.

Isaksen, S. G. (1995). CPS: Linking creativity and problem solving. In G. Kaufmann, T. Helstrup, & K. H. Teigen (Eds.), *Problem solving and cognitive processes: A festschrift in honour of Kjell Raaheim* (pp. 145–181). Bergen-Sandviken, Norway: Fagbokforlaget Vigmostad & Bjørke AS.

Isaksen, S. G. (1998). *A review of brainstorming research: Six critical issues for inquiry* (Monograph No. 302). Orchard Park, NY: Creative Problem Solving Group–Buffalo.

Isaksen, S. G. (Ed.). (2000). *Facilitative leadership: Making a difference with creative problem solving*. Dubuque, IA: Kendall/Hunt.

Isaksen, S. G. (2004). The progress and potential of the creativity level-style distinction: Implications for research and practice. In W. Haukedal & B. Kuvas (Eds.), *Creativity and problem solving in the context of business management* (pp. 40–71). Bergen, Norway: Fagbokforlaget.

Isaksen, S. G. (2007). The climate for transformation: Lessons for leaders. *Creativity and Innovation Management, 16,* 3–15.

Isaksen, S. G., & Akkermans, H. (2007). *An introduction to climate*. Orchard Park, NY: Creative Problem Solving Group.

Isaksen, S. G., & DeSchryver, L. (2000). Making a difference with CPS: A summary of the evidence. In S. G. Isaksen (Ed.), *Facilitative leadership: Making a difference with creative problem solving* (pp. 187–249). Dubuque, IA: Kendall/Hunt.

Isaksen, S. G., & Dorval, K. B. (1993). Changing views of Creative Problem Solving: Over 40 years of continuous improvement. *International Creativity Network Newsletter, 3*(1), 1–4.

Isaksen, S. G., & Dorval, K. B. (2000). Facilitating Creative Problem Solving. In S. G. Isaksen (Ed.), *Facilitative leadership: Making a difference with creative problem solving* (pp. 55–76). Dubuque, IA: Kendall/Hunt.

Isaksen, S. G., Dorval, K. B., Noller, R. B., & Firestien, R. L. (1993). The dynamic nature of creative problem solving. In S. S. Gryskiewicz (Ed.), *Discovering creativity: Proceedings of the 1992 International Creativity and Networking Conference* (pp. 155–162). Greensboro, NC: Center for Creative Learning.

Isaksen, S. G., Dorval, K. B., & Treffinger, D. J. (1998). *Toolbox for creative problem solving: Basic tools and resources*. Williamsville, NY: Creative Problem Solving Group–Buffalo.

Isaksen, S. G., Dorval, K. B., & Treffinger, D. J. (2005). *Toolbox for creative problem solving: Basic tools and resources* (2nd ed.). Orchard Park, NY: Creative Problem Solving Group.

Isaksen, S. G., & Ekvall, G. (with Akkermans, H., Wilson, G. V., & Gaulin, J. P.). (2007). *Assessing the context for change: A technical manual for the SOQ—Enhancing performance of organizations, leaders and teams for over 50 years* (2nd ed.). Orchard Park, NY: Creative Problem Solving Group.

Isaksen, S. G., & Gaulin, J. P. (2005). A re-examination of brainstorming research: Implications for research and practice. *Gifted Child Quarterly, 49,* 315–329.

Isaksen, S. G., & Geuens, D. (2007). Exploring the relationships between an assessment of problem solving style and creative problem solving. *Korean Journal of Thinking and Problem Solving, 17,* 5–27.

Isaksen, S. G., & Lauer, K. J. (2002). The climate for creativity and change in teams. *Creativity and Innovation Management Journal, 11,* 74–86.

Isaksen, S. G., Lauer, K. J., & Ekvall, G. (1999). Situational Outlook Questionnaire: A measure of the climate for creativity and change. *Psychological Reports, 85,* 665–674.

Isaksen, S. G., Lauer, K. J., Ekvall, G., & Britz, A. (2001). Perceptions of the best and worst climates for creativity: Preliminary validation evidence for the Situational Outlook Questionnaire. *Creativity Research Journal, 13,* 171–184.

Isaksen, S. G., Murdock, M. C., Firestien, R. L., & Treffinger, D. J. (1993). *Nurturing and developing creativity: The emergence of a discipline*. Norwood, NJ: Ablex.

Isaksen, S. G., & Shephard, W. J. (2008). *An introduction to facilitating Creative Problem Solving*. Orchard Park, NY: Creative Problem Solving Group.

Isaksen, S. G., Stein, M. I., Hills, D. A., & Gryskiewicz, S. S. (1984). A proposed model for the formulation of creativity research. *Journal of Creative Behavior, 18,* 67–75.

Isaksen, S. G., & Tidd, J. (2006). *Meeting the innovation challenge: Leadership for transformation and growth.* Chichester, UK: Wiley.

Isaksen, S. G., & Treffinger, D. J. (1985). *Creative problem solving: The basic course.* Buffalo, NY: Bearly.

Isaksen, S. G., & Treffinger, D. J. (2004). Celebrating 50 years of reflective practice: Versions of creative problem solving. *Journal of Creative Behavior, 38,* 75–101.

Isaksen, S. G., Treffinger, D. J., & Dorval, K. B. (1997). *The creative problem solving framework: An historical perspective* (Idea Capsules Report No. 9009). Sarasota, FL: Center for Creative Learning.

Jones, L. J. (1987). *The development and testing of a psychological instrument to measure barriers to effective problem solving.* Unpublished master's thesis, University of Manchester, UK.

Kanter, R. M. (1983). *The change masters: Innovation for productivity in the American corporation.* New York: Simon & Schuster.

Katzenbach, J. R., & Smith, D. K. (2003). *The wisdom of teams: Creating the high-performing organization.* New York: HarperCollins.

Kaufmann, G., Helstrup, T., & Teigen, K. H. (Eds.). (1995). *Problem solving and cognitive processes: A festschrift in honour of Kjell Raaheim.* Bergen-Sandviken, Norway: Fagbokforlaget Vigmostad & Bjørke AS.

Keller-Mathers, S., & Puccio, K. (2000). *Big tools for young thinkers.* Waco, TX: Prufrock Press.

Kepner, C. H., & Tregoe, B. B. (1981). *The new rational manager.* Princeton, NJ: Princeton Research Press.

Koestler, A. (1969). *The act of creation.* New York: Macmillan.

Kouzes, J., & Posner, B. (2007). *The leadership challenge* (4th ed.). San Francisco: Jossey-Bass.

Lewin, K., Lippitt, R., & White, R. K. (1939). Patterns of aggressive behavior in experimentally created "social climates." *Journal of Social Psychology, 10,* 271–299.

Littlejohn, W., & Mayfield, N. (2005). CPS in the classroom: Blumberg Center brings programs to students. *Communiqué, 14,* 6–8.

Loos, K. (1994). *Managing organizational change: How leading organizations are meeting the challenge.* Cambridge, MA: Arthur D. Little.

MacKinnon, D. W. (1975). IPAR's contribution to the conceptualization and study of creativity. In I. A. Taylor & J. W. Getzels (Eds.), *Perspectives in creativity* (pp. 60–89). Chicago: Aldine.

MacKinnon, D. W. (1978). *In search of human effectiveness.* Buffalo, NY: Creative Education Foundation.

Magyari-Beck, I. (1993). Creatology: A potential paradigm for an emerging discipline. In S. G. Isaksen, M. C. Murdock, R. L. Firestien, & D. J. Treffinger (Eds.), *Understanding and recognizing creativity: The emergence of a discipline* (pp. 48–82). Norwood, NJ: Ablex.

McCluskey, K. W., Baker, P. A., O'Hagan, S. & Treffinger, D. J. (1995). *Lost prizes: Talent development and problem solving with at-risk students.* Sarasota, FL: Center for Creative Learning.

McCluskey, K. W., & Treffinger, D. J. (1998). Nurturing talented but troubled children and youth. *Reclaiming Children and Youth, 6,* 215–219, 226.

McCluskey, K. W., & Treffinger, D. J. (Eds.). (2002). *Enriching teaching and learning for talent development.* Sarasota, FL: Center for Creative Learning.

Michalko, M. (1998). *Cracking creativity: The secrets of creative genius.* Berkeley, CA: Ten Speed Press.

Mintzberg, H. (1994). The fall and rise of strategic planning. *Harvard Business Review, 72,* 107–114.

Newell, A., Shaw, J. C., & Simon, H. A. (1962). The processes of creative thinking. In H. E. Gruber, G. Terell, & M. Wertheimer (Eds.), *Contemporary approaches to creative thinking: A symposium held at the University of Colorado* (pp. 63–119). New York: Atherton.

Noller, R. B. (1979). *Scratching the surface of creative problem solving: A bird's eye view of CPS.* Buffalo, NY: DOK.

O'Quin, K., & Besemer, S. P. (1989). The development, reliability, and validity of the Revised Creative Product Semantic Scale. *Creativity Research Journal, 2,* 267–278.

Osborn, A. F. (1942). *How to think up.* New York: McGraw-Hill.

Osborn, A. F. (1953). *Applied imagination: Principles and procedures for creative thinking.* New York: Scribner.

Parnes, S. J. (1961). Effects of extended effort in creative problem solving. *Journal of Educational Psychology, 52,* 117–122.

Parnes, S. J. (Ed.). (1992). *Sourcebook for creative problem solving: A fifty-year digest of proven innovation processes.* Buffalo, NY: Creative Education Press.

Parnes, S. J., Noller, R. B., & Biondi, A. M. (1977). *Guide to creative action.* New York: Scribner.

Pasmore, W. A. (1988). *Designing effective organizations: The socio-technical systems perspective.* New York: Wiley.

Perkins, D. N. (1981). *The mind's best work: A new psychology of creative thinking.* Cambridge, MA: Harvard University Press.

Place, D., McCluskey, K. W., McCluskey, A., & Treffinger, D. J. (2000). The Second Chance Project: Creative approaches to developing the talents of at-risk native inmates. *Journal of Creative Behavior, 34,* 165–174.

Prajogo, D. I., & Ahmed, P. K. (2006). Relationships between innovation stimulus, innovation capacity, and innovation performance. *R&D Management, 36,* 499–515.

Puccio, G. J., & Murdock, M. C. (1999). *Creativity assessment: Readings and resources.* Buffalo, NY: Creative Education Foundation Press.

Puccio, G. J., Murdock, M. C., & Mance, M. (2007). *Creative leadership: Skills that drive change.* Thousand Oaks, CA: Sage.

Raudsepp, E. (1988). Creative climate checklist: 101 Ideas. In R. L. Kuhn (Ed.), *Handbook for creative and innovative managers* (pp. 173–182). New York: McGraw-Hill.

Ray, D. W., & Wiley, B. L. (1985). How to be an idea generator. *Training and Development Journal, 39,* 44–47.

Reid, D., & Dorval, B. (1996). CPSB tips the scales in Indiana. *Communiqué, 2,* 5–7.

Rhodes, M. (1961). An analysis of creativity. *Phi Delta Kappan, 42,* 305–310.

Rogers, E. M. (1995). *Diffusion of innovations* (4th ed.). New York: Free Press.

Rothenberg, A. (1971). The process of Janusian thinking in creativity. *Archives of General Psychiatry, 24,* 195–205.

Rothenberg, A. (1979). *The emerging goddess: The creative process in art, science and other fields.* Chicago: University of Chicago Press.

Rothenberg, A. (1996). The Janusian process in scientific creativity. *Creativity Research Journal, 9,* 207–231.

Rothenberg, A. (1998). *The creative process in psychotherapy.* New York: Norton.

Rothenberg, A. (1999). Janusian process. In M. Runco & S. R. Pritzker (Eds.), *Encyclopedia of creativity* (Vol. 2, pp. 103–108). New York: Academic Press.

Rothenberg, A., & Hausman, C. R. (Eds.). (1976). *The creativity question.* Durham, NC: Duke University Press.

Selby, E. Treffinger, D., & Isaksen, S. (2002). *VIEW: An assessment of problem solving style.* Sarasota, FL. Center for Creative Learning.

Selby, E. C., Treffinger, D. J., Isaksen, S. G., & Lauer, K. J. (2004). Defining and assessing problem-solving style: Design and development of new tool. *The Journal of Creative Behavior, 38,* 221–243.

Selby, E. C., Treffinger, D. J., & Isaksen, S. G. (2007a). *VIEW: An assessment of problem solving style: Technical manual* (2nd ed.). Sarasota, FL: Center for Creative Learning.

Selby, E. C., Treffinger, D. J., & Isaksen, S. G. (2007b). *VIEW: Facilitator's guide* (2nd ed.). Sarasota, FL: Center for Creative Learning.

Service, R. W., & Boockholdt, J. L. (1998). Factors leading to innovation: A study of managers' perspectives. *Creativity Research Journal, 11,* 295–307.

Spearman, C. (1931). *The creative mind.* New York: D. Appleton.

Spitzer, Q., & Evans, R. (1997). *Heads you win: How the best companies think.* New York: Simon & Schuster.

Stead, S., & Dorval, K. B. (2001). Master Blaster: The power of the evaluation matrix. *Communiqué, 11,* 24–27.

Stevens, G. A., & Burley, J. (1997). 3000 raw ideas equal one commercial success. *Research Technology Management, 40,* 16–27.

Straker, D., & Rawlinson, G. (2003). *How to invent almost anything.* London: Spiro Press.

Taffinder, P. (1998). *Big change: A route-map for corporate transformation.* New York: Wiley.

Thomson, K. (2000). *Emotional capital: Maximising the intangible assets at the heart of brand and business success.* Oxford, UK: Capstone.

Torrance, E. P. (1979). *The search for satori and creativity.* Buffalo, NY: Creative Education Foundation & Creative Synergetic Associates.

Treffinger, D. J. (1992). Searching for success zones! *International Creativity Network Newsletter, 2*(1), 1–2, 7.

Treffinger, D. J. (1996). *Creativity, creative thinking, and critical thinking: In search of definitions.* Sarasota, FL: Center for Creative Learning.

Treffinger, D. J. (2000). Understanding the history of CPS. In S. G. Isaksen (Ed.), *Facilitative leadership: Making a difference with CPS* (pp. 35–53). Dubuque, IA: Kendall/Hunt.

Treffinger, D. J. (2008, Summer). Preparing creative and critical thinkers. *Educational Leadership.* Retrieved July 24, 2009, from. http://www.ascd.org/publications/educational_leadership/summer08/v0165/num09/Preparing_Creative_and_Critical_Thinkers.aspx

Treffinger, D. J., & Isaksen, S. G. (2005). Creative Problem Solving: History, development, and implications for gifted education and talent development. *Gifted Child Quarterly, 49*(4), 342–353.

Treffinger, D. J., Isaksen, S. G., & Firestien, R. L. (1982). *Handbook of creative learning.* Williamsville, NY: Center for Creative Learning.

Treffinger, D. J., Isaksen, S. G., & Stead-Dorval, K. B. (2006). *Creative problem solving: An introduction.* Waco, TX: Prufrock Press.

Treffinger, D. J., Isaksen, S. G., & Young, G. C. (1998). Brainstorming: Myths and realities. *National Inventive Thinking Association Newsletter,* 1–3.

Treffinger, D. J., & Nassab, C. A. (2000). *Thinking tool lessons.* Waco, TX: Prufrock Press.

Treffinger, D. J., & Nassab, C. A. (2005). *Thinking tool guides* (Rev. ed.). Sarasota, FL: Center for Creative Learning.

Treffinger, D. J., Nassab, C. V., Schoonover, P. F., Selby, E. C., Shepardson, C. A., Wittig, C. V., et al. (2006). *The Creative Problem Solving kit.* Waco, TX: Prufrock Press.

Treffinger, D. J., Selby, E. C., & Isaksen, S. G. (2008). Understanding individual problem-solving style: A key to learning and applying creative problem solving. *Learning and Individual Differences, 18,* 390–401.

Treffinger, D. J., Selby, E. C., Isaksen, S. G., & Crumel, J. H. (2007). *An introduction to problem-solving style.* Sarasota, FL: Center for Creative Learning.

Treffinger, D. J., Young, G. C., Selby, E. C., & Shepardson, C. (2002). *Assessing creativity: A guide for educators.* Storrs, CT: National Research Center on the Gifted and Talented.

VanGundy, A. B. (1992). *Idea power: Techniques and resources to unleash the creativity in your organization.* New York: AMACOM.

VanGundy, A. G. (1984). How to establish a creative climate in the work group. *Management Review, 73,* 24–38.

van Leeuwen, M., & Terhürne, H. (2002). *Innovation by creativity: 50 tools for solving problems creatively.* Dordrecht, The Netherlands: Kluwer.

Wallas, G. (1926). *The art of thought.* New York: Franklin Watts.

Ward, T. B. (2004). Cognition, creativity, and entrepreneurship. *Journal of Business Venturing, 19,* 173–188.

Ward, T. B. (2007). Creative cognition as a window on creativity. *Methods, 42,* 28–37.

Welsch, P. K. (1980). *The nurturance of creative behavior in educational environments: A comprehensive curriculum approach.* Unpublished doctoral dissertation, University of Michigan.

Wertheimer, M. (1945). *Productive thinking.* Chicago: University of Chicago Press.

Witt, L. A., & Beorkrem, M. N. (1989). Climate for creative productivity as a predictor of research usefulness and organizational effectiveness in an R & D organization. *Creativity Research Journal, 2,* 30–40.

Womack, J., & Jones, D. (1996). *Lean thinking.* London: Simon & Schuster.

Index

About the Authors

Scott G. Isaksen, PhD, is President of the Creative Problem Solving Group, Inc., and Senior Fellow of its Creativity Research Unit. He is also a Professor of organizational leadership and management at the Norwegian School of Management and was Director of SUNY's (State University of New York) International Center for Studies in Creativity. He has authored or coauthored more than 185 books, articles, and chapters in books. He has conducted more than 1,800 programs and courses by working with more than 250 organizations and groups in more than 36 U.S. states or Canadian provinces and 26 different countries. He has served as a consulting editor for the *Journal of Creative Behavior* since 1983. In 1996, he was awarded the State University of New York Chancellor's Award for Excellence in Teaching.

His main interests and areas of expertise include building capabilities for leading innovation, applying Creative Problem Solving to business, establishing the climate for innovation and creativity, and understanding and leveraging style differences. He holds a master of science degree from Buffalo State College in creativity and innovation (1977) and a doctorate in curriculum design from the University at Buffalo (1983).

K. Brian Dorval is Founding Partner and President of Think First Serve®, Inc., a management training and consulting company specializing in the use of creative-thinking, problem-solving, and performance improvement methods to help groups and organizations figure out new ways to grow. He has more than 23 years of experience helping people, teams, and organizations significantly improve their personal performance and business results. He has delivered more than 450 Creative Problem Solving, management coaching, and performance training sessions for companies in 20 countries around the world. He has also published more than 50 articles, chapters, and books on topics related to creative thinking, problem solving, and performance improvement.

In other performance-related areas, he is a USPTA (United States Professional Tennis Association)-certified tennis professional, who specializes in the mental game. He has worked with regionally and nationally ranked junior and college tennis players, as well as adults of varying levels, to improve mental toughness and enhance performance during competition. He conducts research on the topics of creative thinking, problem solving, mental imagery, and sports performance and applies the results to help people, teams, and organizations develop high-performance practices that stimulate growth and success. He is also Head Tennis Professional for Western New York's Shining Stars adaptive tennis program for children with autism. He holds a master of science degree from Buffalo State College in creativity and innovation (1990).

Donald J. Treffinger is President of the Center for Creative Learning, Inc., in Sarasota, Florida. His work focuses on the areas of creativity, Creative Problem Solving, problem-solving style, and gifted and talented education. He has authored or coauthored more than 60 books and monographs and more than 350 articles in a wide variety of professional journals in education and psychology. He began his career as a mathematics teacher in Buffalo, New York, and has subsequently served in several positions at the university level. He was a member of the Educational Psychology and Research faculty of Purdue University, Professor and Chairman of the Educational Psychology and Research Department at the University of Kansas, and Professor of Creative Studies at Buffalo State College. He has received the National Association for Gifted Children's Distinguished Service Award and the E. Paul Torrance Creativity Award. In 2005, he received the Risorgimento Award from Destination ImagiNation, Inc., and the International Creativity Award from the World Council for Gifted and Talented Children. In 2009, he received the Executive Director's Award from the Future Problem Solving Program International. He has served as editor of the *Gifted Child Quarterly* (1980–1984), as Editor-in-Chief of *Parenting for High Potential*, NAGC's quarterly magazine for parents (1999–2007), and as a reviewer for numerous journals, and he is currently a member of the Editorial Advisory Board for the *Gifted Child Quarterly*. He holds an MS degree and PhD degree in educational psychology from Cornell University and an honorary LLD degree from the University of Winnipeg (Canada).

Supporting researchers for more than 40 years

Research methods have always been at the core of SAGE's publishing program. Founder Sara Miller McCune published SAGE's first methods book, *Public Policy Evaluation*, in 1970. Soon after, she launched the *Quantitative Applications in the Social Sciences* series—affectionately known as the "little green books."

Always at the forefront of developing and supporting new approaches in methods, SAGE published early groundbreaking texts and journals in the fields of qualitative methods and evaluation.

Today, more than 40 years and two million little green books later, SAGE continues to push the boundaries with a growing list of more than 1,200 research methods books, journals, and reference works across the social, behavioral, and health sciences. Its imprints—Pine Forge Press, home of innovative textbooks in sociology, and Corwin, publisher of PreK–12 resources for teachers and administrators—broaden SAGE's range of offerings in methods. SAGE further extended its impact in 2008 when it acquired CQ Press and its best-selling and highly respected political science research methods list.

From qualitative, quantitative, and mixed methods to evaluation, SAGE is the essential resource for academics and practitioners looking for the latest methods by leading scholars.

For more information, visit **www.sagepub.com**.